COP
in a Small City

Examining Mission and Integrity

G. Michael Sanborn

NEWMAN SPRINGS PUBLISHING
320 Broad Street
Red Bank, NJ 07701

First originally published by Newman Springs Publishing 2019

ISBN 978-1-64096-693-2 (Paperback)
ISBN 978-1-64096-694-9 (Digital)

Printed in the United States of America

For my granddaughter, Riley,
who persistently demanded to hear these stories.

Contents

Preface

I decided to write these stories to share with others. I hope that it gives some insight to those who wonder about police and how they work and feel. I hope to give information to those who are thinking about a career in law enforcement.

I also hope to influence law enforcement people. I hope that you have honor and commit to a higher level and motivate your peers similarly. If you lack high standards in this profession, I hope that you either develop some or find another career.

Disclaimer: These stories describe real events. Of course, names have been changed, and many stories are amalgamations. If you think you have figured it out, I will confirm nothing.

CHAPTER 1

The Beginning

Why I Became a Cop

I was born into a family where my grandparents dominated our lives. My grandfather continued his dominance of my mother even though she was an adult. He extended her dependence on him. My grandmother was quietly more effective on the children. They were French-Canadian Catholics with strong religious and personal values. They are the foundation to my ethical standards.

Everyone in my family called my grandfather "Pop," which was started by my uncle, their youngest child and only son. French-Canadian fathers were usually called Papa or Père. Uncle Bernie wanted something more modern for those times. My mother, aunt, and uncle called Gramma "Ma," short for Mamère.

I spent my summers on my grandparents' vegetable farm beginning when I could hold a hoe. They spoke always about family, neighbors, and their customers. They valued people who worked hard, were reliable, helped others, never took advantage of anyone, and always spoke the truth. I attended church with them every week. Though I tuned out most sermons, the message still sunk in, which was how my grandparents lived. Their life was very structured and dedicated to family and community.

In school, I excelled in math and science. I struggled with creative writing. I thrived with verifiable facts. Science requires accurate procedures with structured, verifiable reporting. These values aligned perfectly with what I learned from my grandparents. Not surprisingly, science was my college major. I went to a Catholic college that further enforced these values.

It was the Vietnam era. Young men my age were being drafted. I also had a draft card but start with a IIs (2S) student deferment. It meant that I could go to college, and my draft availability would be suspended until I graduated or dropped out. I also got National Defense Student Loans (NDSL) and National Defense Student Grants (NDSG) to attend college. The idea was that college education made our country stronger. Our military readiness saw it as an investment. After the Vietnam War, the acronyms changed to National Direct in place of National Defense.

They did away with the student deferments as started a lottery system. My college friends and I spent a late night in the college dormitory watching the live lottery drawings. They drew birth dates. The first one hundred would most certainly be drafted. My number was 280, likely not to be drafted.

After graduating college, I felt guilty for having avoided the draft. The twenty-year retirement from the military appealed to me. I spoke with a recruiter who told me that I could get a guaranteed position in Officer Candidate School (OCS) because I had a college degree. I had to go through basic training first. As I started the process, he suggested that I start running. I should have taken his advice. Nonetheless, I was strong and managed basic training like most others. OCS was much more physically challenging. I managed there, also like most others.

My commissioned service stressed "integrity" in all ways. An officer's word is more than just character; it is his or her very being. Officers must report accurate information and carry out orders with utmost accuracy, reliability, and thoroughness. It fit well with the ethics foundation I got from my grandparents and strengthened through college.

We were expecting our first child about the time I would be expected to do a lengthy overseas unaccompanied tour. Though the twenty-year retirement still appealed to me, separation from my new family did not. I investigated civilian opportunities and realized that the police also had a twenty-year retirement. I believed that police officers also had a high value for integrity that fit well with my personality and experience so far. I decided to leave the army after my commitment was fulfilled.

It took only a few months to find a position on the Claremont Police Department. Very soon, I struggled with conflicts of integrity within the police department. I managed to tolerate these incidences over six years until another opportunity arose in the public works department. I have worked in other professions, especially teaching. I sadly report that my experience with the police was where I had the most conflicts of integrity. I do not regret my law enforcement service to the community. I learned a lot and found even better ways to serve my community because of this experience. I hope that by sharing my experiences, I will help move this and other professions and the understanding of community in a positive direction.

Police Academy

Municipal police are hired and must wait for the next available opening in the police academy. This usually takes several months, four months for me. Newly hired officers are put into service with in-house training. Within three days, I was assigned a beat. So I had some experience before going to the Sixty-fourth Class of the New Hampshire Police Academy in 1982.

When officers describe the challenges of the police academy, they typically speak about the physical demands. The standards vary according to gender and age. The most demanding category is, as one would expect, younger men. They are expected to run one point five miles in twelve minutes and fifty-three seconds. They must complete thirty-seven sit-ups within a minute and twenty-seven push-ups with no apparent time limit other than they must be continuous.

The army has loosened standards and allow two minutes to complete each thirty-five push-ups and forty-seven sit-ups. The two-mile run must be completed in sixteen minutes and thirty-six seconds. During my tenure, Basic Infantry Army Officer Candidate

Course (BIOCC)—also called Officer Candidate School (OCS)—demanded maximum possible scores: thirty-six sit-ups and fifty-four sit-ups, each within a minute and the two-mile run in fourteen minutes. There was a "run, dodge, and jump" course that had to be done in less than twenty-three seconds. We also were expected to do fifty-four hanging bars in one minute. Intense physical activity was worked in daily, and we often ran five miles. BIOCC or OCS is not to be confused with police officer or military police. It is for becoming a commissioned officer in the United States Army, a much higher standard.

The first morning formation assembly noticeably had some missing people. Basic training in the army had a high sick call list, but these people were missing. They quit. The commandant made a remark that he felt guilty for scaring them off. He had promised a five-mile run this day. I was looking forward to it. Though he said he felt guilty, I sensed that he was pleased. There seems to be some people who find making others look inadequate a way for them to look better. I would certainly smoke this guy and give him a taste of his own humiliation.

Compared to any educational setting I have been in, neither is very challenging. Both seem to like requiring some pointless memorization. I say pointless because being able to recite something doesn't prove understanding. The program supervisors use it to justify having taught it to release them from some perceived liability. By the time I went to the New Hampshire Police Academy at the Pease Air Force Base in Portsmouth, I had completed basic training, OCS, and two college degrees. I had four months of training and experience from my department. Though there was something for me to learn, nothing about the police academy was challenging for me. Apparently, one of the adjunct cadre took it personally.

The police academy had no physical challenge for me. I realized this right away with the first physical exam meant to be qualifying. It was necessary to pass this to continue in the academy. They lined us up for the one-and-a-half-mile run around an old airfield. I was an average, middle-of-the-pack runner in the army. I let other jockey for the front positions. I started at my normal army pace and started passing others. I was soon in the front. I was not comfortable in this position because I had never been there in the army. I worry that I may be adrenalin driven and would burn out. I slowed my pace. Still, no one caught up. I slowed some more. Glancing over my shoulder, I realized that I was still gaining on the crowd. I listened to my body as I did in the army. I evaluated my breath and strength. I felt that I was running under my ability. I decided to ignore everyone else and just run as I felt best. Sadly, I became the subject of distain from peers. It's something I have seen many times. For some, it's easier to bring someone down than to rise to the challenge. The commandant threatened to bring us on his five-mile run. He was a short man with an oversized belly. I indicated my acceptance of his challenge since five-mile runs in the army were at least weekly. He never delivered on his threat.

One day, we were standing in formation during an inspection by a cadre from Belmont, Lieutenant Hackley. His department wore a lighter-blue uniform with a broad-brimmed hat. As he stepped in front of me, he was so short that it was difficult for him to see above my chest. He did the prescribed look up and down my uniform and said, "I hear that you think this academy is a walk in the park." I answered honestly, "No, sir, I never said that."

The lieutenant looked up a little, but I couldn't see his eyes hidden under his broad-brimmed hat. He said, "Are you smiling?" I didn't think I was and tried to suppress any indication and replied, "No, sir."

Lieutenant Hackley continued his barrage that had nothing to do with the purpose of this inspection, saying, "Good because I would have to kick your ass."

After a moment, he said again, "Are you smiling?" I replied, "Yes, sir. I am trying hard not to, but I am smiling." He asked, "Why?"

I replied, "Sir, I know you won't kick my ass for two reasons." He seemed puzzled and asked for an explanation. I said, "First, it would end you career. Second, you would lose."

Lieutenant Hackley didn't seem to have an intelligent response to my reply. After a pause, he turned to the next candidate. I believe that he was just trying to bring me down. I try to be humble and still do not necessarily perform to my best but a respectable showing. I will never yield to any intimidation tactics.

I was somewhat disturbed about some conversations I was hearing from my academy peers. One was "choir practice" on Friday before going home for the weekend. It was immediately obvious that it did not involve singing. It took a couple of weeks, but I listened and learned. It was a gathering at the end of the runway to have a few beers before driving home.

This bothered me greatly. I didn't drink at all. This was my choice based upon my childhood experiences. I fully accepted that others make a different choice, but to drink then drive was very wrong, especially for police officers. If someone wants to drink and do risky acts, that's his or her business. However, drinking and performing risky acts such as driving is very different. No one has the right to risk another's life. Over and above this, I wanted membership in a corps that held high standards for itself. These are police officers whose duty is to prevent drinking and driving. From what I overheard, it wasn't one beer but several that each were consuming in a short period of time. It also appeared that this was a long tradition from other classes, and cadre knew it. I was powerless. If I protested, I would more likely be labeled as one who couldn't be trusted to back up my fellow officers; hence, the "code" was taught right from the beginning at the academy. Do not report other officers who violate laws.

None of the cadre officers ran with us. They simply stood at the start and finish and timed us. We would assemble at the starting point and told to stretch. The army never did stretching, so I just stood and waited to begin the run. Once, one of the cadre told me to stretch. I declined. When he continued to insist, I replied, "What do you do when someone runs away from you? Do you yell, 'Wait a minute, dirtbag! I got to stretch!'?" Since I always finished first and never had a problem, no one bothered me after that.

As I said, the commandant was short and visibly out of shape. Candidate Patrick from Keene had a similar build. He was also a jerk, which was evident in how he talked about his work and the way he spoke to others. I expected him to drop out, but he managed to make it through the academy. As a group, we typically marched between destinations. Someone had to call cadence so we could remain in step. Patrick liked to call it.

The greatest hold the commandant had over us was releasing us on Friday. We all wanted an early release. I wanted to get home while others wanted choir practice. Whatever the motive, we all tried to work together to get this early release. This jerk from Keene thought that he would be funny with calling cadence. "Oh, I wish I was a short, fat runt. Then I could be a commandant." We wanted to pummel him. Fortunately, we didn't repeat his call. He wasn't happy and repeated it. Several of us tried to tell him to stop. A part of me wanted to slam this jerk on the ground, but I held my values. Fortunately, none of the cadre heard him.

CHAPTER 2

Community Policing

Ossipee Ladies

To maintain a police presence in the community and avoid other officers who hang out at the police station, I often wrote my reports parked in a highly visible place with traffic flowing. On this winter evening, I chose a parking lot on West Pleasant Street, the main entrance to the city from the south. At night, people driving by would assume that I am watching for violators. The truth was that I was paying no attention to them and focusing on my report. Only a loud, unusual sound would gain my attention.

It was a warm summer night, so I had my window down. I was somewhat startled when someone drove up to me. Police shouldn't let their guard down like I did. This car was beside me before I noticed it. He rolled his window down, and I could tell he was upset about something. He said, "You gotta go get that car."

I put my report aside and placed my fingers on my car's ignition as I looked at him. I asked, "What's it doing?" Already, I am running through possibilities in my mind. Most complaints are about speeders and possible drunken drivers.

He explained, "It's all over the road. It goes from crossing the center line to driving on the sidewalk."

I was anxious now, knowing I would have to be quick to catch the car before someone got seriously hurt. "Where was it going?" I asked. He said that it was going down Maple Avenue. I was somewhat relieved that it didn't drive by me, and I was too zoned out to notice. I reached to start my car, indicating that I would hurry to catch it. He said, "You'll have no trouble catching it. It's going less than twenty miles per hour." I asked for a description of the car. He said it was a big brown sedan, then emphasized that I would have no trouble finding it.

I thanked him and drove away. He was correct about catching it easily. I saw it as soon as I turned onto Maple Avenue. It was driving down the center, straddling the double yellow line. That was plenty of reason to stop it and a writable offense. Any driving left of center on a highway marked with a double yellow line is prohibited.

As I came up behind the car, traffic approached from the other direction. The driver suddenly and overly corrected, driving up onto the sidewalk. This is classic drunk driving and to the extreme. I was now preparing mental notes for what would be a very long DWI report.

I was close enough now and turned on the blue lights. Surprisingly, the car pulled right over neatly against the curb. I walked up to the car. An elderly woman was in the passenger seat. The only other occupant was another elderly lady in the front passenger seat. She greeted me pleasantly.

She was stopped with her foot on the brake, but the car was still in drive. She was glad to see me, reporting that she was lost. As the headlights from another approaching car shone on us, she attempted to steer the car to the right. This immediately concerned me as she had to know that she was stopped as she was speaking to me standing beside her car. I reached in and shifted her car into park.

I asked her where she was going. She replied, "To Ossipee." Then she added that she started from West Ossipee. She was taking her sister into town so that she could do some shopping. I knew Ossipee was on the other side of the Lakes Region of New Hampshire, which is at least two hours with normal driving. Clearly, she wasn't driving normally with speeds less than twenty miles per hour.

I asked, "When did you leave?" She replied, "About nine o'clock. I must have made a wrong turn, and I am trying to get back."

It was about six o'clock in the evening now and dark. I knew it was impossible to get here in an hour, so she left that morning. That would mean that she would have been driving more than nine hours. I wondered why she hadn't run out of gas. At these low speeds, the car was probably idling most of the time. She kept trying to steer the car, so I reached in and put her car into park.

As we spoke, more traffic approached us. Each time headlights shone into her face, she tried to turn her car to the right. She still had her foot on the brake and pressed harder. I was glad that the car was in park, but she grabbed the selector and wiggled it. That alarmed me. I was afraid that she might still drive away from me. I felt even luckier now that she stopped in the beginning. I wasn't sure that she would remain and what it would be like trying to stop her again. I reached in, turned her car off, and removed the keys.

She sensed my concerns for her well-being. I told her that she was a long way from Ossipee. I asked her if she had made any stops. She replied, "No, and my sister and I need a bathroom." I noticed the wetted area on the seat by her sister.

Never had I encountered anything like this. What do I do with them now? I decided that there must be something seriously wrong with them. They obviously have immediate medical needs. I was also concerned about their state of mind. I called for the ambulance, code 1, which is without lights and siren. It is the ambulance company's standard police to operate the lights whenever responding to such a call or when carrying a patient. I was relieved to see their lights coming, code 2.

I quickly briefed the EMTs. I explained that these ladies left Ossipee early this morning and have been driving since. I was most concerned about their state of mind and warned them about the incontinence. They decided to bring them to the hospital for a more thorough assessment. I was glad. Technically, I could have left all responsibility for them and the hospital at this point. Since my wife worked there and I knew the emergency room nurse well, I retained responsibility. I just had to wait for the wrecker to remove the car.

When I got to the hospital, the ladies were the favorite patients of the evening. The nurses and doctor liked their charm and innocence. They had them all cleaned up and dressed in hospital gowns. The emergency room nurse had already tried to call a friend they identified, but there was no answer. I decided to contact the Ossipee police. We had all those numbers at the police station. The dispatcher could look it up for me, and the sisters were in good hands for now, so I went to the police station.

I managed to contact the Ossipee police chief right away. As police officers, even when someone hasn't broken a law that would cause their license to be suspended or revoked, we could write the Commissioner of Motor Vehicles and ask for administrative action against their license. The police chief knew them but hadn't done anything like this. He explained that they drove a short distance to the market from their home and back. It hadn't been a problem. He too was a very pleasant guy. I told him about my experience this night. Since I saw the serious problem, it would be me that should make this request of the commissioner. He agreed and assured me that he would meet with the driver in the next few days. He also assured me that he would get into contact with their family and someone would come get them. I gave him the contact information to the hospital and left the coordinating to him.

I returned to the hospital. The sisters and hospital staff were enjoying their time together. I explained to the nurse and the driver of my plans to request action against her license. She was disappointed but understood. She was mostly concerned that she may have placed her older sister in danger.

One more short report, a letter to write, and I was done. I still dwell on how lucky it was that no one got hurt. If it wasn't for that concerned person, they would have driven through Claremont and farther.

Charlotte Abandoned

While patrolling on a Saturday morning, dispatch called be to go to the IGA (International Grocers Association) store for an abandoned child. As any call, thoughts go through a police officer's mind on the way to the call. It's a way to prepare oneself on how to handle it. We remember past calls and how they were resolved. We try to recall department policies and procedures and how they might apply. My previous experiences involved defiant elementary and middle school children who refused to leave with the parent, who left them behind. Mostly, they were expected to walk home. Though not my style of parenting, there is nothing wrong with it if the child can do this, especially if home was a reasonable walk away. I was not prepared for what I found.

I parked the police car in front of the store. As I walked into the store, a woman called me. She was standing by the checkouts and holding a child about eighteen months old. I walked over to her. All my mental preparation got flushed. Now what do I do? Is this really the child for whom I was called? The woman, wearing store clothes and name tag, assured me this was the child. They found her wandering around the checkout area. She went on to explain that they announced over the intercom several times. They also went to everyone in the store. They were positive no one there was related to this child. I radioed dispatch who assured me they had no reports of a missing child.

What do I do with this little girl? I asked her for her name. She just looked at me. The woman explained that they had tried to speak with her, but she didn't respond to any of them. They have been with her for more than a half hour and very confident the parent was no longer, if ever, in the store. She handed me the child, which further increased my anxiety.

As luck would have it, a woman checking out with her groceries thought that she recognized the child. She explained that she works at WIC (Women, Infants, and Children) and was somewhat confident she knew who the mother was. She added that the child's name is Charlotte. She offered to go to her office and look up the mother's address. She agreed to call the police station when she got it. This was great news. At least I could see an eventual positive outcome. I still had the problem of what to do with this child. I decided to bring her to the police station and wait for the call.

Police cars are not equipped with child seats, which is required by law to transport such a small child. I decided that we were exempt.

I strapped her firmly in the seat beside me. I was happy but surprised how compliant she was. I had daughters older and younger than her. They would have been screaming in terror. Little Charlotte looked wide-eyed all around her and frequently at my face. I spoke with her often, telling her what I would be doing next. Though she looked at me as I spoke, I didn't sense that she understood. She remained nonverbal throughout my time with her.

I brought her to the dispatch center to wait for the call. The dispatcher wanted to interact with Charlotte. At this point, I welcomed it. I took over dispatching while she looked after Charlotte. Soon, the WIC volunteer called. She told me the mother's name and address. The dispatcher assured me that she could watch the child while I went to the apartment to find the mother, Aimee.

It was a relatively large apartment building with twelve apartments. Her apartment was down a short flight of stairs. I knocked on the door for some time but got no response. I returned to the police station.

It was now time to involve the state social agency, DCYS (Division for Children and Youth Services). It later changed its name to DCYF (Division for Children, Youth, and Families). The number we had was the supervisor on call who answered immediately. He came right over and took the child. He asked, and I assured him that we would keep checking for the mother.

I stopped every hour or two throughout my shift. I checked one last time a few minutes before the end of my shift. Much to my surprise, the door opened within seconds of my knocking. A very unattractive person opened the door and looked up at me. I was struck by her gender-neutral appearance and dress. Clothes were oversized. Her hair was ear length, dark brown, and uncombed. Behind her, I could see many people in the apartment, adults and children. The apartment was also very cluttered. Sadly, this is typical of most apartments in this building.

I told this person that I was looking for Aimee. With a voice that wasn't easily recognized as feminine, she acknowledged that she was Aimee. I told her that we have Charlotte. She seemed very puzzled and looked around the immediate area in the apartment.

As she looked, I explained that I got her from the IGA store. She turned back to me and said, "I could have sworn that she got in the car with us."

This was unconscionable to me. My daughters, at that age, were always in physical contact with us in a public place such as a store. In the grocery store, they either held our hand, were carried, or rode in the shopping cart. Nearly seven hours have passed, and Aimee was surprised that Charlotte wasn't with them. She explained that they drive a Gremlin, a small Rambler-made car, and seven people were riding in it. This was a car designed for five people. Again, our daughters went from hand or shopping cart directly into a car seat. There was no chance for them to wander off or run in front of a car, yet this parent had no idea the child wasn't with her.

I gave to her the number the DCYS supervisor wanted me to give to her when I found her. I learned later, very much to my surprise and disappointment, that supervisor simply returned the child to her, and no case was opened.

Where's Daddy?

Pete and I were a great team. A good shift is any one that he and I were assigned to the same car. These times were infrequent since we were most often understaffed. When we were together, we were the team that would serve warrants recently issued by the court. These were usually tougher cases. Most warrants were failure to appear or to pay a fine on time. Though they avoided court, their reasons were lack of money and seldom resisted arrest. If the amount was small, we arranged a deal that they would pay the fine within a few days. The tougher ones were those recently issued arrest warrant from the judge or justice of the peace. The offender usually knew we were looking for him or her and, if we got him, he would be going to jail with a high bail or no bail.

Our evening shift started out busy with calls as usual. When things became quiet, we started serving the warrants. When we find them, we brought them in for processing and called for bail. For the routine ones, bail was typically low enough for them to post it. If they had a history of failing to appear in court or resisted our arrest, the bail would be higher. Bail is meant to assure one's presence in court. If they fail to appear, the bail could be forfeited to the court. If they were on one hundred dollars personal recognizance bail and failed to appear, they were released without having to deposit any money. However, if they fail to appear, they automatically owe one hundred dollars to the court, and the bail would be much higher. In the end, the court rarely kept the money. Often, the bail money was applied to a fine.

We had five warrants to serve this evening. We found two right away, and processing was quick and easy. They were released on a fifty-dollar bail. We went to serve a third one in a large twelve apartment building. We parked the car in the front of the building and walked upstairs to the apartment listed on the warrant. We stood on each side, and Pete knocked on the door. We could hear movement inside, but no one came to the door. We knocked again, more intently.

The door opened quickly. I little girl about five years old stood with the open door in her hand and looked at Pete and me as we peered around the side of the entrance. She was remarkably cute. Pete and I both had daughters about this age. Pete asked, "Is your daddy home?"

We were stunned when this cute little girl, much like our own daughters, looked up at us and said, "F—— you," and slammed the door closed.

Pete and I looked at each other in disbelief. This time, I knocked on the door. The same little girl opened it. She took the same stance with one hand on the door. I said, "Can you show us where Daddy is?" She held her finger next to her mouth, nodded, and said, "Uh-huh."

She walked from the door a short distance into the kitchen as we followed. She then pointed to the cabinet doors under the sink. Pete cautiously opened one door, exposing Daddy crunched into the small area under the sink. He surrendered to arrest. We asked if there was anyone around to watch his daughter. He called someone's name. Another man and a woman came from the bedroom area. He said that they could watch her.

I think back at what we did. What first came to mind is how obedient this little child was in doing what her daddy told her to do. Daddy didn't anticipate the second knock. With no conflicting instructions from Daddy, she was happy to please us. Technically, we took this child into protective custody by arresting her father. We then placed this child with people we did not know. The proper process is to bring the girl with us, call child protective services, and have them place the child. We could have left her with pedophiles. The other way of looking at it was a legal alternative. A parent or guardian can place a child with someone without any government approval. However, we didn't give this parent much choice. None want to involve child services.

This dad was held on the bail predetermined on the warrant, one thousand dollars. He was held in county jail overnight.

We didn't get to the remaining two warrants and left them for the day shift. The night shift doesn't go knocking on doors in the middle of the night to serve routine warrants. Of course, there is no hesitation to wake people when we are looking for an active criminal.

Though this was one of our most memorable nights, we sometimes worked alone and in competition. When we were bored, we would go to the warrant file and find some in our respective beats. When one of us found someone, we announced, "Coming in with one." With one officer processing the prisoner, the other needed to remain available so he couldn't be making a simultaneous arrest when it could wait. As soon as Pete cleared, I would sign off looking for an arrest as soon as possible before he could.

It went back and forth one night. Pete and I were each tied with two arrests. I got lucky with my next stop and found wanted husband and wife together. I took both and proudly announced, "Coming in with two." Pete responded asking if I needed any assistance. I sensed a sound of defeat in his voice. These two were very cooperative, and I assured him that I would be "all set." It didn't take long to process them, and I returned to patrol, letting Pete know the game was back on, "ten to one," returning to patrol.

Five minutes barely passed. Pete announced, "Coming in with five." I was stunned and defeated. No way could I beat that in the time remaining in our shift. Then Pete announced, "Can you assist me in the sergeant's office?" I acknowledged that I could, though I was very confused. It must be some very strange arrest to process in the sergeant's office. When I got there, I learned that the five that Pete had in custody were coffees for everyone, including the dispatcher. It was a good night. We had a good team. We worked well together and respected and cared for each other.

Tower Lounge Fight

It was not unusual to get called to bar fights. I remember my first one. It was the bar under the Winner Hotel. We used to say that the Winner was full of losers. It was a dingy hotel with narrow hallways. The bar was in the basement. The entrance was directly off the street.

I walked in with my backup. It was so dark in there it was hard to see who was there, especially in the darker corners. There was no active fight when we arrived. It was too dark to see who might be injured. We talked to the bartender. He was not happy to see us. He said that there was no problem. We walked around the bar. No one seemed to be in any distress, so we left.

There were other bar-fight calls. Most were over when we arrived. It was our policy to not accept formal statements and assault charges from intoxicated individuals. We made certain that the fight would not resume when we left. We strongly encouraged those involved to go home. Sometimes when they were intoxicated, refused to go home, and indicated they would resume the fight, we took then into protective custody. It was rare that anyone wished to bring assault charges once they sobered.

Sometimes when a major call came in during shift change, both shifts will respond, so there are double the number of officers. There was one such call on a Saturday night, "fight at the Tower Lounge."

The Tower Lounge was a large higher-class bar above the Pleasant Restaurant, also considered to be higher class. It was the first and only fight I responded to at the Tower Lounge. It is directly in front of the police station, next to city hall, so we all ran to it.

The stairway to the second-floor lounge was long, straight, and wide. The fight seemed to have just stopped as we ran up the stairs. When we entered the barroom, there were several people standing out of the melee, against the walls. They seemed to be the nonparticipants. There were several men standing nearer the bar. They appeared to be the participants. They had bloodied lips and knuckles. We wanted to establish the severity of potential charges.

We also had two supervisors for each of the shifts. My supervisor asked generally to the group, "What's happening?" Everyone was silent. My supervisor said to us, "Get their names. We'll hash this out separately."

I looked around and approached the closest one that was obviously involved. He was breathing hard, standing with his fists clenched, his knuckles bloodied, looking glaringly at some other men. I was standing on his left side and slightly behind him. The tables and chairs were in disarray, preventing me from being in a better position to interview him.

I took out my notepad and asked his name. He ignored me. I asked more intently. He turned slightly toward me and said over his left shoulder, "I ain't got a name." I warned him that if he did not give me his name, I would arrest him for disorderly conduct. He ignored me, increasing his breathing rate, and glared more at the other men.

I stuffed my notepad and pen in my shirt pocket and told him that he was under arrest. He still ignored me. I placed my hand to cup it around his left elbow and told him to come with me. I was taken completely by surprise when he suddenly exploded. He jumped up, and he turned toward me with fists flying. I stepped back and attempted to draw my baton and tripped over a turned-over chair. We both fell to the floor with him on top of me. On the way down, his first punch didn't land but was close enough to break my glasses. Fortunately, my friend Bob was right there. Bob grabbed him and slowed his advance enough that I regained my footing, and we pressed him to the floor. He was faced down, with his hands tucked tightly under his chest to prevent being handcuffed.

This is a tactic that we practiced a lot at the police academy. When your prisoner is on his belly and resisting, they often have their fists clenched and held tightly in the center of their chest. Approaching from their head is ineffective. With this guy, it was a setup. Once we lift him to get to his hands, he would be able to reattack. We are taught to reach in from their side, along the inside of an elbow, and up to his hand. We encompass his clenched fist and pull it downward along the center of his body. This effectively bends his wrist backward, which hurts.

I was just beginning to realize that this guy was unusually strong, built like a weight lifter. He had very muscular shoulders and arms. I was no weakling either, and I had leverage advantage, with at least as much adrenalin flowing. When he resisted my effort to bend his right wrist, I pulled progressively harder and upward while holding him down with my knee on his lower back. He eventually released his arm, and I put it on his back, holding it with both hands and one knee. Bob pulled his second hand to a point that I could grab it. I took out my handcuffs. He still struggled, but I was able to get the handcuffs on.

I kept my knee in his back and looked around to assess the room. The other officers were interviewing the other participants. We stood him up. He struggled some, but we thought his fight was over, so Bob went to assist the other officers. I directed him toward the stairs. He started trying to kick me. I held him down, pulling on the handcuffs, a technique that usually works. By pressing them down with more weight, they need to keep their feet more firmly planted. This guy was strong enough to stand on one leg and hold my entire weight too. I pushed him toward the stairs.

We stumbled around the toppled chairs and tables. As we approached the stairs, his kicking became more intense. He kicked my shins several times. It hurt. Pressure on his wrist was ineffective in discouraging him. I was making progress toward the stairs, but I realized that I would not be able to safely get him down the stairs if his fight continued. I considered my authority to use whatever force is necessary to make the arrest. I saw the wall at the top of the stairs. I can keep my anger in check and function logically. My actions were deliberate. He was hurting me with all his might. I needed to gain control for both our safeties. With his hands cuffed behind him, I drove him face-first into the wall. It was effective. He stopped kicking. Then I got the "Oh, shit, who's watching?" thought.

With the expectation of having to answer to complaints of police brutality, I looked around the room. This was the first time that I gained an appreciation for how crowded the bar was. People were lined shoulder to shoulder all around the outer walls of the room. I felt doomed. Much to my surprise, everyone started clapping and cheering. I felt absolved.

The wall stunning effect on my prisoner was temporary. He resumed trying to break my grip on him and kick me. John joined me and took the other arm, and we forced him down the stairs. The stairs only reduced the frequency of his attempts to kick us as we stumbled down together. Once outside, I pressed down more upon him and pushed him fast enough to reduce the attempts, but he continued through the alley to the police station.

When we passed through the door into the police station, John and I could no longer be on each side of him. He took advantage of this. Since I was reasonably guarding his kicks, he abruptly turned and managed to get a high kick toward John's head. This is deadly force. I acted almost on reflex to protect John, pulling him from being off balance from that high kick and to the floor inside the police station, just out of the camera view. I held him on his side and pressed my knee into the side of his abdomen so that I knew it hurt. I also knew that his side with my weight on the handcuffs partially under him must hurt. I placed my fingers on his throat, gently squeezing and releasing his trachea. I then place my face close to his ear and said with a low growl, "If you kick me one more time, you are going to die." As I said this, I continued flexing my grip on his throat, still gently.

Only John saw this. I wasn't proud of it, but I felt that I had to do something to stop this all-out battle. I am sure that John had seen much worse from other officers, just as I have. Much to my surprise, I obtained complete compliance after this. We brought him down the elevator to the processing room.

He identified himself as Blane Richards. He remained calm and cooperated through all the processing. He explained his relationship to a former police officer. Ted was his stepfather. I had heard of Ted's reputation. He was a large man and had many complaints of police brutality. He eventually left the department. We all assumed it was about his brutality but officially reported from the "Sugar Shack incident." He and other officers were drunk, driving a jeep on the snowmobile trails. They crashed into a warming hut called the Sugar Shack and destroyed it. It was also rumored that Ted was brutal with Blane during his teenage years.

I brought five charges, including assault, resisting arrest, disorderly conduct, damage to my glasses and torn pants. I called for bail, which was personal recognizance, and released him. His arraignment was in two weeks.

In court, I noticed Blane was wearing a cast on his right arm, the one that I pulled. I knew that he was strong and resisted all he could. I didn't think that I broke his arm, but I did. When his case was called, he stood with his lawyer. The lawyer spoke, "Your honor, we wish to change our plea to guilty on all charges." The judge ordered a one-hundred-dollar fine on each of the five charges, six months in jail suspended on good behavior, and nearly five hundred dollars in restitution for my broken glasses and torn pants, payable to the Claremont Police Department. I was satisfied. Blane paid his fines and restitution in full immediately after court. The city reimbursed me. This protects my privacy so that he would not learn of my bank account through his canceled check.

I had another interesting experience with Blane five years later. I transferred to the public works department. I made this transfer for a variety of reasons, one of which was it fit better into my science and management education and my leadership experience. As the water and sewer superintendent, I advertised for a vacant position in the workforce. It is a highly sought position due to its competitive pay and benefits. Blane walked into the office and past the secretary, who tried her best to intercept him. He came directly into my office and sat in the chair in front of my desk. I recognized him immediately and assured the secretary that it was OK.

Blane said, "Do you remember me?" I replied, "Yes." He seemed a little disappointed but asked, "Any chance for me to get this job?" I replied, "No chance in hell." As he stood, Blane said, "I didn't think so." He walked out of the office.

I can be very forgiving for what he did to me. The problem I had was how he would interact with the other city employees and the public. He has an explosive temper and quickly jumps into physical conflict during an argument. I didn't want to expose coworkers to violence, who worked together well. The employees who knew him supported my decision.

Working with the Secret Service

New Hampshire's first-in-the-nation primary status brought many presidential candidates to our state. Many even came to Claremont. I became involved in some of the security. A few Secret Service agents came a few days early to look at the facilities, traffic patterns, and emergency services and coordinate with local law enforcement. A few hours before the arrival of the candidate, the Secret Service arrived in command. They were very polite and respectful but left no doubt who was in charge. They carefully planned the arrival and departure routes, which were different. They planned alternative routes with equal detail. They planned emergency evacuation methods by air and car. First responders and all three area hospitals were placed on alert. I was proud to be a part of it.

Most of the time, I was assigned an area along the route. I would see the black limousine but could not see the candidate inside. I got a much more exciting role when Jesse Jackson came to the city. He came to the high school and spoke with the students and staff. Just before his arrival, there was a huge influx of people to attend, press, and protestors. News vans filled the street around the school, and helicopters were flying above.

My designated place was to guard the hallway in the high school through which Reverend Jackson would enter the assembly. I was dressed in plain clothes, a sport coat covering my service weapon and radio to our dispatch. Our communications with the Secret Service was through our dispatch with an agent in the dispatch center. I stood alone in this hallway. Others guarded the entrances on each end of it. I stood with uncertain anticipation.

Suddenly, I saw a mass of people all wearing black suits enter the hallway. I recognized Reverend Jackson in the center of six people. Though he walked briskly with his protectors past my position, I was most impressed when he turned toward me, smiled, and thanked me. I was too surprised to give an intelligent response.

I listened to Reverend Jackson's speech. I remember his great compassion for all people. Reverend Jackson left by a different planned route. That was the closest that I ever got to protecting a presidential candidate.

I knew that it was not the time that we would elect a black president, especially one so outspoken. People were just too afraid of a minority coming to power. I was happy that Jesse Jackson was well received by the crowd, with many cheers and applause. Walter Mondale got the democratic nomination. Ronald Reagan was reelected. Since then, I have listened to Reverend Jackson and grew to admire him, his honesty, boldness, and genuine concern for everyone.

Thefts from Cars

One of the more frustrating things is catching those who steal things from cars. They can hit several cars in a small area, then walk away. The greatest deterrent is locking the car. It's frustrating to find so many people fail to lock their cars. Occasionally, thieves break windows. They do this most often when something very valuable is visible from the outside. Valuables should be in the trunk or at least out of sight.

Most frustrating is that I have caught people who I am certain are trying to steal from cars. One I caught was walking down the street and would bend over and shine a flashlight into the car as he walked by. He seemed to be especially looking for cars with keys left in the ignition. What's frustrating is that there is nothing illegal about shining flashlights into a parked car. At best, I can stop and question, just to try and discourage him.

Another time, I was dispatched to a take a report of a stolen radar detector. I found the middle-aged man standing by his car at the address. He described the radar detector with some uncertainty, which is not unusual. Few people have perfect memories of their things and can't find the owner's manual. I looked for any damage done to the car. He said that he had left the window open, making easy access for a thief. Another thing we record is the value of the stolen object. For it to be a crime, the object must have value. Another reason is we like to track the data of the value of stolen articles and the value that is recovered. It's data that is reported in our monthly report and to the state for their data tracking.

When I asked this victim the value of the radar detector, he replied, "I don't really know." When I expressed some doubt, he added, "I bought it from some kid for ten dollars."

I couldn't resist laughing. He seemed annoyed with me. I explained that he bought a stolen radar detector. The kid sold him a stolen radar detector and returned to steal it and sell it again. I told him that it would be highly unlikely that I would be able to find it and return it to him.

We also had a problem of thefts from cars in the shopping plazas. The best we could do is to watch these plazas for people walking among the cars. One night, I found a car driving from row to row. It wasn't looking for a parking space as it drove by several. The proactive thing is to stop the car and at least identify who is driving and possibly others in the car.

When I was temporarily assigned to the detective division, I was working on a bunch of stereos, CBs (citizens band radios), and radar detectors. I was manually comparing serial numbers, model numbers, and descriptions since the computer technology hadn't been fully developed. One of these radar detectors was recovered from a troubling youth, the son of a local businessman. He felt some privilege. He was also in one of those cars that I stopped patrolling the plazas. I was confident that the radar detector he requested to be returned to him was stolen. I just couldn't prove it. I assumed the person never reported it. We can't solve crimes unless people report them.

I expressed my frustration to the supervising detective, Walt Beam. I had lots of respect for him as he seemed knowledgeable and professional all the time I worked with him in the patrol division. When I said that I was going to have to give it back to the thief, his recommendation crushed my concept of his integrity. He replied, "Unless you can find someone to lie and say it's his."

This comment stunned me. I had no reply. I returned it to my suspected thief. I would have to wait for another day to find a chargeable offense.

Please Not in Front of My Kids

I had been involved with Dennis for several years since he was twelve years old. He was involved in many things, such as truancy, shoplifting, stealing from cars, and was suspected in several burglaries. Every time I went to arrest him, he wasn't at home. Often, it was because they didn't live there anymore. I would eventually find him on the streets. Every time it was a chase, and when I caught him, he tried to resist. He was small but fought his hardest to get away. Like most, he never tried to hurt me; he just didn't want to get caught.

No one in Dennis's family or their friends valued education. Most didn't even make it into junior high school. None ever came close to graduating from high school. Their vocational skills were simple, such as painting. They didn't work regular forty-hour shifts for very long. It was too long and tedious for them. It's very hard to impress on their kids, like Dennis, how important it is to go to school and prepare for a vocation. They lived very much in the moment. Their lives were very unstable.

Dennis soon grew into adulthood. He was nineteen now, and there was a warrant for his arrest. His last-known residence was a second-floor apartment on North Street. Remembering and expecting to have to chase him if I found him, I parked the car around the corner, out of immediate view of that apartment. It was dark, so it was easier to make the police car less obvious.

The stairs to the apartment were on the outside. I walked quietly up the stairs to the entrance. The door had a large window, providing a good view into the kitchen. I looked through the window and saw Dennis sitting at the head of the table, less than five feet from me. They were eating dinner. A woman sat at the side of the table. There was a small child sitting in the chair between them. There was another child in a high chair close to the woman.

Dennis noticed me immediately when I tapped on door. His expression was surprise first, then seemed odd calmness. I was ready to give chase but didn't get signals that he was going to run. Instead, he invited me in. Dennis introduced me to his girlfriend and her kids as he stood. He asked, "You want me to come with you?" I replied, "Yes." Dennis then asked, "Can we not do this in front of my kids?"

I thought for a moment and looked into his eyes. I thought about all those times I chased him, his struggles to get away from me, and that I eventually got him to the police station. While processing, we always had a pleasant discussion. I had always encouraged him to get some education, develop some skills, earn a living in a way that is consistent with societal expectations. He listened. He always had excuses why he couldn't. He did show me respect as we differed. I was remembering this part of him and realizing that I have never seen him in any stable relationship in his home until now. He may still be committing crimes, but he is making progress for himself and people who cared for him. This is more than I have ever seen with him.

Dennis was serious when he said that he would meet me outside if I would let him. To do so is contrary to all my training. He could not only attempt an escape, he may have a weapon somewhere and get it to use against me. Still, I wanted to trust him and agreed. I told him to take a minute with his family, and I would meet him by the car.

As I waited, I continued to wonder if I had done the right thing. Less than two minutes passed, and Dennis came down the stairs. Since I had the car out of sight of the apartment, I knew that we were out of sight of the kids. Dennis was cooperating. I still wondered if this would last. Department policy was that all prisoners should be handcuffed before placing them in the car. I felt that I had stretched procedures far enough so far and handcuffed him.

It was a short ride to the police station. Dennis immediately thanked me for not handcuffing him in front of the kids and letting him say goodbye. As I processed him at the station, we talked about how things were going for him. He explained that the warrant was for a burglary he participated in months ago. He had a job, cleaning businesses after hours. He has been with this girlfriend since before the youngest was born. The kids aren't his, but he feels like they are.

I completed the processing feeling good about how Dennis seemed to be finally getting what we had been discussing and now hearing it from someone who cares for him. I also know that if something goes wrong, like his girlfriend leaving him, all progress could be lost. Nonetheless, I maintained hope that he would continue and be strong enough to keep it together during life's normal struggles.

Police have a lot of influence on establishing bail. Bail has two purposes. Primarily, it is to assure the defendant's appearance in court. The secondary consideration is for public safety. Had Dennis resisted or tried to run away, we would ask for a high bail. I called the bail commissioner and asked for personal recognizance. The bail commissioner knew Dennis as I have. He remembered all those times he resisted arrest and didn't show up for hearings. With Dennis sitting beside me, I looked at him and said to the commissioner that he had changed, had a job, and was supporting a family. I explained that it was an old charge, and Dennis surrendered without incident. He reluctantly accepted my recommendation.

I followed Dennis's case through the courts. Dennis wasn't directly involved in the burglary. He participated more in using the stolen objects. The charges were eventually dropped as it was difficult to prove that he knew the objects were stolen, though we knew he did know.

I never saw Dennis get involved in any more criminal activity. I saw him a few times, and he always greeted me very pleasantly and told me things are good. When I see someone who greets me and tells me how well things are going, I accept what they say and feel good. When they see me and avoid eye contact, I assume that things are not going well for them.

Party Crasher

As we patrol around town, we take note of where there are gatherings. I always paid closer attention to the more densely populated areas of town. If it's a large gathering at a downtown apartment building, it's likely we'll get a call later. Usually, it's a loud noise complaint, but it can be other reasons, such as a fight or to remove an unwanted person.

I noticed that an apartment building near the beginning of Washington Street had many more cars than usual and the upstairs apartment was well lighted. It wasn't one of our usual but had the potential. Later that night, the call came. I was surprised that it wasn't for loud noise. It was for a man that fell over the bank and was hurt.

The Sugar River runs close behind these apartments. Its bank is very steep. As I drove to it, I started considering scenarios for a man falling over the bank. I thought that it may have happened during a fight or maybe someone pushed him. I was wrong on all accounts.

I got there as the ambulance arrived. It was easy to find him. He certainly saw out lights and called for help. We found Marty about halfway down the thirty-foot bank. The brush was thick and hard to move through. Getting down to him without sliding into him or getting hurt ourselves was a real challenge. The EMT gear and backboard made it even more challenging.

We got to him with no additional injuries. I stood by while the EMTs checked him out. He complained about his neck and back. I knew then that we were going to have to carry him out on that backboard. Marty was of average height but had a noticeably large belly, so I knew he wasn't going to be light. The EMTs weren't in the greatest shape either. I called dispatch and asked for assistance from rescue, the fire department response team.

As they worked on him, the EMTs asked how he got into this predicament. Marty explained that there were a lot of people in the apartment. It wasn't his apartment. He was one of the guests. The apartment had only one bathroom, and it was busy. He had to "take a piss real badly," so he decided to pee over the bank. He said it was because it was dark. I expected it was likely also because he was very drunk. Whatever the reason, he took one step too many and fell down the bank. As they sought a better understanding of his injuries, they asked about his fall. He went face-first, then rolled "head over heels." They asked if he still needed to urinate. He said no. He explained that he had already started before he took that extra step and fell.

Rescue arrived. The large truck with even more flashing lights got Marty's attention, and he asked, "Who's here now?" He didn't realize that I had called for them while he was talking to the EMTs.

I said, "It's the fire department." He asked, "Why are they here?" I explained that we would need their help to get him up the bank. He said, "That's OK, just as long as there are no f——ing cops."

In the dark, Marty couldn't see my uniform. He probably also didn't expect that a cop would work so closely with the EMTs. With little thought and wanting to respond to Marty's prejudices, I replied, "Just this f——ing cop that is going to help carry your fat ass up this hill."

Marty was stunned and a bit taken back. He said, "Oh, I'm sorry. I didn't mean anything." I assured him that I was not offended.

I developed an image in my mind to compensate for Marty's crassness. He's this fat guy who walks up to the end of the riverbank, unzips, reaches under his fat belly, aims, and starts urinating. Since he was drinking heavily, his bladder is extremely full, and since he is drunk, he staggers around some as he urinates. In the shuffling of his feet, he moves too close to the edge and starts to slip. He reacts, trying to right himself with the other foot, then slips. He starts to slide down the bank, still urinating. He tries to right himself but then falls face-first. Now he's tumbling in a forward rolling motion, still urinating. The urine would be making a stream into the air with each roll. I was thinking how hilarious it would have been. Imagining this scenario, I was certain that regardless of the actual details, this guy must have urine all over him. I was glad to take one corner of the backboard as we carried him up the hill and not having to touch him.

Marty checked out OK at the hospital, just bumps and bruises. He was able to return to the party.

Animals

No police officer likes dog calls. Nothing causes more friction between and among neighbors than their dogs, and we are being dragged into it. Dog owners think of their precious dog as a member of the family. The extreme ones believe their dog can do no harm as a family member and fault their neighbors for intolerance. They don't seem to realize that a dog is a dog without the attributes that make us human. When the dog challenges neighbors, he is doing his canine job, protecting his family. That loving, never-will-hurt-anyone member of the family will attack a perceived threat. Two or more dogs develop an exponentially greater pack mentality. Dogs also do not understand property lines.

All animals are only animals. There's a fable of a scorpion and a fox. The scorpion persuades the reluctant fox to carry it across the stream. The scorpion promises the fox that it will not sting in exchange for the ride. Halfway across the stream, the scorpion stings the fox. As the fox sinks from the effects of the poison, it asks the scorpion, "Why did you sting me? Now we will both die." The scorpion replies, "I couldn't help it. It is my nature."

Anthropomorphizing is giving human characteristic to animals. People who see their pet as a member of the family attribute family characteristics and values onto an animal. They have great difficulty accepting that it is still just an animal with its basic behaviors.

There are state laws and city ordinances about animals. Dogs as a menace, leash laws, and licensing requirements are apparently straightforward. However, judges want people to be notified before they are brought into their courtroom. So the Claremont police have established a procedure. First call, they give a verbal warning. Second call, they give a written dog abatement order. Third call is a summons to court. The problem is that this procedure doesn't differentiate among annoying barks, defecating on the lawn, or a vicious attack. A single dog can be problematic, which seems to be the basis of this procedure. The procedure is fine for barking and trespassing dogs. It doesn't apply well to two or more dogs that take on a pack mentality and can be far more dangerous. Small wonder that dogs mauling someone, even their owner, is a surprise and believed impossible by their loving family member.

Another factor that the police with whom I have worked encounter is people ask for the identity of the complainant. The standard response is to refuse to identify the complainant. Realistically, the beat cop doesn't know. The caller is known by the dispatcher, but the name is not transmitted by radio. By not identifying the complainant, the responding officer has no credibility to the complaint they are delivering. Properly challenged, the complaint is invalid without a verifiable complainant. The responding officer has a bluff at best. Without a victim, there is no legal standing. Citizens have a right to face their accusers.

There are often calls about dogs when no one is home. In these cases, the first step of the three-step process has not begun. The same problem arises if the dog owner refuses to answer the door. At least, the officer can make some observations and can validate the complaint, if she or he chooses to make the effort to record these observations. Remember, no one likes dog calls and would like nothing more than to dispense the call as quickly and easily as possible. This is a disservice to the taxpayers as dogs are the greatest problem in neighbor relations. I have even heard police officers report the case as "unfounded." "Unfounded" means the officer investigated and found the complaint had no merit when they simply didn't find the dog running free.

Cops can become a victim in these calls. I was never bitten but have been close. Several officers shot dogs that attacked them. The most vicious attack I had was from a black dog late one night. We had several calls from the neighborhood. When I arrived, the house was dark. As soon as I got out of the car, I was challenged by a large black dog, barking loudly, with lips rolled back exposing the teeth. I tried to get it into the back of the police car, but it wouldn't cooperate. Often, dogs like to ride and will jump into the police car, giving me a chance to control it. It continued its vicious challenge, and I could neither capture it nor escape it. I did not want to shoot it. There are always bad public repercussions from killing a dog, especially on its owner's property. I tried to fight it off with my flashlight.

The problem was that each time I pulled my arm back to prepare a strike, it ducked. I tried several times to strike the dog to get safely away from it but missed each time. Finally, for no understandable reason, the dog ran off. I left a note on the owner's door but never heard from them. So this dog problem continued unresolved.

There was a time that coaxing dogs into the car worked very well. I had a call of three Dobermans running about a neighborhood and scaring everyone. The complainants identified the house from which the dogs escaped and added that the owners were not home. When I arrived, the three Dobermans immediately challenged me in the street. I looked at the house and saw that the dogs had jumped through a window, breaking the glass and screen. I opened the back door of the police car and whistled, saying, "Come on." Much to my surprise, the dogs' viciousness immediately subsided, and they ran into my car. I then left a note on the owner's door, saying that the police had their dogs.

There was no way that I would be able to get a rope on three active dogs in the back of a police car. I decided to bring them to a jail cell. I drove into the sally port. With the garage door closed behind me, I let the dogs out of the car. They were much friendlier inside the building. They happily followed me through the processing area and into a cell. I was able to lock them in.

The owners came after a couple of hours to collect their dogs. They were somewhat privileged in that they avoided the kennel charge. They had more serious problems to repair the damage and to decide how to contain these dogs that have learned to jump through a closed window.

Another time, I was attempting to serve a warrant on someone. I knocked on a porch door, and a small dog started barking from inside the porch. No one came to the door. Many people do not hear the knocking on a porch door, and it is necessary to go to the inner door. When I entered the porch, the little dog attacked me. Being so small, it couldn't bite through my boot or reach about it. I was able to brush it away. It was a determined, dumb animal and kept coming. Each time I brushed it away with the side of my boot, it returned. I didn't feel much danger as it was only able to bite my boot, not higher. There was still no answer, so I left a note on the door. As I left, the dog increased its vicious attack. I brushed it harder than usual, sliding it all the way across the porch. This gave me a chance to escape the porch. I thought about this dog like an annoying mosquito. It was as persistent as a mosquito with barking instead of buzzing and biting with teeth instead of sucking blood.

I encountered the absolute opposite of this ankle biter during a different call. I responded to a home to take a report of a stolen lawn ornaments. I knocked on the door. A man said, "Come in." It was bright sun outside, and the house was dark inside. I could barely see my way as my eyes adjusted to the change. Just as the door closed behind me, a large Great Dane appeared in front of me. It jumped up and, like Marmaduke, placed both front paws on my shoulders. It was taller than me. Its head was huge. He was so large that I couldn't hardly see around him. I know Great Danes are mostly friendly. I was aware that a pair of Great Danes had chased down and partially ate a ten-year-old boy in England a few years earlier, so I also knew they could be vicious. I felt this one was being friendly. Police also need to be on guard even in places that appear to be benign. I assessed the dog as likely harmless and overly friendly. I couldn't assess the safety of the house with him blocking my view, so I was still a little uneasy. I heard the man speak. He was sitting at the kitchen table a few feet farther into the house. He laughed and said, "He does that to everyone." I could see better now, felt relieved, and gently removed his paws from my shoulders, lowering him to the floor. I pat him and scratched around his ears and back that was up to my waist. I was set up for this overwhelming affection, which I didn't mind. I enjoyed the remainder of my time with this huge dog and his master. We never found his missing lawn ornaments.

One of my fellow officers, Bradley, told me about an encounter he had when he killed a dog. The complainant described a vicious dog that kept circling their house. Bradley observed this behavior and described the dog's aggressive posture, bared teeth, hair on its back up, tail straight out. Officer Bradley shouted and waved his arms at it, but the dog's aggressive behavior continued. I was suspicious that I could explain this behavior and asked, "Did the caller have a bitch in heat?" He was surprised that I asked and said that she did. The dog was on a chain on the yard. I inquired further, "Was the other dog a male?" Again, Bradley confirmed my suspicion. I told Bradley that the male dog was only doing what male dogs do when there is a bitch in heat. I joked that the dog saw him as a competitor to mate with the bitch. The problem could have been easily resolved by bringing the female dogs in the house and waiting a few minutes for the male dog to calm down.

We also got calls about farm animals loose in the road. These can be a serious hazard to motorists. A notable call was about a pig that was in the road. My grandfather raised pigs, and I spent the summers on his farm, so I understood their intelligence and their stubborn nature. I also know that they can be dangerous.

I didn't see the pig as I drove up to the Stocker Farm. I knew this John Stocker and had confidence that he would take care of it if he knew. I stopped at the farmhouse. I parked the Ford Crown Victoria police car in the driveway and walked the fifty feet to the door. Not surprising, there was no answer. I wrote a note that his pig was loose and in the road, then placed it on the door. I turned around, and there was the pig between me and the car. I heard stories from my grandfather about how big his boars used to get when he bred them before I was born. Some weighed eight hundred pounds. I had never seen one that big until this day. The Crown Victoria with police suspension sits high. This pig's back was several inches taller than the hood of the car. It was more than half the length of this full-sized car. It also had testicles like a half basketball hanging from its rear. It watched me as I approached and started a low growling grunt.

I have been in a pen with pigs that weighed two hundred to two hundred fifty pounds. I could push them away. I knew to be careful as they bite very differently than a dog. A dog will bite by coming straight at you. A pig's snout is in the way. They get their best bite on you by turning the head sideways at you. Pigs are also omnivores. They eat everything. Farmers know not to place the pig pen next to chickens because they will eat them.

I stopped as soon as I saw this huge boar between me and the safety of the police car. I had no safe alternatives close enough should he charge me. I was also too far away from headquarters for my portable radio. I was feeling somewhat confident knowing that the .357 Magnum that I was carrying could stop a charging bull. I waited, watching the boar's body language. It seemed to be enjoying a day out and searching for new varieties of food. There wasn't much to eat here, and it continued its slow steady pace, smelling for other food. I calmly walked around it and got into the car, much relieved. I only worried that it might go back into traffic. If someone hit it, it would demolish their car and likely seriously hurt the occupants. There wasn't much that I could do.

In the springtime, when the river water was high, we often saw beavers and muskrats moving to new locations. One night, Mike and I watched a large muskrat walking down North Street late one evening. Mike had never seen one before. This was a special treat due to its unusually large size. As it walked along the edge of the road, a cat approached it, then stopped in the center of the road. The cat was crouched as cats do when they are ready to pounce on its prey. The funny thing was that this muskrat was twice the size of the cat. My partner and I watched from our police cars and started to make a bet. Unfortunately, we both bet on the muskrat. So we decided to bet on whether the cat would be dumb enough to attack it. This went on for several minutes. The muskrat continued its unsteady start, stop, and waddle pace. The cat remained crouched as if to be hiding in the middle of the road. Occasionally, the cat advanced to remain in striking distance of its prey. Finally, my partner said, "I just want to beat that rat." I said, "I want to beat that stupid cat," though I really wanted to see it regret an attack. Finally, the muskrat made it to the intersection of the street and river. When it went out of sight in the shrubs, the cat turned and ran in the other direction. Perhaps it felt that it had successfully protected its territory.

Another night during this season, Officer Jim Doyen assigned to the opposite beat from me received a call about a beaver in someone's garage. The dispatcher added that the beaver was being aggressive. The Jim signed off on the call. I listened with interest. I have a bachelor's degree in biology, so I tend to prefer letting natural things return to their environment as much as possible. We humans are the intruders in their natural world, building in natural nesting sites. After a few minutes, the officer called the supervisor. He asked for permission to shoot the beaver as it wouldn't leave and was being threatening. The supervisor gave the permission. I asked for a chance to solve the problem. I was given a temporary stay on the beaver's execution.

When I arrived, I saw Jim standing in the center of an open garage door with his car in the driveway directly behind him. I parked in the street, a few feet from the driveway. When I walked up to the door, the average-sized beaver was against the far wall. It was chattering rather intimidatingly and moved back and forth against this wall. It stopped periodically to intensify its threatening sounds, raising its head and showing its very large teeth. Jim said, "See, there's no way except to shoot it."

I told him that the beaver feels trapped and is doing what trapped animals do. They defend themselves as best they can. Jim agreed with me but still saw no solution other than to kill it. I asked him to move his car into the street and stand back. A clear path to escape was now available. I suggested to the homeowner that the animal would find its own way out if we just left it alone. The home-owner was not at all willing to consider this option. I said, "Stand back so that it can't see you." I approached the open garage door but as close to one corner as possible. The beaver protested loudly, raising its head and looking at me. I walked slowly into the garage along one side. I made slow steady steps. The beaver went to the corner farthest from me. As I continued, the beaver's protests became fewer and less intense. When I got just beyond the halfway point, it darted for the open door. I was a little surprised that it didn't go across the driveway, which would have been directly to the river. Instead, it turned and ran behind the house. It had a clear path to the edge of the wooded area. I suspect that it was being driven out of its home along the river, which is why it went in another direction. It would also explain why it unintentionally ended up in the garage.

Racoons are also frequent violators of human concepts of peaceful coexistence. They like to go dumpster diving. Unfortunately, they can't always climb back out. We get called when someone brings their trash to the dumpster and gets frightened by the racoon scurrying among the trash. My preferred solution was to find something as much like a tree branch as possible and place it in the dumpster. I would then leave and let the racoon climb out. To be certain, I would come back later to make sure that it made its escape. It worked most of the time.

Sometimes I couldn't find a branch, or the racoon wouldn't climb out. Perhaps it was too frightened or lacked the intelligence to figure it out. Most residential dumpsters are small enough to tip over. If I had a reluctant racoon or couldn't find anything for it to climb on, I just tipped the dumpster over. The racoon remained hidden in the trash but, left alone, would eventually scurry off.

The biologist in me favored the wild animal. Humans invaded their world and offered free lunches. Even we wouldn't pass up free food. Late at night, I would pass the time watching racoons at the banquet tables around the city. We humans call these trash cans. Burger King is located on the busy commercial Washington Street with the forest behind it. Racoons loved Burger King. Unlike the police who got half-off privileges, racoons got their dinner for free. The only problem, the racoons were very messy and scattered trash around all the trash cans. I often wondered why Burger King didn't take up all the trash before they closed. I found out when a manager called me one evening.

The restaurant manager requested extra patrol at night because he felt it was vandals who spread the trash at night. I laughed and told him that it was racoons. He didn't believe me. He felt that their heavy, concrete containers made it impossible for animals to do such a thing. I assured him that it was no deterrent to the raccoons and suggested that he watch some night to dispel any doubts. Now convinced, he asked for the police to shoot them. I said that the police would not and told him to just take up the trash when they closed. He said that the company policy was that employees do not go outside after dark. I told him that he would have to contend with the trash in the morning so long as they maintained this policy. I suggested that they could amend their policy requiring that no one goes out alone after dark. He said that he would have to seek corporate approval. I told him that it's his problem and not a police problem. I offered Fish and Game services from the state, adding that they would likely suggest the same. Score one for the racoons.

Skunks are another frequent critter problem. I had several close encounters and was very fortunate to never had been sprayed. I attribute it to being as much of a surprise to the skunk as it was to me. One dark rainy night, a skunk suddenly appeared in my headlights. I slammed on the breaks, skidding the car. I realized that I would not stop in time and then reacted to reduce the contact time and the amount of spray on the car. I floored the accelerator, spinning the tires. I passed directly over the skunk. I heard it tumbling against the floorboards. I started thinking how I would get the smell out of the car.

I looked in the rearview mirror after clearing the skunk. I saw it hobble away in its typical skunk way, seemingly unhurt. I waited for the intense odor that never came. My luck was with me that night. I was even more lucky another night.

Prowlers in a backyard are common calls. If you respond with lights and siren, the prowler will be long gone before you get there. Even the blue lights can be seen from a great distance at night. The siren can be heard all over the city. I never used the siren for simple prowler complaints and turned off the blue lights far in advance of arriving on the scene. I also parked one or two houses down the street and ran into the caller's backyard. I waited until the latest possible time to turn on my flashlight. My night vision was good coupled with—I don't mind—uneven ground and crashing into minor obstacles. I left my gun holstered with my right hand ready to draw, if necessary. Still, I rarely caught the culprit. When I did catch them, it was usually a racoon or a neighbor's dog.

One night, I was feeling particularly happy about my response. I ran down the sidewalk and along the side of the caller's house and into the backyard. I ran around the corner of the house and into the backyard. Just as I was getting ready to turn on my flashlight, I tripped over something soft. It moved as I fell into a forward roll over it. I came up out of my roll facing in the direction of what tripped me, simultaneously turning on my flashlight. I illuminated a skunk that was now only about four feet from me. It ran back and forth and circled around. I backed up as quickly as I could, keeping my light on it. The skunk seemed to get its bearings from being unexpectantly rolled over and blinded by the bright light, then ran off. Lucky again, I went to the front door and knocked. The caller answered. I explained that I found a skunk in his backyard. I was too embarrassed to share that I had tripped over it.

A couple of my fellow officers told me how they entertained themselves with skunks. They would bring a BB gun with them and look for a skunk in a neighborhood they didn't like. They would then shoot the skunk with the BB gun until it sprayed, left, and drove away.

I have twice been attacked by a farmer's bird. One was a turkey; another was a goose. Geese are known by many to be very aggressive. Sometimes they attack as a group. Often, there's one that takes the lead. They charge with their necks low and extended, honking and hissing while opening and closing their bill as if biting before they get to you. A goose's bite is only a hurtful pinch because they have no teeth and their bills are rounded. To "get goosed" is to get pinch in the buttocks, which is a common practical joke played among farmers' children.

I'll take a goose attack any day over being attacked by a turkey. Turkeys will fly up at your head. They peck hard with their sharp beaks, beat you with their wings, and claw at you with their feet. It's a far more vicious attack than a goose attack, though geese can be quite effective too. I remember one delivery truck driver recount a turkey attack, "I was never so scared in my life."

I grew up on farms and often encountered geese and turkeys. What I learned from my grandfather paid off as a police officer. To stop the attacking fowl, make a quick grab for its neck. Try to grasp it a few inches below its head, but getting a firm grip is more important than a precise location. Once you got the bird's neck in your hand, expect it to thrash violently. It's important to maintain your hold. Pulling it close to your body will help reduce its thrashing. With the other hand, cover the bird's eyes. It will still thrash around a bit but will start to calm down. Though it may greatly reduce its effort to fight, it will not likely completely submit. Releasing the animal with a push away will usually result in its running off in protest. Sometimes it will resume its attack. Repeating the process will persuade it to strut its dominance some other place.

Bats are very different and require great care not to get bit as they have a high incidence of rabies. You should always assume a warm-blooded animal acting out of character has rabies or distemper. Both are serious diseases that transmit to humans and our pets. The best way to deal with a bat that has gotten into a house is to open doors and windows and step back. If it has landed somewhere, you'll likely have to coax it into flight. Be sure to leave a clear path to the open door. Only when there is no other alternative, a bat can be wrapped in a towel and brought outside. Be very careful not to hurt its wings. Its survival depends on being able to fly and catch its food. If you kill a bat, Fish and Game will want the carcass to examine it for rabies and fungal infections.

A mouse can be gathered up in your bare hands, but wear gloves if you want. Mice can't open their mouths wide enough with their nose in the way to bite you. Just keep your fingers together so it doesn't have access to the webbing between your fingers, which it can bite. Mice don't have rabies because any rabid animal that would infect them eats them. Mice can't bite, but you better be certain it's a mouse. Shrews and moles can bite you. Worse yet, shrews have a poisonous bite. They are one of the few poisonous mammals in the world and the only one in North America. They need to eat every few hours or they will starve, typically dying of hypothermia because they need a steady supply of food to maintain their body temperature even in the summertime. They constantly hunt for this reason, whether they are hungry or not. They will bite and poison their prey and store it in varied cubbies. This way, when hunting is less productive, they have stored reserves.

There was a directive that the police cars were to be washed on Sunday mornings. I didn't mind washing the car and did it whenever it was dirty and I had time. Like most of us, I didn't like the directive, being told when to do it. Worse yet, on one Sunday, the person who was going to relieve me and take this car was a jerk that I could barely tolerate. I did what was expected and washed the car. I then thought about how I could get it dirty and make it look like it just happened naturally as I did my work. As I drove through the center of town, I saw a particularly large flock of pigeons in front of the parking area in Tremont Square. Because I knew birds often lightened their load by dumping their waste loads upon taking to a panic flight, this could be the opportunity I wanted. As I entered the square, I sped up and took the turn wide into the center of the flock. The birds responded just as I had hoped they would, and I didn't hit any. The car got sufficient droppings and even on the windshield. I was thinking how proud I was and lucky to find this perfect concentration of pigeons. Then as I drove out of the square, I wondered why so many birds were so closely together. I looked in my rearview mirror. There was an unusual number of cars parked in the square for this early on a Sunday morning. Then it occurred to me that there were so many birds because people were feeding them. *Oh, crap*, I thought. Now I am going to get some complaints. Much to my relief, I never heard of any complaints. Maybe there were, and the administrators couldn't figure out who to blame or just didn't care.

Animal encounters are frequent with small city police work, but how to deal with them is not covered at the police academy. The only department policy is the dog abatement procedure.

Drunk on a Bench

Seems like some of my more interesting experiences were when I least wanted them. I was enjoying the nice weather on a Saturday afternoon when the dispatcher assigned to me a complaint of an intoxicated person on a bench on Broad Street. I thought that I could resolve this call quickly by just sending the person on his way. If necessary, I would give him a ride home; then I could return to enjoying the nice weather.

Broad Street is wide as the name implies. It has a large grassed area between the roadway and the sidewalk. The city had several benches in this grassed area. The street separates with a medium and has Broad Street Park dividing the two lanes near the city hall.

The dispatcher told me that it was the bench near the Moose Club. I drove down Summer Street by the high school and turned right onto Broad Street. I easily found the bench with a person lying facedown on it. As I parked the car, I noticed the person appeared to be a small woman.

I signed off and got out of the car. As I walked around the car, she called out to me with an exaggeratedly long "F——k you!" As I stepped onto the grass, I replied, "Sugar and spice and everything nice." It was my typical response to divert anger with women. It didn't work this time; she repeated her greeting even louder and longer. She added more inciteful language along with a few "pigs" interlaced in it.

I saw the open wine bottle in her left hand, under the bench, in violation of Claremont's open-container ordinance. She is not only in public, she is on city-owned property. I pointed this out to her, hoping to gain some compliance. I was standing beside her now. She replied, "I don't give a f——, you f——ing pig."

I warned her that she could not remain here and if she was not willing to move along, I would have to arrest her. I got only more profanity mixed with her clear intentions to remain. The dispatcher was vigilant and called to see if I was "all set." I responded that I was with my portable radio.

I gave my final warning and got a similar response. She was already facedown on the bench, so I grabbed the nearest wrist, the one with the wine bottle. I pressed the bottle out of her hand and lifted her wrist to her back where I applied the handcuff. She shouted profanities and tried to resist. Her size and state of intoxication left her unable to launch a successful escape. I moved slowly so as not to hurt her. She was trying to kick me. I stood her up. She tried to kick me some more. I was able to control her kicking by bearing some weight on her so that she needed to keep her feet on the ground.

I turned her toward the police car and gently pushed her in that direction. I held her to the right of me so she was unable to kick me. She was quite prolific with her obscenities and name-calling to me over her left shoulder, which could easily be heard by anyone nearby. My supervisor now called to check on my status. To answer him, I had to take out my portable radio. I was able to control her with my right hand. My original intention was to offer a quick reply that I was "all set." Something atypically devilish came over me. I placed the portable radio near her face, keyed it, and allowed a few seconds to transmit obscenities, knowing scanner land would enjoy it. I then gave a quick reply that I was "all set."

I suddenly heard sirens. I knew that it had to be my supervisor and the other patrol officer coming to my assistance. I felt guilty for my impulsive action and retransmitted an assurance that I was all set. My prisoner was now resisting with greater resolve. She extended her feet forward and pushed back against me. I grabbed her upper arms for better control. She was so small and light that I easily could pick her up and carry her to the police car. The dilemma was when I picked her up, she could kick me. It turned into a combination of pushing, lifting, and holding downward as we advanced to the police car.

Whenever an officer uses physical force on a citizen, it is wise to bring criminal charges. Police officers have no right to touch someone unless they are placing them under arrest or at least taking them into protective custody. I charged her with the open-container violation and resisting arrest. I would have gladly dropped these charges if she decided to become civil, but she didn't. She didn't want to call anyone to take her, so she spent the night in jail.

I was surprised that this case went to court. I expected the prosecutor to approach me with her apology and a request to drop the charges before court. Since she wished for a trial, I only wanted a suspended sentence. I left the stand, and she testified to her defense. She complained that she had bruises on her arms from where I beat her with the nightstick. She was seeking sympathy from the judge, and it seemed to be working. I reached over the bar, grabbed the prosecutor's shoulder, and demanded that he put me back on to rebut this claim. My personal reputation and integrity were being challenged.

I took the stand again. I explained that I did not, would not, and could not have beaten her with a baton. I explained that my baton remained in the car as it usually did. I added that the only time I have ever used it was to break windows in a car or to gain access to a building. The judge asked, "Then how do you explain the bruises on her arms?"

Of course, this hearing was weeks after the arrest, so any bruises would have healed. I replied to the judge's question, "If there were any bruises, I didn't know how she got them." I continued, "She struggled when resisting arrest. I grabbed her by her upper arms. Perhaps I grabbed hard enough that my fingers made those bruises." The judge found her guilty and fined her fifty dollars. Now she had a criminal record, and resisting arrest shows a violent history.

It's too bad that she didn't just comply from the beginning. I would have helped her get to a safe place had she cooperated. Now she has a criminal record. I would rather have enjoyed the sunshine.

Hanging on the Streets

A constantly impossible situation for police was the antagonistic relationship downtown businesses had with people who hang on the streets to socialize and meet friends. Granted, not everyone on the streets is there for benign reasons. Some are seeking an opportunity to commit a crime, but these are an extreme minority. I also recognize that the group appears unruly and likely to discourage some potential customers to walk past them to the businesses.

I remember a complaint one shopkeeper made about me to the chief. I lived in the downtown area at the time and walked to work. As I walked by one business, a shopkeeper stopped me and complained about a suspicious person hanging around the area. I explained to the shopkeeper that I carried neither radio nor service weapon and was on my way in to work. I asked her to call the dispatcher, and an officer on duty would respond. When I got to work, I asked the dispatcher if the shopkeeper called. She said that she had not. I asked the dispatcher to tell the patrol officer to make an extra sweep through the area.

The chief called me to his office the next day. He had what appeared to be a discipline action in his hand. He described the complaint from the shopkeeper and that I did nothing. The shopkeeper obviously expected me to seek out the individual. The chief's body language appeared to be that he was preparing to issue this action against me. I explained to the chief that I was on my way in to work. He didn't seem to back down. I then referred to the department policy forbidding off-duty officers from engaging as a police officer and that they must call for an on-duty officer. I told him to check the log because I relayed the complaint to the dispatcher. He paused for a minute, then agreed to call the shopkeeper, and explain the situation.

Foot patrols helped maintain order in the downtown area only when the officer was very active. If the officer stood reliably in one position, problems could arise in others. Police danced a fine line of keeping order to conservatives' expectations and individual rights of freedom.

A regulatory tool police used was loitering. One could be charged for loitering if they were at a place and time for no reasonable purpose. Judges did not like this charge. It required people to explain why they were in a public place. If they refused to disclose their purpose or their reason wasn't good enough in the police officer's judgment, they could be charged with loitering. Judges mostly found people innocent or dismissed the charge upon motion by an attorney. It encroached on citizens' basic freedoms. The judges preferred a charge of disorderly conduct. One would be disorderly for several reasons, including blocking the sidewalk or building entrances. Disorderly also covered loud and unreasonable noises, obscene and derisive language, and threats. It was a much better charge than loitering, which was eventually found to be unconstitutional.

The city passed ordinances that made it a violation to block business entrances or the entire sidewalk. They added ordinances to prevent bicycles, skateboards, and other such things on sidewalks in the downtown area. There were ample legal tools an officer could use on people causing any real problems in the downtown area. The difficulties were with the businesses that felt people just hanging around in front of their businesses deterred customers.

Some police officers tried various methods to appease the shopkeepers when there wasn't enough cause to arrest someone or to request that they move along. Officer Kent stood across the street from a group he felt were troublesome, drew his baton, and held it on his shoulder with his crossed arms while staring at them. His technique was to intimidate them into moving out of the area. It only increased the animosity between them and the police and the shopkeepers.

While on foot patrol one evening, I noticed Officer Vincent with a similar us-against-them-attitude driving frequency through my foot patrol area. It became obvious that he was monitoring a group of six teenagers. They spoke loudly, waved to friends in cars, and use language that some say is free speech while others find it offensive. This officer was obvious in his approach, as he drove on the opposite side of the street so that he could roll down his window and glare with his head partially out the window. I didn't see anything wrong with their behavior, so I did nothing to intervene, yet this officer kept driving by in this manner every few minutes. Finally, someone in the group said something to him that I couldn't hear. He suddenly turned the car into the lane opposing traffic and into the parking spaces, facing the wrong way. I could hear him say, "What did you call me?" Again, I could not hear what the person said, but I heard the officer's response, "Don't make me have to get out of this car." To describe this officer as a jerk would be kind. I didn't have a great relationship with this officer. My gut response was a desire to say to him, "Get out of the car if you want, but you may regret it." He eventually drove off.

As time went on, I reflected a lot on police working directly with the community. My substitute teaching helped a lot, and I got to know many of these young folks who spent so much time on the street in a very different environment. I started to mingle with the groups for short periods of times. I developed short friendly conversations yet didn't remain too long to respect their rights to be free from police interference. With this relationship, when a shopkeeper complained, I could go to the group and explain why the shopkeeper felt that they were discouraging his or her business. In every case, they were very understanding and changed their behavior or moved to another area.

I had some interesting conversations with some groups. I asked one group of young men why they spent so much time standing on the street. His response was that they were hoping to meet girls. I chuckled and said, "So you are looking for a girl that would pick up a guy off the street." He thought about it for a second and saw my point. He then said that they had nothing else to do and blamed the people of Claremont for not having anything for them to do. I would challenge this reasoning. It is not for the taxpayers to find things to entertain them in the manner they wish to be entertained. I pointed out that Claremont had many parks, recreation centers, and opportunities for them to get involved and develop more. I never found any with the initiative to consider that option.

There was another group that had cars. They too were trying to meet people. Again, it was hard for me to understand how driving back and forth in the same area could achieve this goal. On the street, people tried to look good with their grooming and dress. Cars brought in a whole new realm. The car itself had to be cool. It also had to play the right music loudly. Exhaust systems, lift kits, decals, and other vehicle displays were important. Driving technique was the next means to demonstrate the proper level of coolness. The driver had to slump down so that he could barely see over the dash, looking through the steering wheel. The hand had to hang over the steering wheel so that only the wrist was in contact with it. The other hand would often be holding a cigarette as a necessary part of being cool and looking mature.

These drivers went from the downtown area out to the shopping and commercial plazas on Washington Street and back, again and again. They drove slow through the plazas and in the downtown area with music blaring to attract the maximum attention. In between, they often sped and otherwise tried to out maneuver to outcool one another. Citizen complaints on these vehicles included the loud stereos and the manner of operation. The city passed a sound ordinance limiting the decibel levels of cars, but it was so high that it's unlikely they exceeded it. Besides, we didn't have a decimeter. It was difficult to bring viable charges from complaints, but the complaints were sufficient reason to stop these vehicles and find something else wrong with them. I focused on finding defective equipment.

It was easier for me to control these drivers by focusing on any defective equipment. Most of the time, I issued a "fix-it ticket" that required verification of the repair by a licensed inspection station. They could also return to the issuing officer for verification. The reason for returning to the officer is that there was no system to track these "fix-it tickets." The officer maintained his or her own copy until it was resolved. The instructions were that if the correction wasn't made within four days, a citation would be issued. It fit my purposes well because it usually took the car off the road for the remainder of the night.

Now and then, I would be in the right place and the right time and catch a moving violation, such as speeding or spinning tires for a smoke show. Smoke shows also had varying levels of achievement and honor status among these drivers. A smoke show with raw power achieved the greatest status. Smoke shows done by holding the brakes, called brake stands, were lesser. The braking smoke shows could be ranked a little higher if there was a significant amount of smoke.

Being in the middle of business owners wishing to make their businesses attractive to customers and individuals wishing to use the public ways to socialize in their own way was always challenging. Most of my colleagues preferred the intimidation tactics. Many times, I felt that the officer dispatched to a complaint of disorderly conduct exhibited worse, more disorderly than the mischief maker. It seemed that they believed that it was necessary to overwhelm the person to gain compliance.

When responding to street fights, many officers responded with their batons. Several times, there were unfavorable news articles. I couldn't make sense of stopping people from beating on one another by beating them. I liked using pepper spray. At first, I thought that spraying the person dominating the other would control the situation. I quickly learned that disabling one gave the advantage to the other. So I learned to spray both, then separate them. I also learned that pepper spray almost paralyzed some while having little effect on others. A correctional officer friend shared his observations. He said dark-skinned white men were more tolerant. This described him and me, and we both function reasonably well despite the irritant. As a science person, I recognized that there is insufficient data to confirm this.

We had a very different and a bit unnerving street patroller. When he was cruising the streets, we would find him showing up at our calls. Oliver had a scanner and followed us to our calls, sometimes getting there ahead of us. I felt intruding into police business was by itself enough cause to stop him as a suspicious vehicle. He frustrated me because he would often fix the problem and resume his activities. I found other ways, warning him about obstructing traffic in the area, making it harder for him to find legal parking to observe me. He was just a pain and eventually grew bored of the mundane calls.

There was one officer's technique that caused me great concern. Officer Turgeon was on a call that was down a short alley. When he came out, he found that Oliver had legally parked his car but got out and was standing at the entrance to this alley. Officer Turgeon grabbed the front of Oliver's shirt and lifted him off his feet, pressing him against the wall. Officer Turgeon held Oliver with one hand and took his glasses off with the other. He placed his glasses in his shirt pocket, then brought his fist up to Oliver's face. He said, "If I see you following me one more time, I will beat the shit out of you." Oliver was frail compared to Officer Turgeon. He stood no chance in a physical confrontation.

Oliver rightfully said that it was his right to be in a public place, and this infuriated Officer Turgeon even more. I was afraid that he was going to beat him then. He had already committed an assault just by grabbing Oliver. An officer has no right to touch anyone unless he or she is making an arrest. Officer Turgeon had no reason to arrest Oliver. He was trying to intimidate him. I was in a very uncomfortable position and suggested to Officer Turgeon that Oliver has gotten the idea and we should leave. He reluctantly agreed.

I found respectful communication to be more effective. Asking questions and directing the agitated person to a more neutral space nearby helped. On a few occasions, nothing was going to work, and an arrest was necessary. Sometimes there wasn't a clear charge that could be brought. I found that my calm, controlled demeanor was best and looked much better if the case went to court. The incorrigibly angry ones expected me to react like my colleagues and try to overpower his anger with more anger. He wanted a physical confrontation. As some got angrier, I got calmer. This seemed to infuriate them more, something they didn't understand, and they attacked me. It was never a great physical challenge to take physical control over someone so intoxicated that he could hardly stand. It ended the situation with an arrest that was easily won in court. Testimony was never embarrassing and showed calm professionalism for me. Justifying physical force to protect myself was easier than justifying force to control a person's behavior in a public place.

I recently discussed some human behavior by a popularly published psychologist. As a biologist, I learned that all animal behavior has a purpose. It may be challenging to discover the purpose of the behavior, or I may not be able to understand it. Animals do not waste effort. If there isn't an obvious goal, it may simply be practice or an effort to better coordinate a set of behaviors. The psychologist disagreed with me that all human behavior has a purpose. He eventually agreed that it if there wasn't an immediate physical goal, it was at least an expression of emotions or an attempt to communicate these feelings.

For the people on the street, some expressed directly to me their desire to meet people. In doing so, they communicated with their dress, their posture, and even where they were located on the street. It has always amazed me how important a hat and how it was placed on the head could be so important to some. "Don't mess with the hat" was a typical warning. Their identity and self-esteem were so wrapped up in that hat.

Tattoos and their location on the body communicate many things, including a mate's name, children, heritage, and gang membership. Most important identifying tattoos are displayed on the neck.

One's car also communicates much information. The make, model, color, and modifications are a display of personality and communicates as much as one's dress and posture. The operation, music type, and volume all mix in the complex human behavior to communicate to people listening.

Some dress, behavior, etc. is intended to demand attention. Most of the time, whether police or private citizen, ignoring it is best but may be intolerable to the person seeking attention. It may lead to even more seemingly bizarre behavior from the communicator demanding attention. Still, I chose and choose to ignore most of it, thereby sending my own communication that tends to establish a confidence and perhaps dominance.

Human behavior is extremely complex. Anyone who believes they understand all or dismiss some as meaningless deceives only themselves, regardless of their credentials.

Look in Your Rearview Mirror First

Before you do something stupid, look in your rearview mirror. There might be a cop right behind you.

One night, I came up behind a built-up Dodge Charger. Its paint was black and dull, perhaps a work in progress. It had a rear lift kit, large rear tires, and bright yellow stabilizers intended to keep the rear wheels from hopping when they spun on pavement. The windows were tinted, and the back window was small and angled, so it was difficult to see the people inside. I felt sure the driver saw me as we drove through the rotary Tremont Square because he was driving slowly. I could tell the exhaust was loud and assumed he kept the engine at low revolutions per minutes to keep the noise down. We came out of the square and onto Pleasant Street where many young folks were standing. Much to my surprise, the challenger's engine suddenly roared, and the back tires spun, producing a great smoke show. It excited the people hanging on the street. Some tried to get the driver's attention while pointing at me.

I felt like a present was just handed to me. A quick, easy, and very justified violation to write that would help quiet groups for much of the evening. I turned on the blue lights and hit the siren. We had a choice of several siren tones. I liked the one that, when you hit it quickly, seemed to announce, "You..." The buildings downtown directed and echoed the siren very effectively.

The car pulled over immediately. I was quite surprised when I approached the driver. I expected a young man and several people inside. Instead, I found one young lady driving this car alone. She had long hair and held her hands on her face, fingers over her eyes, facing downward and crying almost hysterically. She appeared to be high school age.

I know. People think cops have a soft heart for a crying woman. Well, it's true. It's especially true when it's a high school girl who we expect to protect, not prosecute. Still, I asked her for her license and registration. I recognized her last name right away. It was the same as our assistant fire chief. The address confirmed their relationship. The car's registration was to a young man. I asked her reason for driving someone else's car. She explained that it was her boyfriend's. She cried the entire time she spoke with me.

OK, my heart was softened with the surprise of a young crying woman that was technically still a child. She is the daughter of the assistant fire chief. His reputation is that of being very unpleasant and disrespectful of police officers. Given this combination, I wanted to just warn this young driver because I was quite confident that she wouldn't do it again. I also thought that it was likely that, with just a warning, it might give the assistant fire chief a better perspective of local police officers. I returned her license and the car registration and offered the cliché "Drive carefully, or at least check your mirror before you do something dumb." I returned to patrol, leaving her to regain her composure before driving.

About an hour later, I was called to the supervisor's office. As I approached the door, I saw the assistant fire chief sitting with him. I thought that perhaps he wanted to apologize for his daughter's behavior like most parents do. Parents who come into the station to speak with the officer typically want more details of what happened so that they can exercise their parental supervisory responsibilities of their child. I couldn't have been more wrong.

The assistant fire chief accused me of "hitting on" his daughter. I just couldn't believe how he maintained this position even after I explained what she did. He firmly demanded that I do not stop his daughter again. I stood my ground and told him that I would stop and write her the next time I saw her do a smoke show downtown. I pointed out that it was impossible to see who was driving that car and I hadn't previously met his daughter. His vicious attack continued as he was convinced that I was trying to develop a sexual relationship with his daughter. My impulse now was to write the ticket for what I saw this evening and bash him in court.

I had to emotionally step back for a moment. I had to remember my purpose and objective of the traffic stop. I made a deal with his daughter, and I was going to honor it. He was picking a very different fight with me that wasn't his daughter's. I don't know what she told him. My daughters were much younger than her, but I considered what I wanted my relationship to be with them at this age. If his reputation among us was any indication to what she endured at home, my sympathy was still with her. I left that office by assuring him that I acted professionally and would not hesitate to stop his daughter any time she violated the law. I concluded with that it was my discretion not to write a ticket and would write one the next time. This one was a warning. I think she learned her lesson.

I don't know her relationship with her father, but his relationship with me was not good. Oddly, years later, he did the first fire inspection for my home when we applied for a foster care license. The fire escape plan is reviewed during this inspection. My daughters were four and six years old. He was wonderful with them as they very happily demonstrated our escape plan. People continue to amaze me. We all have different responses to different situations. We all love our children and want to protect them, always.

Drug Raids

There are two no-knock drug raids that stand out to me and for different reasons. The first one was at the Claremont Arms, when it was promoting luxury apartments for the midlevel social class in Claremont. These apartments were intended for people who had good jobs but weren't able or interested in having their own home. This raid was officially a state police search with the drug task force. Raids are timed based on information from informants. The idea is to hit them when they were likely to have the most drugs and money.

It was four o'clock on a Friday morning. I was called in early to assist in the raid. I knew very little about what to expect. The five-minute briefing was that the drugs were kept in the headboard of the bed. We expected everyone to be in bed. We each had specific roles. The fast entrance was to prevent the destruction of evidence and to quickly secure the apartment for officer safety. The search would be conducted after the apartment and its occupants were secured. I wasn't expected to take photographs this time. I was to follow two state police drug task force members into the bedroom to provide backup as necessary.

We lined up in the hallway on each side of the second-floor apartment with guns drawn. Those tasked with the master bedroom were on the left. On the right side, there were one for the kitchen, one for the bathroom, one for the living room, and one for the second bedroom. We bedroom raiders would follow the officer who opened the door.

We quietly made our way to our positions. The trooper who was going to open the door was carrying a sledgehammer. This surprised me. I thought that he would kick the door open. My favorite partner Peter and I used to take turns kicking open doors. This trooper carefully checked to confirm the door was locked. He stepped back and, with a single motion, knocked the locking mechanism out of the door, which then flew open. He then ran to the bathroom. We entered the apartment like an explosion. I followed my colleagues through the small ordinary living room and into the bedroom. I could see and hear the trooper with the sledgehammer smash the toilet. I thought this odd at first, then realized he wanted to remove any opportunity to flush the evidence. Later, he explained that even if someone started to flush evidence, smashing the toilet could keep some of the evidence from going down the drain.

I couldn't get a clear view into the bedroom past the troopers ahead of me. I followed them semiblindly, trusting their bodily language signals as they moved quickly and to each side of the bed. The couple were already sitting up in bed as I entered the room and took my position near the foot of the king-sized bed. The man was on the left. He was bare chested, wearing red shorts. I was grateful for the red shorts. It's a bit gross to dress a naked person with handcuffs. The trooper next to him took verbal control. Though confused and reacting as someone waking unexpectedly, he cooperated and placed his hands behind him. He complied with every instruction. The trooper holstered his weapon and removed his handcuffs from his belt. The woman sat still beside him. The other trooper was telling her not to move.

I wasn't told about any kids in the apartment. I could hear them screaming now. They were running around the apartment and trying to get in to their parents. Officers were blocking their way. The three kids were all preschool age. With the man secured in handcuffs, the other trooper handcuffed the woman. She expressed concern for her kids as they kept screaming and running around the apartment. The trooper on the man's side slide open the headboard compartment. He pulled out a large ziplock bag of yellow pills I recognized as Darvon. The other trooper pulled out a plastic bag on the woman's side. It had several prescription bottles in it. The trooper asked the man, "Where's the money?" He said that it was under the mattress. The trooper instructed and assisted the man out of bed and into a chair. The trooper pulled a zippered bank envelope and a handgun from under the mattress.

The kids were still screaming and running around. The woman was again expressing her concern and asked if they could come in. The trooper denied her request. The oldest child managed to get past the trooper blocking the door and ran up to her mother. None of us stopped her. She hugged her and climbed into her lap. The other two kids followed. They clung to their mother as best they could. It was one of the saddest moments I have ever experienced as a police officer. I wondered why I hadn't been told about the kids. Worse yet, I wondered why there were no plans for their safety and feelings. I hated that these parents chose a way of life that placed their kids in this position. This is a traumatic event that will affect them for the rest of their lives. It is equivalent to any other abusive trauma they could experience. The kids were brought to the police station, and the dispatcher brought them into an office. She did well trying to console them for the three hours until a social worker came for them after their office opened.

The couple were arraigned in court that morning. The woman was released on personal recognizance. The kids were returned to their mother. He was held for lack of ten-thousand-dollar cash bail. I assumed that the evidence supporting the search warrant was against him. The money taken from under the mattress was evidence and could not be used for bail. If the case was one, that money would go to the state's drug task force.

The Spofford Street search was in sharp contrast to the Claremont Arms Luxury Apartments. Spofford Street is a neighborhood dominated by houses in disrepair. People renting these apartments lack an established credit and reliable employment history. The landlords live out of the city and likely own similar dilapidated properties in other communities.

Real Ward rented one of these apartments, which he shared with his girlfriend and their four kids. I had some experience with Real—small things like shoplifting and minor neighborhood disputes. I had no experience with his girlfriend or their kids. The kids were of school age, twelve and younger.

I was part of the search team. Like with the Claremont Arms team, it was headed by the New Hampshire Drug Task Force of the state police. My role was to photograph the evidence. We executed the warrant during the late morning. Unlike the Claremont Arms search, this was much calmer. This family has experienced such searches before.

There were two large plastic bags of marijuana and a few prescriptions pills. I photographed over three thousand five hundred dollars in cash. I also photographed a welfare check payable to Real's girlfriend. One trooper asked me to photograph several pieces of jewelry. They were not part of the search, so they couldn't take them as evidence. The trooper wanted to compare the pictures to reports of stolen jewelry. If he could match them, he would get another warrant.

Only Real was taken into custody. Like the Claremont Arms arrest, the money was evidence and could not be used for bail. Real was held for lack of one-thousand-dollar cash-only bail. He could not plead guilty at his arraignment in district court because he was charged with a felony. When his superior court case came before the judge, he plead guilty and went to prison for three to five years. He had a lengthy criminal history, including other drug sales, burglary, and theft. Prison time was simply a way of life with him.

It's hard for me to understand the thoughts and motives for both these families. Like most people, I have a strong work ethic. I achieve satisfaction by being constructive. These people who sell drugs have a distorted work ethic from my view. They work hard to establish a customer base, not unlike many businesses. They follow an entire set of rules that obviously conflict with rules established in law that describe how our society works. They also have rules in how they interact with their customers and competitors. They compete with one another by providing a dependable and quality product. They expect a level of loyalty from their customers. They expect that their customers will not report their illegal activities to the police or other authority. When a customer violates this rule, they will not only lose this supply, word gets out to other dealers, who will also refuse to sell to them. Violators still manage to get their drugs by enlisting a friend to get it for them. Only when a customer faces serious criminal charges will they turn against their supplier.

It's a complex subculture that is very much a way of life. They teach this culture to their children, who never learn the work ethic as we know it. They also lack motivation in other areas of society, especially in school. There is no magic to break this cycle. Very few escape it. There seems to be more joining this culture than those escaping it.

Can I Shoot Them?

Our schedules were to work five days and have two days off. There were three patrol cars. One patrolled beat number 1, the area north of the Sugar River. The other patrolled beat number 2, south of the Sugar River. The third car was the supervisor's, who patrolled both and often was the backup for calls. There was a beat number 3 that included the downtown walking beat. After two days off and provided there was a full complement of officers, that returning officer did the walking beat. If the downtown became quiet, the beat number 3 officer would get in the car, usually with the beat number 2 car, because that was usually the busiest beat. The beat number 3 officer relieved the dispatcher for his or her evening meal. Most officers hate this duty, but I didn't mind.

One evening, while covering dispatch, a familiar call came in. Albert is a respected, hardworking contractor. He was a deacon in the Catholic Church and a major contributor to all their programs. His faith was unquestionably strong. I understood him with my family's Catholic heritage.

Albert also owns a farm. His common complaint was that someone was on his property. Sometimes they are mischievously around his barns and equipment. However, the majority just parked on the edge of his field for some private, intimate activity. Albert felt offended by this immoral activity, especially on his property. This is the call that I received this evening.

Albert identified himself on the phone, but I knew him well enough to recognize his voice. He reported that there was a car across the field behind his house. I acknowledged his call and prepared to dispatch the patrol officer. He continued to describe the car, which wouldn't be necessary. The officer would find the offending vehicle easily. Albert expressed his anger about them being on his property. He continued to speak, describing what he saw and why he didn't want them on his property. If Albert wanted us to catch the offenders, I had to get the car rolling in his direction, so I asked him to stand by and dispatched the beat number 1 car.

After dispatching the call, I resumed my conversation with Albert. He said, "I can see them in the car." I assured him that the officer would take care of it. Normally, we make certain it's mutual consent and don't even bother to get the trespassers' names but just get car registration number and ask them to leave the area. We all knew Albert was more insistent than most, so we usually got their names and wrote a very brief report. This would give the chief enough information so he could be prepared to speak with Albert, who often came in the next day.

Albert was growing concerned that it was taking too long for the officer to get there. I tried to assure him; then he said, "I can see them. Can I shoot them?" This surprised and worried me. For a good Catholic, he seemed to have a low regard for life. What also worried me is that Albert, known for his temper, is also known to be a good shot. I said, "No! No! Please don't shoot at them. The officer will take care of it." I radioed the responding officer and asked for an ETA (estimated time of arrival). He was two minutes away, which seemed to satisfy Albert for the moment.

The officer signed off with the call, calling in its registration. I recorded the number in the log. The officer signed back on, reporting the car had left.

There was another time that I was covering for the dispatcher that was much more surprising and rewarding. Jefferson Milton was wanted for sexual assault upon an eight-year-old boy. I was one of the patrol officers who checked his house and other known locations several times throughout our shift for several days. We finally gave up, and a year had nearly passed. We assumed that he was far away, living with a new identity. Unfortunately, like other such hard-core sex offenders, he was probably still assaulting other children.

The caller's identity surprised me. He said that he was a member of the Canadian Royal Mounted Police. My grandmother was born in Canada and told many stories of her youth. I had visited Canada many times. We knew very well the reputation and status of the mounted police, though few were horse mounted these days. Nonetheless, they have worldwide respect.

Sergeant Potvin said, "You have a warrant for Jefferson Milton." Of course, I remembered that we have a warrant and immediately confirmed what he had already known from his own research. He added, "We have him in our custody." Now I was worried about extradition. I had been involved in a few across state lines but never out of the country. Sergeant Potvin immediately relieved any extradition concerns, saying, "He will be at your Route 27 border crossing in Maine at ten fifteen in the morning," in three days. I was quite confident that our sheriff would be there. I recorded these details and Sergeant Potvin's contact information in the log. I thought, *Damn, don't mess around with the Canadians*, feeling some of that family heritage pride. They don't let silly things like extradition get in the way when they expel someone from their country.

When we finished our conversation, I notified the supervisor, who called the chief. He decided to send our own officers to get him. Many, if not all of us, felt some pride and satisfaction about working with an elite police agency to bring this child predator to justice.

Albert has an odd low regard for the life of those he feels transgressed upon his dignity. Jefferson Milton uses children like objects to satisfy his desire. His actions cause psychological harm for the victims' entire lives. It's around us in many forms. There are far too many individuals, and there are whole groups of extremists—the white supremacists, some religious extremists, and human predators that devalue the humanity of another person. I find this very hard to deal with. I have not been successful in finding empathy where there is none in the other person. I retain hope in knowing that we are not born this way. It's a learned behavior. Anything learned can be relearned. It is possible to stop this cycle. How is the problem.

I often think about white supremacists as a biologist. I occasionally reflect on our position among nature and how we evolved. The definition of a species is a group of like organisms with similar characteristic that can mate and produce viable offspring. For example, a mule is a cross between a donkey and a horse. Mules are mostly sterile, incapable of producing offspring. Therefore, a mule is not a species, though very much a living, feeling organism.

So many human groups have developed opinions of the humanity, intelligence, etc. of the different races. Since we can all mate and produce viable, fertile offspring with similar characteristics, we're all the same species. The word "race" is used in biology, but a more accurate description is "variation" within the species.

Because I may look like a well-tanned Caucasian, I can challenge white supremacists more effectively. Most claim to be strongly Christian. I can easily get them to accept some science, then accept the idea that humans began in Africa. When I have them trapped in this line of reasoning, I remind them that their religion (and mine) says that God created man in his own image. Africans are black;

therefore, God must be black. Typically, this stuns them, and they are unable to answer.

I toy with others by telling them about the reports that Neanderthal genes have been found in some European descendants, who are white people. When they accept this report, I like to tell them about the definition of species again. Most everyone thinks about Neanderthals as being much more primitive than modern humans. How then could they mate with modern humans and produce fertile offspring? By strict definition, they are the same species. So Neanderthals are only a variation in the species.

There's also some report that Denisovans, native to Siberia, have DNA found in modern humans. The idea that these could all be the same species is unlikely to be accepted. Still, I wonder why do we worry so much about different levels of melanin (brown pigment) in our skin? We all have the same number of melanocytes, cells that produce the melanin pigment, in our skin. It's the melanocyte-stimulating hormone that the base of our brain produces that causes the different shades. Skin transplanted from a person with different "color" will change to the recipient's "color" as it responds to new direction to produce melanin. The way our skin got lighter was when we moved out of Africa where the sun was less intense, we needed to maximize our exposure to synthesize the vitamin D needed to build our bones. The reason our eyes became "slanted" is the extra fat in the eyelids making them thicker to protect against the cold climate. Without these adaptations, we would not have survived. Those with the adaptations survived better in these climates and produced more offspring.

Over time, isolated groups varied more from our original ancestors. We all descended from our early African ancestors, and we are only variations in the species. Our real differences are in our customs, which I find fascinating and not so differentiating. Our differences are cultural with insignificant biological differences. Our strength is in our diversity. The more we mix our genes, the better chance our human race will survive. Life has existed on earth for five billion years. Humans have been here for only a few millions, modern humans only a few thousand years.

So to all those like Albert and Jefferson who think they a better than others out there, get over your lack of regard for another's life. For the extremists, get over any belief that you are greater than any other group of people. We all need one another to survive. I counter their racism by telling them that their primitive Neanderthal genes are showing. When worse, I accuse them of having the more primitive Denison gene dominance.

A college professor teaching urban ecology earned my utmost respect. I signed up for the course thinking it dealt with ecology of organisms in urban environments. I should have read the course description better that described urban race relations. He impressed me right away, and I decided to stay in the course. I learned a lot about the different cultures and respect for them. I also learned about what he called classism. This is practiced far more universally and cruelly in our societies. It's directly related to economics and the slippery, steep slope that maintains these divides. All one needs do is to listen and you will find it in many social interactions, especially among police. It fuels that "us against them" mentality.

Manley Brothers

Stan and Chaz Manley were brothers who dominated the people around them. They were six feet four inches, strong, and heavy. They drank a lot of beer and were loud. They had been to prison for assaults while enforcing their domination. Anytime someone opposed them, their preferred means to gain compliance was to physically shove the perceived offender out of the way or into a wall. Occasionally, they would punch people. The occasion that sent them to prison involved a baseball bat.

Stan and Chaz enjoyed intimidating police and parole officers but quickly assessed those who wouldn't tolerate it. I encountered Stan while on foot patrol during one of his infrequent walks around the city. He and his girlfriend and children completely dominated the sidewalk, expecting others to walk in the street to pass by them. During my foot patrols, I communicated my unwillingness to be intimidated by walking directly at him as he and his entourage approached. Obstructing the sidewalk is a simple violation, but anyone on parole must remain on good behavior. It's a difficult charge to win in court since it is hard to identify who among the group is obstructing. I locked eye contact with Stan and walked briskly at him. He soon understood but maintained his dignity by commanding others in his group to make way for the police officer.

Stan and Chaz also liked to use their prison experience to intimidate people. It somehow helped to instill fear due to their prior violent crime and prison experience. Their "real prison tattoos" are a badge of honor. They lived on the second floor of a three-story dilapidated apartment building. There were eight apartments in this building. Stan boasted to be friends with everyone in the building and was welcomed into all at any time. I felt confident that it was his bullying tactic and suspected that there was more to it, such as taking whatever he wanted from them.

For a parolee, all police involvement, even if you're a victim, must be reported to parole immediately. Three violations of the good citizen rules could send a parolee back to prison. One unreported police contact, being caught drinking or missing an appointment with the parole officer could send him back to prison. Stan and Chaz likely had at least two violations.

Cruz was also a prison parolee who recently moved into the building on the third floor. He served time for a burglary. He rented an apartment alone and worked for a drywall contractor. He worked long hours and was paid well. He was doing well with his parole.

Early one evening, we were called to the Manley apartment for a report of a stabbing. We responded with all units, knowing that this must be an extremely serious incident. When we arrived, I found both Stan and Chaz in their apartment, waiting for us. There was a significant amount of blood on their torsos. Stan was sitting on the edge of a chair. He had several cuts in the front of his shirt and one that went diagonally across his back. Chaz sat in the corner with several small cuts in the front of his shirt and one along his right leg. Stan said that Cruz had attacked them and ran off. It seemed odd that this gigantic bully now appeared helpless and quite scared. Seeing the extent but not knowing the depth of the lacerations, I thought that he might die from his injuries. We cleared the EMTs to come in. They transported them to the hospital.

I interviewed Stan's girlfriend. She explained that Stan and Chaz confronted Cruz in his apartment when he returned from work that evening. They went to talk to him about violating the rules of the building. Stan was the lead person in the discussion while Chaz was his backup. She watched from the hallway. The discussion almost immediately went bad with Cruz attacking Stan and Chaz with the utility knife from his tool belt he used at work and was still wearing. She said that he attacked Stan when he grabbed him. Cruz cut Stan several times on his chest and abdomen. When Stan bent over, he cut the full length of his back. When Chaz stepped in to help his brother, Cruz cut his chest, abdomen, and leg several times, then ran off. They returned to their apartment to call for an ambulance, who notified the police. The trail of blood in the hallway confirmed the location of the incident.

Other neighbors thought that Cruz had a friend living in an apartment they described on Pleasant Street, closer to the center of the city. There were twenty-eight apartments in this building. Undaunted, I started knocking on each door. Few received any response. Those that answered said that they didn't know Cruz. I didn't expect to find him but was quite surprised when he responded to my knocking on a third-floor door. He was expecting to be caught, just not so soon. He surrendered, fully complying. Cruz described the attack as I expected. The Manley brothers were the aggressors. Cruz was small. The Manley brothers were each more than twice his size. Stan had him against the wall and lifted his feet off the floor. They demanded money from him, which he didn't owe. He denied involvement with drug dealing, insisting that he will test clean in any drug test.

I brought Cruz in and processed him on second-degree assault charges. It's a charge that I felt necessary due to the extent of the injuries he caused to the Manley brothers. I felt that it was more than necessary to have been in self-defense. However, a part of me hoped that he would be found innocent for self-defense. He had served his time for the earlier conviction. He was now dutifully employed and performing as a good citizen until the Manley brothers interfered with his life. The bail commissioner set bail at ten thousand dollars, far out of Cruz's ability to pay.

I went to the hospital to check on Stan and Chaz. They were in much better spirits. The cuts were all superficial, thanks to the short length of the utility knife blade. Stan received hundreds of stitches. The doctor measured the cut on Stan's back at thirty-seven inches long. It went from his right hip to his left shoulder in a straight line that a drywall installer could make. It seemed that they had learned a valuable lesson about bullying people. I suspect that they would only be more cautious about who they bullied. I also suspect that they ran a sort of protection ring in the building. The timing of the incident fit well with trying to extort Cruz's paycheck.

The parole officer and the county attorney brought several more charges against Cruz, including possession of a deadly weapon by a felon and violation of parole. The weapon charge seemed unfair because it was a tool of his employment. The unempathetic parole officers said that it was a deadly weapon when he took it off the job-site. Cruz returned immediately to prison for the violation of parole while awaiting a hearing on the other charges. It doesn't seem fair. Had it not been for the Manley brothers, Cruz was likely to do well. Now he was looking at many more years in prison and less likely to transition so well back into the community again.

Nasty Pictures

It was a mostly quiet Sunday afternoon. I was patrolling the south side of town while my favorite partner patrolled the north side. Pete got a call to "go speak with the lady" at an address on West Terrace Street. It was a familiar building with many apartments on a corner lot. The building across from it was also a relatively large apartment building. I had lots of confidence in Peter and that he would transmit a calm request for me if he needed a backup.

After a period, Peter signed back on. He then asked to meet with me. We parked driver to driver. He was holding a photograph film canister. I did much of the police photography. The department had a darkroom where I developed the pictures that I took. It was an excellent chain of custody. I took the pictures, developed them, and made prints. On the back of the prints, I wrote the case number, the date that I printed it, and signed it. I initialed the developed negatives. I usually filed the completed ones in the locked photography room outside the darkroom. It was as secure as any evidence room. I sometimes made extra prints for the investigating officer to supplement her or his report.

Peter held the film canister up. I could tell that it was thirty-five millimeters, which I typically used. He asked, "Do you think that you can do anything with this?"

I took it from him and opened the canister. I first noticed that it was color. I use mostly black-and-white film because it is cheaper, easier to develop, and more than adequate for most of what we do. I used color when it is important, such as to show injuries to people or blood at a crime scene. I then noticed that it was color slides. I had never done color slides. Color on the negatives is the opposite of the print. The film blocks the projected colors and allows only the intended ones through to be printed. Slides are the opposite of color negative. They are the actual colors as they are intended to be projected into or by a viewer. I told Peter that I didn't have the materials to develop color and would check with Smith Photo in the morning.

Peter explained the importance of the film. Sandy had two children, Harvey and Diane. Harvey was seven years old, and Diane was eleven years old. Leon is a grandfatherly type in the apartment building across the street. The kids in the neighborhood often hung out in his apartment. Sometimes he looked after kids while parents worked, shopped, or did other things. He was kind and trusted.

Diane ran to her mother, Sandy. She said, "Leon is taking nasty pictures of Harvey."

Sandy was a short woman. Leon was large. That didn't deter this mom from charging into Leon's apartment to confront him. She demanded the film from his camera. Leon complied, but he opened the camera, exposing the undeveloped film to the light. He then closed it and wound up the film. He took it out and gave it to her. She gave it to Peter. Peter was wondering if the film had been destroyed and what might be on it if I could recover anything.

Our chain of custody was still secure. Sandy could testify her part of the chain. Peter brought it to me, and I secured the film in the photography room.

The next morning, I went to Smith Photo and asked the owner, Don Smith, if he had a kit to develop slides to print. I was surprised that not only did such a thing exist, he had one. I bought it with my own money and went into the department darkroom on my own time to see what I could do with it.

Color slides would appeal to child predators back then, before the digital age. Film can be developed in a black bag. You can take it out of the canister and roll it into the developer canister all by feel. It doesn't take much practice to be proficient at this. The developing canister is light secure, so you can take it out of the black bag and develop it in the lighted room. Once slides are developed, you're done. The results can be viewed with a viewer or projector. This way, they can avoid a commercial developer who hopefully would report what they have to the police.

I didn't need the black bag. I had a darkroom. Still, much is by feel. I can't use the regular black-and-white light. I did it in total darkness. It went easily into the developer canister I could turn on the lights. The temperature of the developer is important as is the timing. After rinsing and fixing, I was ready to remove the film to see what I got, if anything.

I nervously and anxiously unrolled the developed film. I immediately noticed white blotches caused by the exposure to light, and my heart sank, feeling that I may have wasted my time and money. As I unrolled the thirty-six-picture strip, only the first few pictures were affected. The first ones as I unrolled the film would be the last pictures taken.

I held the strip up to the low-level light. The affected pictures were of an older overweight man wearing only a G-string. I suspected that this was Leon. There were several pictures of him in several poses. He was standing in some, front and back. In other pictures, he was lying on a bed. This G-string barely contained his reproductive hardware. The string was around his waist and between his buttocks. It was very disgusting. Though the whited-out film spared me some eye pain, it was sufficient to easily identify this man. I feared that this was the extent of all that was on this film.

I scrolled down the film. Sure enough, there was what we sadly expected. Poor little Harvey in full naked poses. There were front, side, and back views. I scrolled a little farther, and I saw what had to be Diane. There were only two pictures of her. She was mostly dressed. The pictures were of her front, with her holding up her shirt, exposing her undeveloped breasts.

I had to set this down and recompose myself. I had two daughters that were two and four years old. What sort of individual can do this to children? Who gets their jollies taking pictures of kids this way, violating their innocence? I took lots of pictures of my kids but never would I take anything that compromised their dignity. How can he do this? As a science guy, I came to realize that there are things that humans may never understand about the universe, such as what really happens in a black hole, infinity, the concept of nothing, or what is beyond the edge of the universe. Setting aside the theoretical astrophysics, we don't even understand how our own brains work. We know surprisingly little how the genetics, environment, experiences, learning, etc. work to form brain development, connections, chemistry, etc. I can't understand how people can do this to one another and especially innocent children. I am the biologist, but I have friendly disagreements with the local judge when we meet at public events. He says it's in the genes. I say it is learned behavior. Both apply. The degree to which they do is the foundation of our friendly debate. How can we "fix" things when we don't understand how they occur?

After taking a deep breath and gaining my composure, I knew that I had to present this in a manner that would be shocking to a jury. I wanted this guy to go to jail for a very long time. I printed two eight-by-ten-inches pictures of Harvey and labeled the back as I usually do. To preserve the film and avoid crushing it, I usually cut it into lengths that fit in the file. With this one, I wanted to maintain the thirty-six-picture sequence in an easily presentable manner. Certainly, the edge of the film has sequential numbers, but I wanted the shock effect of scrolling past disgusting Leon to many naked pictures of Harvey and little Diane at the end, which would have been his first pictures.

Once dried, I brought these pictures to the detectives. It didn't take much to convince them that this was a high priority. They did a quick criminal records check on Leon. He had been convicted ten years ago trading pictures of a naked fourteen-year-old girl with someone in Texas. He served several years in New Hampshire State Prison but was no longer on parole.

They got a search warrant from what Peter and I developed. They found many more slides, pictures, and videos in his apartment. He was arrested. The extremely high bail assured that he would remain in court until his hearing.

This was an emotional but well-spent effort. I could now leave this with the detectives who would bring it to the county attorney. I could be assured that I and my partner did our parts well. Our reports and chain of custody were tight. I expected to be called as a witness to testify to the chain of custody and the developing. I would be questioned about having done something to enhance or in any way misrepresent what was on the film. I was looking forward to confronting this incomprehensible inhuman in court. I was denied this satisfaction as he plead guilty and went back to prison. I must settle with the satisfaction of having used my skills to protect these and other children he was preying upon. I never met any of these people. I only saw them on the film, yet I have the satisfaction of doing my part in the outcome.

CHAPTER 3

Domestic Disturbances

Domestic Violence

When the dispatcher announces 10-61, domestic, it's one of the dreaded calls. Even though domestic could mean so much more, for police, it means that there is violence between cohabitants or the threat of imminent violence. 10-61s in progress are the worse. It meant that violence was in progress. It could mean loud yelling, serious bodily harm, or gunshots. It was always a dangerous call. The police officer was going into a violent or potentially violent situation. We were at a disadvantage in someone's home. All homes have weapons ranging from steak knives to guns. Many have tools such as hammers for bashing and screwdrivers for stabbing weapons. Even furniture can be a weapon, whole or broken into versatile weapons. Though we learned about the floor plan of many apartments, we didn't know all or how the furniture might be arranged. Many apartments had difficult egresses, narrow halls and stairs. The restricted egresses were often cluttered with trash and other hazardous objects.

When I first started as a police officer, it was necessary to see the violence in progress to make the legal arrest at the time. Though this was very rare, it did happen. When we couldn't make an arrest, we used the protective custody statute a lot. Most often, the aggressor was intoxicated. We could take an intoxicated person into protective custody if he or she presented a possibility of harm to self or others. It was very temporary, only getting us out of the immediate situation. It also involved no charges, therefore no real solution to the problem.

Another method we used was to encourage separation for the evening. Most often, the aggressor was the man. He could spend the night with a friend and return when things cooled down the next day. This was my preferred solution because it relieved me from the responsibility of having him in my custody. I could persuade him to go to a friend's house if the other option is jail. For some though, they preferred jail to the humiliation of letting his friends know they couldn't control his woman.

We had our repeat offenders. The sad advantage to these repeaters was that we knew how to end it. Some had a friend who they always went to. Others preferred to go to jail. There were some who left before we got there.

One thing that often bothered me deeply was a common line of thought from some men that I arrested. It was very disappointing how they tried to gain acceptance from me. They talked about what she did to deserve his response. My colleagues often engaged in such language to appease the agitated man and avoid any confrontation. I hope that they didn't agree with him. This was so much against my core values that I refused to participate in any such discussion and shut it down quickly. I would reply that no one for any reason "deserves" violence. I further warned him that what he said was voluntary statement that would be used against him in court even though I haven't read his *Miranda* rights to him. *Miranda* applies only to questioning. I recommended that he use his right to remain silent because I was going to use his statements against him if we go to court. With this position, I managed better control over his angry state of mind and never had any physical confrontation with these abusers.

The legislature passed a bill into law that allowed arrests for domestic violence if we had evidence that violence had occurred within the last six hours. The evidence could be a victim's statement, bruises, or property damages. This was a major improvement in our ability to find resolution for domestic violence, immediately and for the long term.

When the legislature passed the law allowing arrests within six hours of a domestic assault, it seemed like the tool we needed to make progress against these abusers. It felt good to go in, make the arrest, and remove the bad guy like a superhero. I got many more cases into court. Unsurprising, the person I arrested plead not guilty. I was accustomed to this. Most who intended to plead guilty first plead not guilty at an arraignment to delay having to pay a fine. When it came to trial, they would plead guilty. I still had to be present. A few hoped that the arresting officer would not show up, and their case would be dismissed for lack of prosecution. The judge also wanted some information before sentencing.

I experienced an entirely new phenomenon with this group. On the day of the trial, I noticed the offender and the victim in the back of the courtroom acting like lovebirds, cuddling and even kissing. The first few baffled me. At the time of my arrest, I witnessed a violent scene and a woman in absolute fear, sheer terror of this man. It was inconceivable to me that she would ever admit him back into her life. Now they were acting like newlyweds in the back of the courtroom.

When we went forward with the case, she made it sound like I was the bad guy, intruding into their happy home. Fortunately, the judge understood. Though the judge found in our favor, penalties were minimal and likely suspended. It seemed like a waste of the court's time. Eventually, the prosecutor would notice this behavior and approach the couple before the case was called. It was best to just drop the charges. Eventually, the regulars learned that they could go to the prosecutor as soon as the next day before the arraignment and get the charges dropped.

Frustrating as it all seemed, we did have one more useful tool to help reduce domestic violence. I found engaging Women's Supportive Services, the domestic violence advocates, helped a lot. Eventually, it became policy due to their relentless advocacy. Many officers saw no value in this and hated the advocacy of the leader of this organization, Debbie. I experienced violence in the home as a child. I also studied human and animal behavior in college. I respected Debbie's efforts and welcomed her assistance. She seemed shocked by my acceptance, but soon, we worked well together.

Taking the abuser out of the home by whatever means was always temporary. The woman often depended upon him to provide for her and her children. She would accept his promises to change and let him back in. As he regressed to his old ways, she would sacrifice herself until it became unbearable, and we were called again. Women's Supportive Services provided counseling and support to help the woman become independent of this abuser.

I found that when I charged the man, it almost always got dropped by the woman. I learned to demand that the woman write a statement and sign the criminal complaint herself. Making a good connection with Women's Supportive Services greatly increased the odds that she would follow through with the entire process. The sad part that I still don't understand is how they'll find another man who eventually abused them. Somehow, these guys exhibit the power and strength to which these women are attracted.

Loud Noise Complaints

City cops get lots of loud noise complaints. It's also another dreaded call. The greatest problem is that we have no idea who is calling and of their credibility or motive. We are just dispatched to a "noise complaint." We have no idea if the caller even identified himself or herself to the dispatcher. Charges are rarely brought on the first call. Judges expect someone to be made aware of the complaint first. The disorderly conduct law refers to a noise or language that would offend a normal person. It can come from a private or public place and be heard in another public or private space. It implies they must be warned that they are bothering someone and given a chance to stop the annoyance. Judges do not accept that cops on duty can be the person offended.

Typically, we stop the police car and listen. Some officers roll the window down and listen. Others, like me, like to stand on the sidewalk outside. I want to try and determine the source, if it is just a loud party, blasting music, offensive language, or perhaps domestic violence situation. The other challenge would be identifying the true offender. Typically, we try to identify the apartment renter and hold him or her responsible. If it is domestic violence, I have a duty to protect and lots more authority. All I need is evidence that a domestic assault has occurred within the past six hours.

One call was to a downtown apartment building on a warm summer evening. It has eight apartments in its two stories. It is close to the sidewalk, with a very short front yard. Parking is to the side of the building. As I got out of the car, it was easy to see that several men in the front yard were loud. They were all drinking beer. As I walked toward them, they came to meet me.

They formed a half circle, each holding his beer in his right hand. They were polite and respectful as we discussed what they were doing. I explained that someone was complaining about the noise they were making. They stood in the half circle; they shuffled their feet and looked around. The man at the end of the circle placed his foot on the sidewalk.

Like many communities, Claremont has an open-container ordinance, making it a violation to have an open container of an alcoholic beverage on any public way or publicly owned facility. There were exceptions to some facilities, but they had to have a permit to use them. Even one foot on the sidewalk is a violation of this ordinance. Some officers would react immediately on this opportunity and arrest him. It's only a small fine and such a trivial act. He was clearly testing me and my good nature. In my ordinary style, I looked at him and said, "You know that's not allowed." I explained that my goal was to keep peace in the building and not to make an arrest. He quickly moved his foot, pretending to be unaware that he had stepped on the sidewalk, then apologized. The test was over, and he knew my expectations.

We chatted for a few more minutes, the men still holding their beers, all in their right hands. As we spoke, a toddler wearing only a diaper joined the center of this half circle. It struck me that this child was holding a baby bottle, also in her right hand. The image was enlightening. The grown men all held beer bottles in their right hand. The toddler held a nippled bottle of milk. Perhaps things don't mature that much as members of this group grow. Posture and holding a beverage remain the same. Only the container and its contents change.

I expressed a cop's usual concern. I hoped that I wouldn't be called back. In this case, I wasn't called back. If we get subsequent calls, we would expect the caller to be identified and willing to prosecute the noise complaint. Without that assurance, we have little we can do. Our repeated intrusions can be considered police harassment without a source from which to make an arrest.

Sometimes we get lucky at loud noise calls. If we find someone for whom we know there is a warrant, making an arrest has a very chilling effect. So as we stand at the door, we try to see who else is at the party. Once, a familiar face bounced up behind the person with whom I was speaking. It was Todd Sanborn. Somehow, he thought that he had special influence over me because we shared a last name. It had the opposite effect with me. I have arrested Todd for a burglary. On that charge in court, I made it clear to the judge that there was no known relationship. I believe that all Sanborns shared a common ancestry. Supposedly, three brothers came from a sandy area in England and settled the townships of Sanbornton and Sanbornville. Sanbornton continues today.

So as I am speaking with the person responsible for the party, Todd bounces up with his smiley face and said hello. Since I knew Todd from the previous arrest, I was also aware that there was a warrant for his arrest. I responded, "Hello, Todd. You're under arrest." It was funny to see his smile change quickly to a frown. He then turned and ran deeper into the second-floor apartment. The party organizer wisely stepped out of my way, and I gave the short pursuit into the living room. Todd went to a window, then abruptly changed to sitting into a chair, apparently changing his mind about jumping out of the second floor. He took a firm grip on the wooden arms to the chair. Todd had never resisted arrest with me. He was also much smaller and too intoxicated to present much of a challenge. I easily peeled a single finger from the arm of the chair. As the old cliché goes, get one finger and the others will follow. I applied the handcuff to the loosened arm. Todd began to flail his whole body, trying to escape. I dragged him over the side of the chair, tipping it over. With him, the chair, and me squirming on the floor, I managed to keep control of the handcuffed arm. If he was able to free the arm with a handcuff attached, he could use it as a weapon. I eventually got control of the other arm and applied the handcuffs. Todd mostly surrendered, but I wouldn't describe him as cooperative. He pushed back at me several times on the way to the car.

Todd couldn't post bail and went to jail. He developed into what most people would describe as a career criminal, spending more time in prison than free. Even when free, he was on parole and never in good standing. Years later, I was in court with a foster child, and his case was called. He was in orange jail clothes, handcuffed to a belt and wearing leg shackles. A deputy sheriff was standing on each side. Rarely do you see such security in district court. The arresting officer explained that he interrupted Todd's burglary in progress. He described the subsequent foot pursuit. As Todd tried to get away, he ran past someone walking on the sidewalk. He punched this man in the head, causing serious harm, hoping to distract the officer's pursuit. Fortunately, there were other officers to continue the pursuit. I still emphasize I have no known relationship with Todd despite our shared last name.

Bible Beater

I was called to accompany DCYS (Division for Children and Youth) for the removal of a child. It was an apartment in a typical downtown neighborhood near the junior high school. Two DCYS social workers were waiting for me in the driveway. On contested removals, they try to send two workers. The police are necessary because, contrary to popular belief, state social workers do not have the authority to take a child into custody; only the police and courts have the authority. Police authority is protective custody, which is very temporary, twenty-four hours plus weekend and holidays. DCYS did their homework. A court hearing was already scheduled this morning.

A social worker knocked on the door. Bernard answered the door. The worker explained that they were there to pick up fifteen-year-old Alyssa. Alyssa was ready and standing on the other side of the room. Bernard let her slip by. He wasn't happy, saying, "God will show you the error of your ways." So far, I didn't know what the charges were. I was simply there to keep the peace.

I was a little familiar with Bernard. He claimed to be a pastor. He held services in peoples' living rooms, rotating the location every week. Anyone can call themselves reverend. The separation of church and state prevents regulatory requirements. Most religious organizations have their own criteria for credentialing. Since Bernard was the pastor of his own church, he had no oversight. I've met several of these pastors. Most have good intentions. Unfortunately, they have little to offer for credentials. Sadly, I had more credentials than most self-proclaimed ministers. My bachelor of arts degree from Saint Michael's College included five courses in theology and four in philosophy, twenty-seven credits, more than the equivalent of a minor.

The prosecutor wanted me to come to court, again to keep the peace. Since this was a juvenile hearing, only those who are party to the case are allowed in the courtroom, so it was mostly empty. I listened to Alyssa describe several things that were not good parenting but not likely enough for the judge to remove her from her father at this point. Bernard was getting more restless in his seat, frequently adjusting his position. He held a Bible in front of his chest. He tapped his finger on it as Alyssa and the prosecutor spoke.

Prompted by the prosecutor's questions, Alyssa then started describing beatings. Her father had struck her with pillows, a kitchen spoon, a broom on her behind, etc. Bernard was more agitated now and said, "The Lord will pass judgment."

Judge Stone warned Bernard to be quiet. He stopped speaking but got more restless with his frequently changing positions. He stood up and walked to the back of the courtroom. I thought that he might be walking out, but he stood in the back. As the testimony continues, Alyssa described how her father beat her with the Bible. My sympathy for Alyssa increased as she spoke. Tears were running down her face. I wondered how it took so long to bring this child to safety.

Bernard started pacing back and forth in the rear of the courtroom, waving his Bible high in the air. He was wearing a black suit, blue shirt, and no tie. The jacket was open to accommodate his large round belly, which stuck out past the opened jacket. He looked toward the judge and said loudly, "There is a higher authority!"

The judge looked at him and said something for which I very much admire her. "There may be, but in this courtroom, it is me. Now sit down and be quiet for the remainder of this hearing."

Bernard just stopped and faced her. It appeared that he was about to say something when she continued, "Sit down and be quiet, or this officer will take you out of this courtroom." The judge glanced toward me.

I was surprised by the judge's direct reference to me and her power to control everyone in her courtroom. I shouted in my mind, *Yes!* And I imagined my flexing arm with a clenched fist at my side. The loud thought and fist remained repressed. I only smiled and nodded my head.

Bernard was stunned. He looked at the judge, then at me. He held his Bible outwardly toward the judge, but not as high. He wasn't moving, so I took a step in his direction. He then sat in a chair in a back row. He remained quiet through the remainder of the hearing.

The DCYS worker testified to her evidence. It involved a call from the school guidance counselor and her meeting with Alyssa at school.

The judge found the case to be "true" and placed Alyssa with DCYS, who placed her with her aunt.

Charlie's Nickel Offer

Domestic violence calls come in many forms. They are not always between a cohabitating man and woman. The call for Charlie was between a mother and son. The mom called because Charlie was destroying the apartment, throwing things at her, yelling threats, and disturbing the neighbors, who were the ones that called.

The call was in a compact neighborhood, where the rents are low and the property maintenance essentially nonexistent. These are high-hazard areas for police, who are mostly not wanted here. Backup is standard. The officer assigned to the beat takes the lead.

Backup follows the beat officer's lead. This was my beat. My backup was right behind me.

The walkway and porch were characteristically narrow and cluttered. The wooden door had a window covered by drapes and an additional cloth for privacy. My knock on the door was promptly answered by the mother. Though she hadn't called, she was glad to see us.

The door entered the kitchen. It's difficult to know how much disruption had been caused to the kitchen because many people in these neighborhoods live in congested apartments. Often, more than one family lives in one. Since this was my first time with this family, I didn't know their normal. One thing that really stood out to me was the overturned refrigerator. I knew that wasn't normal. It was leaning forward against the kitchen table and a chair. It didn't see the rest of the apartment.

Charlie was standing next to the overturned refrigerator. Most noticeable about him was how short he was. He stood slightly sideways with his right shoulder forward. He leaned a little toward us and continued with nonstop profanity. He was holding some sort of softball-sized dish in his left hand that was stretched back, ready to be thrown. The mom asked us to remove him. It appeared imminent that Charlie was about to do something that would justify an arrest, but I wouldn't necessarily have to wait for it. A threat of a violent act is enough.

I asked the mom a few quick questions. Does Charlie live here? How old is he? Has he hit you? Just recently? Are you afraid of him? She answered positively to all these questions and told me that he was eighteen years old. These are essential elements to a domestic violence act. If they have occurred within the past six hours, a police officer can make the arrest. As the mom answered these questions, I moved closer to Charlie. Charlie threatened to "punch me out." That was more than enough; I arrested Charlie. He didn't have a chance even if he intended to resist. We quickly overpowered him.

I brought Charlie to the police station and processed him. He spoke very belligerently throughout the processing but mostly cooperated. I placed him in the holding cell and notified the court. I wrote my report and prepared charges of assault on his mother and criminal mischief for vandalizing his mother's apartment.

A few hours later, dispatch called me to bring my prisoner to court. I woke Charlie and informed him that I was bringing him to court. He expressed more unkind words to me and about the judge. I advised him that it would be in his best interest to show respect for the judge, but he didn't seem willing to accept my advice. I walked Charlie from the cell to the elevator. Normally, this would be done with handcuffs on, but Charlie was so small I felt that he was not much of a threat. Besides, I would have to remove them again before he saw the judge. This judge would expect me to have a very good reason to leave them on.

Charlie and I entered the elevator. I pressed the button for the court level, and we faced the door as the elevator rose. Charlie looked up at me and said, "For a nickel, I would punch your lights out." I looked down at this hot-tempered little guy. The top of his head hardly reached the middle of my chest. I was pretty sure that I had a nickel in my pocket and felt myself reaching for it. Reason took over. I had values far greater than this foolish impulse. Later, I thought about how that would look to the judge whose office is just outside the elevator. It would be like one of those police comedy shows, me slamming a prisoner out of the elevator and onto the floor.

Charlie walked ever so slow and looking about from the elevator to the courtroom. I directed him into the audience seats. He slowly sat down as I told him and to wait until he was called. I sat beside him.

This was an arraignment. It's a public reading of the charges that I prepared. He could enter a not-guilty plea, and a hearing would be scheduled. If he pleads guilty, then the judge most often issues a judgment. In this case, I expected a fine, two hundred dollars at the most.

Charlie demonstrated his true form. He stood only because I stood and told him and pulled slightly on his elbow. He showed the judge no respect. Just the opposite, he showed her disrespect and made it clear he had less respect for her gender. I couldn't help thinking that this was much like my offer for a nickel. The judge has a lot of discretion. Bail is primarily to assure that the defendant will appear in court. Bail can also be established to protect the public, even a single person in public, even a relative. These two charges each carried maximum fines of two thousand dollars and a year in jail. Of course, the judge maintained her composure. I so much wanted to tell her about our conversation in the elevator, but it was irrelevant to the charges before her.

The judge asked for his plea. Charlie only shouted obscenities at her. She looked at me, and I tried to give her an assuring posture with a slight forward nodding of my head. I wanted her to feel assured that I would crush this guy if he made any attempt to approach her. She was much more patient than I would have been and waited for Charlie to end his rant. He did not.

The judge said, "All right then. I will enter a not-guilty plea on your behalf. Do you wish to address bail conditions?" Charlie gave her an obscene reply. She asked me to describe the details of the charges before she imposed bail conditions. I told her that he had done much damage to his mother's apartment, including turning over a refrigerator. I added that his mother reported that he assaulted her.

The judge asked Charlie if he had a place to stay so that he would not return to his mother's apartment. With explicative language, Charlie said that he had no place and wasn't interested in any. She asked if he was working, which he was not. He continued with his language as the judge imposed a bail of two thousand dollars, that he not be within five hundred feet of his mother's apartment, and that he remains in good behavior. She asked if he had any questions. He replied with his vulgarity. Clearly, he had no intentions of being in good behavior. She ordered me to take him into custody.

Normally, after someone is arraigned, they sit and wait until everyone else is arraigned and then all leave the courtroom. Court proceeding proceed more orderly and quickly this way. With the judge's order directly to me to take him into custody, she signaled that she wanted me to remove him and bring him to jail, which I was happy to do. Outside the courtroom, I asked Charlie if he had anyone he could call to raise bail, my only requirement. I got the response I expected. I brought Charlie to the car and brought him to county jail where he would wait until his court date six weeks from now.

Charlie spent that time in jail. He was assigned a court-appointed attorney who negotiated with me and our prosecutor. Charlie got a year in jail suspended with credit for time served and a two hundred dollars suspended fine. This jail time and fine could be called forward if Charlie got in trouble again, which I felt quite likely. Two months later, he was arrested during a street fight. The judge imposed the suspended time.

Nefarious Relationships

Because I had done some substitute teaching when it fit my schedule, some students got to know me and trust me. Though it was frowned upon by some police administration, I found it an advantage. The students know that I will assist them to the best of my ability and without judgment.

The dispatcher called me off patrol to speak with someone in the lobby requesting to speak to me. I recognized Matthew who was sitting in the waiting area when I walked in. He was in a math class when I substituted. I knew him only as someone who sat quietly in class. He was one who didn't focus on work very well, and his grades were low. He always seemed to be daydreaming.

Matthew seemed very nervous and had trouble speaking. Though only the dispatcher could hear us, I realized that this bothered him. I asked if he wanted to come back to a private office. He immediately accepted the invitation.

The arrangement of furniture in an office communicates many things, sometimes unknowingly, sometimes purposefully. I don't like the offices with desks. Desks are usually positioned as instruments of power. A desk can also be a protective barrier for insecure interviewers. In either case, a desk discourages free and equal communication.

The office I chose had a desk, but it also had two chairs in front of it. I offered a chair to Matthew; then I sat in the other. We were in equal positions of power, sitting in front of the desk. Still, Matthew seemed very uncomfortable. He shifted in his chair, and though he looked toward me, he avoided eye contact. He seemed scared to me. I wondered if he was about to tell me of bullying he was experiencing at school. If his peers assaulted him, I would have to refer it to the juvenile officer, in whom I had little confidence. I was worried that I wouldn't be much help for Matthew.

I started with some basic questions. Since I didn't know him very well on a personal level, I began with asking how he preferred to be called. He didn't like being called Matt. He wanted to be called Matthew. I remembered his last name but confirmed it. He was fifteen years old and lived in an apartment I also knew well. It was one owned by the mayor, and it was in poor condition.

With a little momentum in our conversation now, I asked Matthew, "What brings you here?" He said it was about Benjamin. I felt that he was going to explain that Benjamin was a school bully. I was very wrong.

Benjamin was his mom's newest boyfriend. Again, I jumped to a wrong conclusion. Teenagers often have conflicts with transient boyfriends. These power struggles often turn violent. It was still worse than anything I expected.

Matthew described their apartment. It had only one bedroom, and he slept on the couch in the living room. Benjamin and his mother would go to bed, and he would then settle in on the couch. After the first week, Benjamin came into the living room when Matthew's mother had fallen asleep. Over the course of several days, Benjamin manipulated Matthew to lie on the floor beside him. My thoughts went wild. I was wondering, "How did I get myself into this?" I wanted to protect Matthew, but I had a very difficult time listening to his story. Never did I doubt that he was telling the truth. This was too real and too difficult for him to tell me.

Benjamin continued to groom Matthew, massaging him, first on his back, then his legs and feet. Eventually, he loosened Matthew's pants and massaged his buttocks, then his genitals. It culminated with Benjamin performing anal sex on him. This sexual assault has been occurring most nights for the past three months.

This was not at all I wanted to hear. This was so difficult for me to see this fragile young person while he explained this abominable act in great detail. He seemed to feel guilt for his participation. This young person, who I knew from a classroom, was experiencing the unthinkable. He was being groomed during the time I had him in class. How can this happen? How could I have protected him? I now understand why he was daydreaming so much. He couldn't focus. I knew that this would have to be reported to the Division for Children and Youth Services (DCYS) and that they could find a safe place. The legality of this is that I would take him into protective custody, and DCYF would place him in a safe home. Matthew explained that he could stay with his older sister for a few days. I assured Matthew that I would have a warrant for Benjamin's arrest tonight. I added that Benjamin would likely be released. I wanted Matthew to come to me or another police officer if Benjamin attempted anything with him. He agreed. I had him call his older sister who came and got him.

As I assured Matthew, I wrote my report, made a copy for DCYS, prepared an affidavit, and got a warrant for Benjamin's arrest. I went to the apartment. Benjamin wasn't there. I spoke with Matthew's mother. I explained only that there was a warrant for Benjamin's arrest. I emphasized the importance of him turning himself in as soon as possible. I also warned her that she could be charged with hiding him if she allowed him to stay there, knowing that he is wanted.

This conversation with Matthew's mother was also difficult for me. I was speaking with a mother that was supposed to protect her child. She allowed a sexual predator into her home and gave him easy access to her son. As much as this troubled me, I couldn't say anything that could in anyway assist Benjamin for his legal defense or to flee.

My shift ended without finding Benjamin. At the beginning of my next shift, I learned that he had been arrested. I was a bit concerned that he was allowed bail, personal recognizance no less. I had to wonder that, if Matthew was a girl, how much different would it have been.

A short while into my shift, I was called back into the lobby. Matthew was standing there, waiting for me. I was beginning to worry that Matthew may be developing some emotional dependence upon me and just wanted some attention. I asked, and he accepted my offer to come into the office. Again, my first assumption was wrong.

Benjamin had gone to his sister's house. He told Matthew that he had to come to me and say that he lied about the sexual assault. I asked Matthew what he wanted. "Do you want to say that you lied?" He seemed to struggle with the decision, but he was only scared of what Benjamin might do to him for not saying he lied. I tried to assure Matthew that he was doing the right thing by telling me about Benjamin's contact with him. I assured him that the conditions of Benjamin's release included that he should not have contact with him. Since he has violated conditions of his release, Matthew will be arrested and will not be released. I asked Matthew if he felt safe enough to stay with his sister. He said he did, especially if I could keep Benjamin away from him. I assured him that I would do my best. Matthew walked from the station to his sister's apartment a short distance away.

I wrote my report, copied DCYS, prepared another affidavit, and got warrants for contempt of court and witness tampering. I found Benjamin and arrested him. Since he was processed earlier, I only had to update this record with the new arrest. Benjamin was wisely quiet while I processed him. He knew very well that he was being recorded. I struggled with my own feelings. I was sitting next to a person that had committed such horrible acts on a naive and innocent child. He violated the child's trust in his mother, who was also deceived. How can anyone do such a thing to a child who will now have to deal with it the rest of his life?

I called the bail commissioner. He set no bail as I expected from these charges. I brought Benjamin to be housed at the county jail. He was arraigned on the new charges the next morning. The judge continued the no bail and invited his public defender to schedule a bail hearing. The judge then set a date for a probable cause hearing, but the grand jury indicted Benjamin sooner. The felonies were transferred to superior court. Benjamin spent the pretrial period in jail. He pleaded guilty and went to prison for three to five years and was ordered to successfully complete the sex offender program before he could be released. He would be registered forever as a sex offender, which requires registering and regularly reporting to the nearest police station. Failure to do so is a felony. He would also be on parole for many years.

I suppose that I should be satisfied for a job well done, but I am not. Matthew never got any services to help him cope with this horrible experience.

CHAPTER 4

Juvenile Justice

Farmer's Restitution

When I was in high school, I had a much-respected math teacher. She was the first one to persuade me to go to college. I admired her so that I shared with her that I would one day be a math teacher. However, I told her that I wanted to do other things first. It was the days of the Vietnam War, but I still felt attracted to the twenty-year retirement possibility in the military, followed by teaching. I did go into the army after college but decided that wasn't the best for me as my first child was about to be born. I looked toward a police career, which also had a similar twenty-year retirement. During my police service, I thought more about the teaching career and started doing some substitute teaching. One of these assignments included a three-week period as a middle school math teacher. I got to know several students, and meeting them while on duty had some advantages.

One of these times was a call that involved a farmer on the edge of the city. A dirt bike was riding through his field. I was fortunate enough to get there and see the bike. It was far across the field and drove into the woods when I arrived. Nonetheless, I recognized the dirt bike and knew it belonged to a student I knew, Perry.

Horace met me outside his house. He was a dairy farmer. I was certainly aware of the work involved having grown up with my grandfather's vegetable farm and working for a dairy farmer through high school and college. We walked into his cornfield where he showed me the damage that was done by the dirt bike today and in the past. The damage wasn't particularly menacing. I had seen others do donuts, tearing up a lot of the crop. It looked a lot like the rider was just passing through the field as a convenience to access preferred trails. The corn was only a few inches tall. Most bent stalks would recover, though leaning stalks are hard to get into the silage chopper.

Horace has a good reputation in the community. He is well respected as someone who works hard for a living and contributes through his church and directly to community charities. I asked, knowing he would be happy to accept, restitution through labor.

Since I knew Perry and where he lived, I went to his home. His mother greeted me at the door and confirmed that Perry was still out riding his dirt bike. She was concerned about why I was there. I told her that Perry had caused some damage, but it wasn't very serious. She agreed to call the station when Perry got home. She called a couple of hours later.

I spoke with Perry and his mother in their driveway. I told her about Horace and the damage to his cornfield. Perry didn't realize the value of his damage though he realized that he had knocked down some corn. Perry readily agreed to go apologize and offer restitution with his labor. I told him that I would check with Horace after the weekend.

When I spoke with Horace, he was very satisfied with Perry's work. He swept out the barn, picked up a few things around it, and mowed the tall grass. I noticed how nice his barn and the yard appeared. I went to Perry's house to praise him. Perry told me that he worked hard. He liked Horace and thought he was a nice guy. Perry had learned a valuable lesson. I was pleased. Then Perry added, "He paid me ten dollars when I finished." That was more than the minimum wage at the time. This was one of the few times everything came out well for everyone involved.

From Domestic Violence to Juvenile Delinquency

Since I did some substitute teaching while I worked for police, it is inevitable that I would be involved as a police officer and a teacher for some young folks. Herbie was one of these kids. He was in a middle school math class I taught for a month in between teachers. He was a polite kid but seemed to crave extra attention. Honestly, he was a bit annoying. I thought little about it.

Several years went by before I dealt with Herbie's family. I was serving a domestic violence petition on his stepfather, George. George was considerably older than his mother, almost twenty years. The petition was because Herbie's stepfather had threatened, pushed, and struck him and his mother, Janet, when she tried to defend him. I had a sense that I was helping to protect Herbie and his mother.

George was in the living room when I arrived, sitting on the couch. I read the petition to him and its conditions. He must leave the residence immediately and remain two hundred feet from the residence and Herbert and Janet wherever they are in the community. I explained that if he was in a store when he saw them, he must immediately leave the store. He expressed his disagreement but complied. He quickly grabbed what he needed and called a friend to come pick him up.

All seemed OK. I remained a few minutes to make sure Janet would call the police if he returned. He would be charged with trespass. It's the one time someone can be arrested for trespassing in his own home. It's because he has a court order to stay away, removing his right to occupy his property. I also made sure she knew how to contact community support services. She assured me that she knew how to contact the domestic violence advocates but would not. I left, relatively satisfied.

Two days later, I was given a juvenile petition to serve on Herbert and his mother. It accused Herbert of assaulting his stepfather. I was also to remove Herbert from his home and bring him to DCYS (Division for Children and Youth Services). They were placing him with his maternal uncle.

I spoke with Herbie and asked what happened. I thought that perhaps he sought out his stepfather and assaulted him. He said that it was all the same incident. When his stepfather assaulted him and his mother, his mother filed the domestic violence petition.

I asked Janet to explain it to me. She said that she dropped the domestic violence petition and let her husband bring the assault charge against Herbie. I asked why, and she explained, "Herbert will be eighteen in a few months. He plans to move out, and I will be all alone."

It was contrary to the values I had about parents' responsibility to their children. Given the decision that the two could not be in the same house, she exchanged her son for this abusive husband. I found this practice all too often. I could never understand how women could sacrifice their children by staying with someone who abused them and even giving up their children when law enforcement came to protect them when others, such as schools, made the report. I also found that even when women successfully separated from an abusive relationship, they soon were in another. There's something about the characteristics of abusers that these women find attractive. I accept that I cannot understand it but will never stop trying to help them.

Herbie was profoundly affected by this. He seemed very depressed when his mother rejected and abandoned him. He ended up dropping out of school when he turned eighteen and moved to Boston to live with friends. I never heard anything more.

Spiteful Neighbor

There's a small compact neighborhood at the bottom of the hill where the airport is located. These are single-family homes. They are contained within an area bound by a steep bank on three sides and the road and river on the other. The side streets through this neighborhood double as play areas, which is fine as cars pass slowly and the kids get out of the way. It's not unusual to see a portable basketball hoop on the edge of the streets in this neighborhood.

Walt called to report damage done to his home. When I arrived, his wife, Joyce, dominated the conversation. They were reporting damage done to their house with lime-green spray paint. There was a mark on the white portion of the front screen door and a strip at chest height on the clapboards around the perimeter of their house. The house was dark brown with peeling paint. Walt added that he was planning on painting soon anyway. He didn't think the damage was serious and expected that he could wash off the paint on the door. Joyce wasn't so calm. She felt that the offenders needed to be punished. In contrast, Walt would accept restitution. He wouldn't want help painting but thought yard work would be a good idea.

I drove around the neighborhood. I saw a Van Halen symbol painted on the pavement around the corner with the same color paint. I saw a group of four boys about thirteen or fourteen years old nearby. I stopped and approached them. Though I didn't remember their names, I recognized a couple from my times doing substitute teaching, so they recognized me. I noticed Sebastian had some of the green paint on his sneaker. I asked him if he painted the Van Halen symbol on the road. He proudly admitted to it, saying, "Van Halen is my favorite band."

I told him that is the same color paint on Walt and Joyce's house. The boys grew nervous. I didn't seek an admission but suggested they go to Walt, apologize, and offer to help with some yard work. Sebastian said that he was the one who sprayed the house. The other boys just threw some things around the yard. Sebastian assured me that he would make the offer of restitution. I returned to Walt who expressed satisfaction in this outcome. I left it with them to resolve and wrote my report accordingly.

A few days later, I saw a juvenile petition for Sebastian. I was more than just disappointed. I felt angry for two reasons. First, it was contrary to the resolution I had worked out. Second and more significantly, the juvenile officer took over my case without consulting with me. Even worse, Joyce was seeking one thousand five hundred dollars in damages—for a house they were going to paint anyway. Basically, she was attempting to get Sebastian's family to pay for painting their house.

I served the petition on Sebastian and his mother, Toni. She expected it. Toni was angry about breaking the agreement for her son to perform restitution. She was also angry about the amount of money her neighbor sought from her. She felt that it was extortion.

Sebastian's mother hired an attorney. The judge diverted it back to the agreement originally made with me. Since Joyce refused, he dismissed the case.

About two months later, when I was assigned to the other beat, there was a call to this neighborhood involving the reckless operation of a motorcycle. It was Walt who rode his large street bike at these boys who were standing in the road. Granted, the boys had been hanging in the street and took a particularly long time to move out of the way when Joyce and Walt drove through. On this day, when the boys took their sweet time moving out of the way when Joyce came home, Walt got on his motorcycle and drove at the boys at high speed. The boys were in danger of serious bodily harm the way he rode at them, even swerving at them on the edge of the street. My colleague brought the reckless conduct charge. Walt was found guilty of this criminal behavior. The reckless operation conviction carried an automatic one-year loss of driving privileges.

Community policing is a concept that requires cooperation of the community with the police. Even more, it requires cooperation within the police department itself. The juvenile officer was a jerk to kids, families, and fellow officers. In this case, his antagonistic behavior amplified a neighborhood problem to a point that risked lives and cost one his license and means of earning a living. He escalated a problem that could have easily been deescalated by simply demanding that Joyce and Walt stay with their original agreement.

Truants

The school district had a part-time truant officer to address the problem of those students who have many unexcused absences. Claire was an older, short, and very pleasant lady. She loved children and wanted them to attend school to have a better life. She went about her business with rare assistance from police. She worked directly with our prosecutor. She could bring a charge of truancy for the child or charge the parent for violating a law called neglecting the duty of the custodian.

This was a case that has frustrated her. Randy, the father, was loud and intimidating. She had spoken with him several times, yet his sons were consistently truant. It had reached a point that she didn't feel safe dealing with him alone. I met her at the police station, and she rode with me to Randy's home on the densely populated section of North Street.

I knew this family. Randy didn't have a regular job. He claimed to be an antiques dealer. He also had a reputation of being good at horseshoes, participating in many tournaments. I knew him when he got intoxicated and people complained about his loud, threatening behavior. I had several dealings with his boys, who were little thieves. I wrote several reports on them but didn't know the outcome because the juvenile officer didn't communicate outcomes of our cases.

Claire knocked on the door as I stood behind her. She was so short that I could easily see over her head. Randy partly opened the door, placing one shoulder against the doorframe, the other against the door. He leaned his head out the door. He looked at Claire then glanced at me. He asked, "What do you want?"

Claire politely asked to come in to talk about why the boys were not in school. I could see the two oldest boys over Claire and past Randy, who was also very short. They were across the kitchen behind their father, looking in our direction.

Randy asked, "You got a warrant?"

Claire said that she did not but wanted to talk about how important it was for the boys to attend school.

Randy reemphasized, "Not without a warrant you won't." Then closed the door.

Claire turned to me and said, "What are you going to do?" She apparently expected me to have some magic that would persuade Randy to let us in.

I told Claire that Randy was correct. We needed a warrant to proceed. I assured her that I saw all that I needed, the boys when they should have been in school. She still seemed distressed. I assured her that I would get the warrant Randy spoke about.

I brought Claire back to her car and went into the police station. I wrote my report and prepared an affidavit for the warrant.

The warrant was for Randy's arrest for a parent failing to perform his duty to send his children to school.

With the warrant and a summons to court in hand, I returned to Randy's house less than an hour later. I knocked on the door, and Randy opened it.

I held up the warrant for Randy's arrest and said, "See the warrant?"

Randy replied, "Yes, come on in." He opened the door and stepped back, allowing me in.

I said, "Too late now, Randy. Here's the summons to court." I handed it to him and walked away. He was later found guilty. They moved out of town, and the process started again in the other school district.

The failure to send one's child to school is only a violation. There is no possibility of any jail time unless it turns into contempt of court. This could happen if Randy refused to pay the fine and/or continued to not send his children to school should the court order him to do so. He reset the process by paying the fine and moving to another school district. His sons never made it into high school.

Dustin at School

There were no cell phones during my police days. You either had a landline or no phone. When a student's behavior at school became intolerable to the point the principal decided to send the student home, she or he called the parent to come get his or her student. If they couldn't locate a parent or the alternatives on their list, they called the police for assistance. I got such a call early one afternoon because Beverly had no phone.

Much information is not transmitted over the radio to protect children's confidentiality. Dispatch requested a 10-9 (phone call) or 10-11 (report to headquarters). Like most officers, I avoided headquarters during regular hours because that is when all the "brass" are there. To get a phone call, we stopped at a phone booth and called the number to dispatch over the radio. She would then call the phone booth, and I would bypass the customary fee for using the pay phone.

The dispatcher told me that North Street School couldn't reach Dustin's mother because the phone was no longer in service. The address was 160 North Street, apartment number 5. It was just a few houses from the school. I parked the police car beside the house and went upstairs to the second of the three floors. I knocked on the door marked number 5. Immediately, a disgruntled female voice said, "Come in."

I was always very skeptical about just walking in as a uniformed police officer. People in this neighborhood often go to one another's apartment. They were not shy about using marijuana or other illegal activities with their neighbors. Part of me didn't want to walk into any criminal behavior in progress. It could be a very difficult court case if the defendant's lawyer said that they didn't realize that I was a police officer and that I was required to identify myself before I entered.

I replied, "It's the police." Her response, "I don't give a f——who you are. What the f—— do you want? Come in." I cautiously opened the door and entered.

The door entered a kitchen. Immediately to the right was the door to the living room that had windows to the front of the building. The TV was between two windows. A soap opera was playing. Beverly was lying on a mattress on the floor, on her left side, facing the TV, her back to me. She was a large, overweight woman, with blonde shoulder-length hair, and dressed only in a pink flower-patterned nightgown.

She turned slightly toward me and spoke over her right shoulder. "What do you want?"

I replied, "The school called. They want you to go get Dustin."

Beverly blurted back, "I can't go. My back is hurting. It's not my problem. It's the school's problem when he is there."

I was a bit taken back by her ease at dismissing her parental responsibilities and giving completely over to the school. "He's not my problem now," she continued.

I replied, "I am just the messenger." She responded, "Then go tell them to keep him there." I said, "No, the message goes one way. I will not go to the school, but I assure you this. If the school calls again, I will go and get Dustin. I will bring him to the police station, and you will have to pick him up there." The police station is considerably farther away than the school. "If you refuse to get him from the police station, I will call DCYS and charge you with neglect."

Beverly was not at all happy with me and let loose a string of profanity combined with pig comments that few people can assemble. She struggled in getting up off the mattress and started to come in my direction since I was standing in the living room doorway. I turned and left, assuring her that I would only be further involved if the school called me. Her final send-off to me was another short burst of profanity. I didn't hear anything more, so I assume either she or someone walked the one hundred yards to the school and retrieved Dustin.

Later, that summer, I got a call from a neighbor in this neighborhood. Two boys were trying to break into her garage. When I arrived on the scene, I found two boys about ten and twelve years old. It appeared that they knew better than to run away, or maybe they didn't know enough to try. I certainly would have been able to catch at least one of them.

I brought them to the police station with the intention of calling their parents and releasing them. For juvenile cases worthy of prosecution, I would write my report later and turn it over to the juvenile officer for final disposition. When I asked their names, they replied Dustin and Gregory. Their address was 160 North Street, apartment number 5, Beverly's apartment. They had no phone. I took their pictures for my report, then brought them home.

I would not let the boys just walk in even though it was their home. I made them wait as I knocked on the door. It was déjà vu.

The rough female voice responded, "Come in." I replied, "It's the police again, Beverly." I heard another string of profanity and sounds consistent with her getting up from the mattress. The door flew open, and Beverly stood there. She looked at her sons, then me.

I explained, "I caught the boys breaking into a garage." She replied, "I can't watch them all the time. When they are out there, it's your job."

I agreed that I was doing my job, which was to catch criminals and bring them to prosecution. I informed her that I would be turning this over to the juvenile officer and she can be expecting to hear from him soon.

The boys went into the apartment. She unleashed her profanity-laced assault upon them for making her life difficult. It was only a few minutes before the boys were back on the street. As usual, the secretive juvenile officer never advised me of any outcome.

Jeter's Canine Passions

Jeter lived at the end of a dead-end street at the edge of the urban compact. His house was literally the end of the street. If anyone kept driving, she or he would drive into the house. I never went far into his house. What I saw from the door was enough to discourage me if I didn't have to go in. It had a dirt floor. Other officers told me that the dirt floor extended throughout the house. The house exterior was an assembly of building materials with inconsistent structure and materials. Part looked like a house that was never finished. Another side of it looked more like a storage shed. There were few windows, and they were always covered with a collection of boards and cloth.

The family had many dogs, cats, chickens, geese, and sometimes goats and sheep. Their lot was not large enough, nor did they have a barn. These animals were kept in the multiple pens in the small yard. They also went in and out of the house like it was a barn.

Other houses in the neighborhood varied from a small well-kept home, mobile homes, and a poorly maintained duplex. One neighbor was a highly skilled mechanic who was well respected throughout the community. Another neighbor was a family that was not well educated and had explosive tempers. This was a mix with many conflicts to which the police were often called.

Most calls were about the trespassing animals. Jeter's mother, Narla, listened to her police scanner and was always ready for my arrival, standing in the door. She was a short, stocky woman with shoulder-length hair, always in a dress that hung loosely on her body. She was always barefoot, regardless of the season. Narla was always belligerent and poised for an argument that began even as I exited the police car. There was little point in engaging in any argument with her. My simple response was that I would serve the warrant if any of her neighbors were willing to sign the complaint.

The neighbors never were willing to sign a complaint. They expected me to arrest her on what I saw. All I saw were animals around the home that occasionally ventured into the street. No judge would convict her for what I saw as small animals walk harmlessly on a dead-end street. No officer liked going to these unresolvable calls.

I dealt with Jeter during his midteens. He was always dressed in clothes that were too big for him. They were always disheveled, dirty, torn, and had holes worn into them. His hair was long and scraggly. He spoke with great difficulty with an unrepaired, deviated septum. He was very hard to understand. No one wanted to get close to him due to his appearance, odor, and strange behaviors. For those of us who knew him, his behaviors were even weirder.

Jeter had a history of bestiality. His family seemed to accept it. There were certainly enough animals in his home for him. The rumor around the department was that his mother only got upset once. It is believed that she got angry when he choked a duck to death during one of these amorous acts.

One day, I was standing behind dispatch fulfilling some administrative paperwork duties when a call came in. It was Jeter's neighbor. Jeter was performing this illegal act on the neighbor's poor helpless dog chained in their backyard. It was my beat, and the dispatcher quickly let me know. She wanted me to rush right out and catch Jeter in the act. My imagination was sufficiently traumatic. Finding Jeter performing the act was not high on my bucket list. Jokingly, I asked her to let me know when he finished, then left without delay.

Jeter was long gone when I got there. I took the report from the poor neighbor. He and his family were understandably most upset. I went to Jeter's home. His mother came to the door. She told me that Jeter had left.

Since he was a juvenile, I wouldn't be taking him into custody or even getting a warrant for his arrest. I simply completed my report and forwarded it to the juvenile officer for him to follow it up. I didn't hear of any outcome, but that is the nature of juvenile cases. I don't believe anything was done, and Jeter was neither punished nor the recipient of any needed services.

To cope with this disgusting sides of humanity, some cops joke and may say something disgusting to one another. When referring to Jeter at shift change, it wasn't unusual to hear someone break into chorus, "Knickknack paddywhack, give a dog a bone." When Jeter was mentioned, someone might say, "Well, f—— a duck." Another one was "Jeepers creepers, it's Jeter's tweeter." There were others, even worse, that I would never repeat.

Community Youth Advocates

When someone says CYA, typically one is referring to "cover your aft" or something similar. I am referring to Community Youth Advocates. This was a nonprofit organization to "street counsel" youths. Lester had served prison time for crimes that he had committed during his heavy alcohol use. He sought similar younger adults to counsel youths. It became tremendously popular and respected. There were several positive newspaper articles reporting its success.

My relationship with the juvenile officer, Darby James, was strained. I can appreciate some level of confidentiality, but he certainly could have given some feedback on cases in which I and other officers were involved. I learned secondhand, mostly when the youth reoffended. Much too often, the youth had no corrective actions imposed for the prior offense. This eroded my confidence in the juvenile officer and thereby my relationship with him.

We also clashed on personalities and dedication to the community. Darby was from a southern New Hampshire town. We understood that his transfer to Claremont was encouraged by that police department. More plainly stated, they were glad to get rid of him.

Darby had a GED (General Equivalency Diploma). I had a master's degree. I was born in this community, attended the local schools, and worked my way through college. I left this community only to attend college and serve in the army. I hoped to apply my education and experience to better my community. I started substitute teaching and providing foster care. Darby didn't participate in the community and was regularly calculating his retirement benefits. He also calculated and ordered all the materials to build his house while on duty. Darby seemed to care only about making his life easier. He had a poster in his office that read, "Hurry up and move out while you still know everything." He communicated openly about preferring harsh punishments over services. The only service he preferred was CYA. It made his life easy to just divert most of his workload to them.

Again, I only learned about which of my cases were referred this way by future encounters with the youth. I began going directly to the CYA staff with my concerns, bypassing Darby. Lester was most understanding, and I felt he followed up to the best of his ability. To the best of his ability is a key issue that I had with the whole agency. Lester's heart was in the right place, and he truly wanted to serve the community in this way. Unfortunately, he too had only a GED and no education on child development or social welfare. The agency did not consult with any professionals in this regard.

Lester hired Andy. His experience involved alcohol, drugs, and prison time. He didn't even have a GED. Andy dressed in worn and torn jeans and T-shirt with prints that stressed normal decency limits. His brown curly hair was shoulder-length and tied back. He rarely shaved. Except in court, his language was filled with obscenities. He and Lester thought this appearance and speech helped him connect with the youth. I disagreed with this, believing that these youths needed role models to raise their standards, not role models who lowered themselves to their standards and even lower.

The New Hampshire Department of Human Services started to monitor agencies that were not directly regulated by law or administrative rules. They could only suggest improvements until rules were in place. Developing rules and the approval process takes many months or years. It was becoming clear that CYA would eventually need someone with some credentials.

Lester hired Roger. At least Roger had a college education, though from a college with low standards. Roger promised to work on a master's degree in counseling, which is what the state rules would eventually require. Roger had not been to prison or ever convicted of any crimes. He presented himself well, neatly dressed and with a neat haircut. He took pride in how he was able to relate with troubled youth.

It bothered me when Roger told me that his conversations with the youths were confidential. He used the example, "I know who stole the twelve gas tanks from the boats in Sunapee Harbor, but I can't tell you." I didn't even know that gas tanks were stolen since it was not only in a different town, it was also a different county. What bothered me is that Roger was defining his confidentiality privilege reserved for licensed therapists, lawyers, and other duly licensed professions. I felt that he was enabling, even encouraging criminal behavior. He wasn't even attempting to encourage restitution, just teaching the thieves how to stay out of the court system.

The administrative rules developed slowly. Eventually, court diversion programs became regulated. It required a board of directors and a diversion committee from the community. Lester managed to comply. Even though these were all volunteers, the operation expenses were increasing. Lester was skillful at fund-raising and managed to keep his organization afloat for a while.

Lester helped establish a group home for adolescents in the city. Previously, youths committed to residential programs were sent out of the community. This was welcomed by local people and the state officials. However, as the state looked closer, it had the same credentialing problems as CYA. It had no real program, no specialized treatment, no way of knowing if the youths attained goals to be returned to their families.

During this time, Andy started drinking alcohol and smoking marijuana heavily again. He was arrested by the Cornish police for a domestic assault. Lester stood by him, which seriously hurt the public opinion of CYA.

As the state pressed for properly credentialed and licensed employees, neither CYA nor the residential program could find sufficient funding to achieve these standards. Though it seemed to leave a hole that was much needed, it wasn't long before another agency started a properly credentialed court diversion program.

A well-operated court diversion program can help with the development of youths while teaching them the importance of restorative justice. The program held the youth to expectations. If they failed to perform, their case was sent back to court. It still doesn't forbid the local beat cop from encouraging youths to make amends for their wrongs without going through the formal diversion process. I felt that it discouraged some officers from using this valuable community relationship tool.

Gravel Pit Parties

We would learn about the parties in a gravel pit when a neighbor called to complain. It seemed that the neighbors grew concerned when the bonfires were too large. When we arrived, people scattered into the woods. There were too many people and too large of an area to have any hope of containing them. Even if we could successfully contain them, our entire department doesn't have the resources to transport and process so many. Our purpose was to disrupt the underage drinking and make sure everyone leaves safely.

These parties were a mixture of teenagers and young adults. Those who were old enough to possess alcohol often remained after the others fled. During my first involvement, I followed my mentor's lead. He drove the police car close to the bonfire, causing panic to the partiers who ran in all directions. He walked around those remaining and verified their age. He then pointed to any unopened beer and asked, "Is this yours?" The intelligent ones denied ownership of it, except for only the beer they held in their hand. If they admitted to possessing the larger amount, they would be arrested and charged with providing beer to a minor. Any such arrest posed significant legal difficulties because we would have to identify the specific minors to whom he provided the alcohol. Upon receiving the negative response, my mentor would say, "Then you won't mind that I take this into evidence." This gave fuel to the popular rumor that the cops took the evidence for themselves. In my early years, I was insulted by this assumption, especially since I didn't drink alcohol. Later, I began to realize that there was an element of truth to it when several officers planned a party involving free beer. Some even called it choir practice, like at the academy.

I decided to handle these pit party complaints alone when they were in my beat. One of my favorites was when I parked the car with others in attendance. I left the hat and baton in the car so as not to be recognized in the dark. I still carried my thirty-thousand-candlepower flashlight in my lower leg pocket. I was able to walk past several people, even exchanging hellos, without being detected as a police officer. I walked up to the edge of the crowd surround the fire. Still, no one noticed that I was a cop. So I took out my flashlight, turned it on, and scanned the crowd. It was the first time that I heard a crowd of about one hundred people gasp in unison followed by the clink of several beer bottles hitting the ground dropped in rapid succession.

The crowd didn't immediately disperse. I was able to express my concern for their safety in getting home. Several assured me that they were fine. Since it was early in the party, I felt comfortable that no one was significantly impaired but still watched for any that might have problems moving. They all seemed fine.

I was left with the usual few that were of legal age. I did as my mentor did and inquired about their ownership of the remaining beer. When they denied it, I said, "Then you won't mind if I dump it on the ground." I then started opening and dumping the bottles into the gravel. I found some special enjoyment in watching their faces as I poured that hard-earned, expensive brew. I told them that they could help me if they wished. All declined and walked away. I found great satisfaction in dispelling the rumor about this cop drinking beer taken as evidence.

More troubling than the pit parties were the parties at homes. There were only so many pits, and we could be alerted during the prime partying times. We had no way of knowing about the teenage house parties until someone complained. Sadly, most of the complaints were around the noise because the neighbors weren't aware that the parents were gone.

I saw several houses trashed by these parties. The normal partying was bad enough with spills and even vomit. Some showed up with intentions to do harm to retaliate for past social interactions. At one party, someone dumped cement into the pool. At another, they punched numerous holes in doors and walls and tore doors off cabinets. When I found these parties in full swing, I typically found a teenager that warranted taking into custody and having the parent come to the police station to get them. Three in one night was my greatest haul.

I was off the night a colleague began what I consider over-zealous in taking a youth into custody. The star football player was called Weasel because he was fast and nimble. He "talked back" at Officer Bradbury when he arrived at the party. It was Weasel's home, and he had invited football players, the spirit team, and others. These were students who did well in school but were not making a wise decision to have this party. Officer Bradbury decided to arrest Weasel. Weasel decided to run. Officer Bradbury was outmatched by Weasel's skills but decided to even the odds with his baton. He beat Weasel into submission.

The family knew me and asked for me to stop by their home when I came on duty. They didn't excuse Weasel's behavior but couldn't understand why Officer Bradbury had to be so violent, especially when he knew Weasel was easily identifiable if he managed to get away. Weasel's injuries were serious enough that he couldn't play for several weeks. It may have not only impacted his ability and desire to advance in football but also his higher educational scholarship opportunities. I hated being in these positions. I explained how an officer can use whatever force is necessary to make the arrest. I also explained that I had no authority to decide on either position and referred them to the chief. I'm glad that they understood. They obtained a lawyer for civil action.

Mailbox Bashers

It was my night to be on foot patrol in the downtown area. It's a good assignment during a warm summer evening. The foot patrol officer rarely had to write reports. Its purpose is mostly for visibility and public relations, especially for the downtown business owners. I was enjoying the evening, walking and talking with people on the street.

I monitored a call to the mobile patrol officers. There was a car riding around the edges of the city. They were smashing mailboxes with a baseball bat as they drove by. This isn't an unusual problem. What made this one stand out is that we had a call while it was in progress. There were subsequent calls. Collectively, we had a very good description of the car, its Vermont registration number, and the four youths inside it. The frustrating part was trying to intercept this car as it was causing damage in different parts of the city.

I thought about asking to take a spare cruiser to assist in the search. Spare cruisers are last year's cars. They have high mileage and lots of wear. They are reasonably reliable, but newer models are preferred for their dependability in emergencies. Spare cruisers are used to attend meetings and out-of-town trainings by officers. They are also handy for backing up the primary patrol cars when additional police presence is desired. Before making this request to my supervisor, I decided to check the downtown parking areas. Much to my surprise, I found the car in the municipal parking lot.

I stood back from the car, remaining in the shadows. I worried that people inside would see me and drive away. I radioed my findings so that the patrol cars could be nearby to intercept it if it drove away. When one was nearby, I approached the car. There was no one inside. The patrol car remained nearby, and I returned to the shadows to observe the car.

It wasn't long before four individuals appeared. I sounded the alarm, and we quickly surrounded them; a patrol car trapped the car in the parking space. The four ran in different directions. I had an advantage, being already on foot and anticipating their reaction. I could only catch one, which I did with a very short run. I easily took him to the ground and applied handcuffs. He was a teenager from Windsor, just across the Connecticut River. I stood him up and walked him to the police car, placing him in the back seat.

I looked around to see if I could help. My other favorite partner, Bob, was calling for assistance. He was between two buildings about fifty yards from me. Assured that my prisoner was safely observed by the officer assigned to this car, I ran to Bob's position.

I found Bob struggling on the ground with a very combative individual. They were between two buildings, which was shaded from the streetlights and very dark. Bob is not very big, thin and slightly shorter than the average officer. The person with whom he struggled was about his size. In the dark, they appeared to be entangled with each other. This is very dangerous as the officer's gun may be accessible to the combatant; hence, there is a potential injury to the officer, my friend.

I searched for the combatant's hand. My intention was to grab it and pull the combatant out from the entanglement, directing him facedown to the ground for handcuffing. I saw a skinny hand move in my direction. I grabbed the wrist and pulled with great energy, physically communicating my dominance to the combatant. Unfortunately, it was Bob's wrist. I was at first disappointed with myself, but it exposed the combatant, and I could see more clearly. As I separated the two men, a dagger fell to the ground. Grabbing the wrong wrist now seemed like a very good thing as I believe he was trying to stick the dagger into Bob. Interrupting Bob's efforts removed him from harm. We quickly subdued this combatant, but he wouldn't give up the fight. He struggled with us and called to his friends to resist. He continued his struggles while in custody, calling to the others to resist.

The other patrol officers easily caught the other two. The combatant who struggled with Bob was the only adult. Since he was uncooperative, we searched him and placed him in a jail cell. Because he fought every bit of the way, we left the handcuffs on. Even in the jail cell, he kept calling to his friends to resist.

The other three were minors, fifteen and sixteen years old. They were cooperative, but we didn't want to dedicate all our police officers to process them simultaneously. We have five adult male cells and the adult in one. We had one female cell and one juvenile cell. I didn't like the juvenile cell because it is too much like a closet. Some kids may have been locked in closets, and this would be too traumatic. The extreme isolation is traumatic regardless of their experiences.

Even though they were arrested together, we now must maintain separation from adult prisoners. We further wanted the separation with this adult's continued efforts to incite them. Two were brothers, so I put them in the female cell while I processed the other.

I collected only basic information and photos. I switched the one teenager with the brothers and processed them together. When finished, I brought all three to an upstairs office and called their parents. I was in no hurry to process the adult. He was still ranting and calling to the boys.

While waiting for their parents to drive from Windsor, I talked with them. They called the adult "Turk," his chosen nickname. It wasn't his heritage at all. It was that he was fascinated in the old knives and swords he attributed to Turkish people.

Turk was a janitor at Windsor High School. They met him there and started hanging out with him after school and on weekends. They decided to come to Claremont this night. The boys didn't seem to have consumed any alcohol or drugs and denied using any this night.

I spoke with each parent when they arrived. Our juvenile officer is unpredictable about what charges he pursues, so I couldn't give any assurance on this possibility. The parents seemed surprised. They knew that boys were hanging out together. The did not know about Turk, nor did they realize the boys had left their town or even riding in a car. I assured them that I preferred to leave this matter in their hands and would make that recommendation. I released the boys to their parents.

I notified Bob that I was available to help process Turk. Technically, Turk was Bob's arrest since he had first direct contact with him. So I stood by to assist. Turk was still mostly noncompliant and calling to his friends. He seemed very disappointed when I told him they had left with their parents. We didn't get very far in the processing. We can hold someone up to twenty-four hours, not including weekends and holidays. Since this was a Friday night, we could hold him until Monday. However, this judge routinely came in Saturday mornings if we had any arraignments. We returned Turk to his cell. We removed the handcuffs at the cell entrance. He walked in, yelled for a little while, then sat on the bunk. He eventually went to sleep.

Bob processed charges of soliciting criminal activity from the minors, criminal mischief, and a felony of transporting minors across state lines without parent consent. Our shift ended. The morning shift completed the processing. He was arraigned the next morning and was being held at the county jail for lack of bail.

I was very concerned about how Turk recruited and influenced these teenagers and that his work at the high school provided easy access to them. I wrote a letter to the Windsor High School principal. I described what they had done and how Turk continued to incite these students while in police custody. I was surprised and deeply disappointed in his response. He stated that Turk was a good employee, and this was not in keeping with his normal behavior. He suggested that the aberrant behavior might have been caused by drugs. I still shake my head. Why would he allow this guy near these children? The fact that he thought Turk was using drugs was just further information confirming my reason to notifying him. Knowing that I did my best and informed competent parents remains my consolation.

Bluff School Break-in

Sunday afternoons are usually quiet. This was a particularly pleasant sunny summer Sunday. At two o'clock, the dispatcher informed me that the alarm was going off at Bluff School. Some places have lots of false alarms, but the schools had great alarm systems. When they went off, it was usually someone who was working at odd hours and didn't correctly enter the code to deactivate the alarm.

We usually drove to such alarms with blue lights only. A siren would tip off a burglar. I was close enough that I didn't even use the lights. I notified dispatch by signing off at the school. I looked for a staff person's car as I approached the school. There wasn't one. I drove around behind the building, assessing doors and windows. On the back side, I found a broken window next to the rear exit. There was a bicycle leaning against the building next to this broken window.

I informed dispatch of my broken window and bicycle finding and went into the building through this broken window.

Once inside, I listened. I heard footsteps as they ran across the second floor. I was game for a chase, but the problem I had was this school has two staircases, and I can only go up one. I asked for an estimated arrival time for a backup. Because he didn't expect anything of substance either, he was ten minutes away. I was worried that my burglar would go out a window or fire escape. I yelled, "Don't run! The dog will bite you!" I positioned myself on the ground floor between the two staircases and intended to wait for my backup. The two of us could have each taken a stairway.

A minute later, I heard a young male voice say, "I'm not running." I saw the sneakers coming down the stairs very slowly. I walked toward him, and he came to me without a problem. I could see that he was a child, but older than the ones that go to this grade school. Kids tend to break into schools they attend. So I thought he may have more serious criminal intent beyond just trespassing. When I asked, he told me his name was Bobby.

I asked Bobby for his last name and address. Bobby was thirteen years old. He lived in Windsor, Vermont. With prompting, he told me that he used to go to this school before they moved to Windsor. Bobby was dressed in old, well-worn clothes. His light-brown hair was cut poorly, probably by someone in the household.

Being a border town, it is not unusual for people to move from one state to another when legal troubles increased. Often, the social service agency is getting too close to taking an unfavorable action, and they just move out of the jurisdiction. After a year, the agency must close its case, and the family moves back. Often by then, the other state agency is beginning to act, and back and forth they go. I didn't have anything to be certain that is what was happening, and I didn't need to know. Bobby has now committed a crime, and I would be making a referral regardless of his residency or legal status.

My backup arrived. I called dispatch to notify the school of the damage and open window. I walked Bobby out the back door where his bike and my car were. This door is not alarmed. The alarm is based on motion detectors, not perimeter switches. Motion detectors are easy to strategically place in a school that are activated by motion in the halls.

Bobby was fully cooperative, but I felt that he might not get the full benefit of the consequences of his actions, so I decided to put handcuffs on him. It might help convince him of the seriousness of his actions. I placed him in the back seat of the police car, then put his bike in the trunk. The bike was old and in poor condition. It didn't appear that the brakes worked.

Bobby was looking around outside the car when I got in. He asked, "Where's the dog?" I replied, "He's in the other car." Bobby replied, "Oh." I think that he had no idea I lied about the presence of a police dog.

I drove into the sally port like I would with any criminal. I brought Bobby into the processing room. I removed the handcuffs, photographed him, and completed a brief juvenile processing. I called his mother, and she was on her way.

After processing, I brought Bobby upstairs to an office to wait for his mother. It's not good practice to place a child in a jail cell unless it's very necessary. Since his mother was on her way, I brought Bobby upstairs to an office to wait for her. While waiting, Bobby spoke freely. He described a lot of petty trouble that he gets into. He explained that he wasn't interested in stealing anything from the school. He was bored and wanted to look around. He'd done some shoplifting. He didn't like school, and it was easy to see that his education was far below his present age.

When Bobby's mother arrived, I brought her into the office. I had Bobby explain why he was here, which he did simply but accurately. I explained that I would be filing a report and referring him to the juvenile officer, who would be in contact with her. She and Bobby met me behind the police station to retrieve his bike. She took Bobby home. It's not likely that this juvenile officer would attempt any charges across the state line.

CHAPTER 5

Motor Vehicle Accidents

Unresponsive with Toddler

Dispatch sent me to a 10-25 with PI, a motor vehicle accident with personal injury, on Unity Road. By the dispatcher's description, it was between the twin bridges, the two stream crossings, before Spring Farm Road, which is about two miles from the center of the city and not far from my home. Unity Road is a minor state-maintained road, so it is one of the better highways through Claremont. The speed limit in this area is forty miles per hour. Though it was near my home, I wasn't worried that it could be a member of my family because my children were in school and my wife was working.

Accidents with known personal injury demand a code 3 run, with lights and sirens as fast as reasonably possible. The dispatcher will dispatch the ambulance and fire department immediately after notifying me. Both monitor police calls and would likely be already moving to their vehicles before being dispatched. I was still well ahead of them.

I found the car that slid sideways against a large maple tree in front of my neighbor's brick home. The operator had lost control around the corner between the two bridges. There was significant damage to the passenger side of the car, which was against the tree. The property owner, my neighbor, was standing by the car. My first responsibility is to keep the scene from getting worse to make sure no one else will get hurt or for the ones already hurt from getting worse.

Since it was well off the road, I could protect the scene by parking the police car on the edge of the road with the lights running.

I ran up to the car. A woman was leaning over from the driver's position toward the passenger's side. She was not responsive. Beside her was a toddler in a car seat, in the front seat, facing rearward. This was the recommended way to transport small children at the time. The toddler appeared to be unhurt. She looked at me with blinking eyes. She wasn't even crying, just looking as though she was wondering what was going on. Knowing the ambulance would be monitoring, I radioed that the driver was unresponsive, and a child seemed to be OK.

I refocused on the woman. She did not respond to my calls. Her eyes were closed, and her eyelids were twitching. She was not wearing a seat belt. Since the car slid sideways into the tree, she would have been thrown from the driver's position and onto the toddler. I looked again at the toddler and the car seat with its high protective sides. The child still seemed fine. I still worried as she was not crying, but she seemed alert, looking at me. The firefighters arrived, followed within seconds by the ambulance. One firefighter checked for hazards with the car while the EMTs and the other firefighter attended to the woman and child.

I stood by if further assist to the injured was needed. With the scene stabilized and the injured being treated, I could start trying to understand how the accident happened. The tire markings indicated that she was driving toward Unity. Just as she approached the final bridge, the car veered sharply to the left. The turn was so violent that it caused the car to rotate into a sideways slide and into the tree. There were no indications of any attempt to regain control. I suspected that the violent left turn was because she was drifting into the guardrail at the bridge. She made a dramatic correction that started the slide. Because she wasn't wearing a seat belt, the sudden change in direction of the car caused her to leave the driver's seat. Once out of the driving position, she would be unable to control the vehicle. Her motion was due to Newton's first law of motion. An object in motion will remain in motion until acted upon by an outside force. The car changed direction due to the force of the turn while she remained traveling in a straight line. Her body stopped its motion when she crashed with the interior of the car, which was likely the child's car seat and the passenger door.

I still wondered why this woman was seemingly having a minor seizure. The EMTs found no serious head injury but worked carefully to get her secured onto a backboard to protect her back, neck, and head. They transported both the woman and the child to the hospital. I continued processing the scene and called for a wrecker to remove the vehicle.

I went to the hospital to inquire further about the injuries. The child was fine, but they learned that she wasn't the driver's daughter. She was taking care of the child for a friend. They were not able to find a medical explanation for the woman's unresponsiveness. Her injuries were just bumps and bruises. I was suspicious that she was faking a medical reason for the cause of the accident. It didn't matter to me. Clearly, she was in control of the car. Loss of control caused the accident. There were no other vehicles involved, just a tree. Not wearing a seat belt could have been a significant contributing factor but after the initial event.

I have often heard an argument that there are times when you could be better off without a seat belt. I chose not to engage directly. I simply respond, "Maybe, though I have never seen one." I have investigated hundreds of accidents. I have seen some when it wouldn't have mattered because the vehicle was destroyed. Never have I seen one where they would have been better off without a seat belt. I realize that people who fixed on this excuse to not wear their seat belt will never be convinced otherwise.

This accident illustrates another reason to wear a seat belt. She might have been able to recover from the overcorrected reaction if she had not left the driver's position. Interestingly, when I got the code 3 call to this accident, I gave my usual tug on my seat belt to hold my butt firmly in the driver's seat. A code 3 run is a violent run. If I slide even a little in the seat, I cannot keep the firm control of the police car to operate at higher speed.

I have heard many cops say they feel the seat belt makes them less safe in the police car. We respond to a variety of calls. Sometimes we drive into dangerous situations. A cop in the driver's seat is a sitting duck, an easy target. We are safer when we get out and can move to safer locations, even if it is beside the car. They say that time it takes to unbuckle the seat belt may be too late.

There is a technique that cops can practice so that the time it takes to unbuckle the seat belt is no longer a factor. Several things must happen in rapid sequence or simultaneously as one brings the fast-moving car to a safe stop. We must quickly determine strategic position for the car as we arrive. We typically turn off the siren but leave the blue lights running. We must sign off, notifying the dispatcher we are at the scene. We may also make additional requests of the dispatcher as we begin analyzing the scene and the situation. We must put the car in park, unbuckle the seat belt, open the door, get out of the car, and close and lock the door or decide to leave the door open.

I found a technique that worked for me. First, I thought about how much is done by my right hand: the radio, siren, steering, moving the shifting lever, unbuckling the seat belt, and reaching across my body to pull the door handle. I learned to unbuckle the seat belt with my left hand. I could do this well in advance of stopping the car. I take my left hand off the steering wheel and place it against my chest. I slide my hand under the shoulder strap and over it to reach across my body to release the button of the seat belt. I raise my arm to cause the seat belt to slide across my body and be retracted into its position or fall beside the seat, out of the way, then replace my left hand to the steering wheel. I turn off the siren with my right hand. This way, the dispatcher can understand me better without the loud siren in the background. I sign off and make any requests. I don't try to hang up the radio microphone in its holder, leaving it on the seat so I can still easily find it. I pull the door handle with my left hand and simultaneously place the vehicle in park. While pulling the door handle and moving the selector to park, I push open the door with my shoulder. If the scene is dangerous, I will roll out of the car, staying close to the ground. Even before my foot hits the ground, I am already drawing my weapon with my right hand. By the time I have both feet on the ground, I am ready to fire my weapon. Practicing this is essential. When it's safe, I practiced skidding the car to a stop. With the wheels locked up, you can place the car in park while it's still moving. There's also no point in trying to steer the car in a safe skid, freeing both hands to coordinate the other tasks.

After investigating hundreds of accidents, I found no valid reason to not wear a seat belt. It is far more likely to protect you than to hurt you. It will also keep you in the seat to better control the car and possibly avoid the accident altogether.

Let me explain science about how seat belts reduce injury and saves lives. In physics, force times distance is work. It takes energy to perform work. Force over distance divided by time is power. The seat belt works on the principle of spreading the force over a distance and increasing the time of the deceleration. If you can stay in your seat as the car slows down, less energy is applied to your body. Even though it's a fraction of a second, it is more time. Time is divided into this force, making it less. Cars are designed to crumble. Again, force times distance. As the car crumbles, it is dissipating energy as it slows you in your seat belt. Without the seat belt, you continue to travel at full speed inside the car as it crumbles to a stop. Your body strikes the inside of the stopped car at whatever speed you were traveling.

Imagine this example. Run into a wall. Now place a mattress against the wall and run into it again. The wall stops you immediately. The mattress stops you over a distance. That is how a seat belt works. The mattress crumbles as the car does. Your body is slowed by its contact with the mattress just as the seat belt slows you.

When I teach physics, I work my students through the math. I let them decide the weight and speed. I show the force of the body, which varies from one thousand five hundred to three thousand five hundred pounds, depending on their choice. I then point out that many people think they can hold themselves by placing their hand on the dash. To them, I say, "Congratulations! You must be able to bench press three thousand five hundred pounds in one quarter of a second."

Another recommendation is to decrease speed as much as you can before a collision. It's easy to show the math again. The energy in the crash is half the mass times the velocity squared. You can't change the mass of vehicle. For every five miles per hour you decrease, energy decreases exponentially. It's not the case that in a head-on collision, the faster vehicle fairs better. Newton's third law states that the forces are equal and opposite. The more either one slows, the less the energy in the crash. Wear your seat belt.

Only in New Hampshire can you not wear a seat belt or a motorcycle helmet as an adult. If you continue to live the state motto, "Live free or die," do someone a favor and sign your organ donor card.

Trucker Not the Cause

It's not unusual to have volatile tempers and arguments in progress when a police officer arrives on the accident scene. Remember, an officer's primary responsibility at an accident scene is to keep it from getting worse. I always felt that this was to prevent another motorist from becoming involved by crashing into the disabled cars. Sometimes I feel powerless when a gawker looks at the entangled vehicles or the theatrics going on and crashes into the car in front of him. So, first, I try to make sure no one is going to crash into the existing accident, then try to scale down and normalize the activities that follow.

Washington Street in Claremont is our busiest commercial area. When I was a kid, it was a simple two-lane road with much of it still farmland. The retail concentration was in the center of town. Traffic grew and slowed on Washington Street as plazas began to be built on the old farms. The road grew in stages too.

The beginning of Washington Street intersects with North and Broad streets. This was the first area to have four lanes. Later, there was a center turn lane extended. As the larger plazas were built farther out, that area became four lanes. For some unbrilliant reason, we now had two four-lane sections separated by a three-lane portion that required traffic to merge into two travel lanes and a turn lane, then back to four lanes. Yeah, I know, it was driven by funds available, not by reason.

It was common to have minor accidents as traffic came into town from the four lanes merging into the center turn lanes area.

Some people just had to be first in line. One of these collision stands out for me. When I arrived on the scene, a tractor trailer was parked safely as far right on the road as possible. There was a shiny Ford pickup truck parked just inside a nearby parking lot. A man in his early thirties was next to this truck. He was pacing back and forth, arms waving as I turned into the parking area. His body language didn't seem to communicate much coherently other than he appeared to be very upset. I saw the truck driver standing calmly near the front of the transport truck, holding papers and small book in his hand. The expression on the truck driver seemed like one of disappointment and annoyance as he watched the other driver's performance. I was very aware that this is going to have a very negative impact on the truck driver's delivery schedule.

The animated pickup driver naturally demanded my immediate attention. He was repeatedly shouting, "He cut me off!" As I walked from my car to the pickup, that driver increased his animation. The pickup had an ugly deep scratch that extended the full length of the driver's side of his shiny new truck. I acknowledged his statement and asked for his license and registration, which he had ready for me. He was a Claremont resident, so he was very aware of these narrowing lanes. I wrote his information into my report along with his statement. I occasionally glanced toward the tractor trailer driver who remained calmly by the front right of his truck, patiently waiting his turn. When I had what I needed from the pickup operator, I told him to stand by, and I would speak to the tractor trailer driver.

I walked the fifty feet from the pickup to the front of the tractor trailer where that driver patiently waited. The pickup operator remained by his truck, still pacing but less energetically. As I walked closer to the large truck, I scanned it for damage. I couldn't see anything other than the broken turning signal. It was one of those that stuck out from the front fender to make it more visible especially in multiple-lane traffic.

The truck driver handed to me his license, registration, and logbook. I glanced quickly at his logbook and handed it back to him. I smiled and said that I was a city cop and only troopers cared about his log. He smiled and took it back. I wrote his information onto my report, then asked, "What damage do you have to your truck?" He pointed to the broken light and replied, "This is it." The height of this broken lamp matched the height of the scratch on the pickup. I told him that I knew what happened now.

I called the pickup truck driver over to us near the front of the tractor trailer. When he arrived, I pointed to the sign where it was still four lanes. Though we could only see the back of the sign, he knew that the sign reads "Right Lane Ends, Merge Left." I showed to the pickup operator the broken turn signal on the tractor trailer. He said, "Yeah. So?" I said, "Notice that it is bent forward." I then tugged on it to show that it would take a force from the rear to the front of this truck to bend it and that it indicated that someone had passed him on his right.

Again, the pickup driver wasn't convinced. I added that the trucker was in the through lane, giving him the right of way. The signs indicated that the right lane was ending and merging traffic must yield right of way to through traffic. The pickup operator's body language started to fade. He was less animated and lowered his posture. I went for the conclusion, telling the pickup operator that New Hampshire rules of the road allow for passing on the right only when it can be done safely.

The tractor trailer driver smiled. The pickup operator admitted that he tried to beat out the truck but felt the truck driver should have let him. I told him that he should talk to his insurance company. He slowly walked back to his pickup. I thanked the truck driver, and we all left.

Truck drivers often get unjustified negative opinions of their work. Sure, there are some who deserve such thoughts, but I have found that the majority are true professionals, like this driver. He maintained composure and professionalism despite a very determined effort of the other driver to discredit him. I feel good that he had a similar confidence in me to conclude in his favor. True professionals, even from different professions, can recognize and appreciate one another. Professional truck drivers earn a hard living yet still show great tolerance to traffic that mostly disrespects them. They have my admiration.

Rear-Ended Telephone Pole

Late one evening while on patrol, I was directed to an accident on Charlestown Road just south of the golf course maintenance building. It was wintertime and the snowbanks were high. Snow in the open areas was about two feet deep. As I rounded the corner near the accident, I saw a single car, a Chevy sedan, that went backward into the snowbank and rearward into a telephone pole from the southbound lane, but it was pointing north. Four people were moving around much more than usual. Typically, people in an accident who are not injured just stand still, waiting for the police. It wouldn't be terribly unusual for a car to collide backward, particularly if they were traveling at high speed and lost control. The car could rotate and be faced in the opposite direction of travel. There was no evidence of rotation. It went directly backward until it struck the pole. The trunk was dented sufficiently so that the center of the lid buckled, leaving an opening into the trunk from the side. The hood was partly open but did not appear to be dented. My initial thought was that the hood likely dislodged from the impact.

I parked the police car to warn traffic and provide some protection to the scene, my primary responsibility at an accident. I must account for traffic safety and other emergency responders, making the scene as safe as possible so that I don't have additional victims. This includes me. I can't help anyone if I become part of the problem. Attending to the injured is secondary. The road is wide enough that parking the police car on the side created no significant hazard. The flashing lights were enough warning to any traffic.

As I approached the car, I saw two young men and two young women, walking about and looking about. Usually, they focused on the wreck. The pole was broken but still erect. Some wires dangled, which naturally caused momentary alarm for me. I called to the four people to beware of the wires. I made a quick assessment of what wires were down. Streetlights were still on, a good sign. I first look at the top wires. They were still attached to the pole and extended to the adjacent poles. I then looked for the power line to the building across the street. It too was intact. I felt some relief. The thick black wire below the electrical wires was the telephone wire. It was intact. The dangling wires were the thinner TV cable wire. It presented only a physical hazard but ruined TV for the neighborhood. There was no electrical hazard. I just needed to be sure that no one got tangled in the TV cable.

All this safety assessment takes only a few seconds. I felt reasonably confident the scene was safe to work in. All four milling about denied any serious injuries, just minor bruises. I informed dispatch that there were no serious PI (personal injury), but I had cable wires down. This would inform the ambulance and fire department so that they would continue to assess more thoroughly my initial assessment. Especially with the broken pole, I wanted the fire department to check it more thoroughly. I also wanted the EMT folks because I still sensed something wrong. These people were too upset to have just minor injuries.

The driver freely came forward when I asked, "What happened?" He said that he was going south when he lost control and hit the telephone pole. I illuminated the tracks into the pole as I spoke with him. I showed him that they went straight into the pole. I said, "What were you doing? Driving backward?"

He hemmed and hawed a bit as I continued to examine his car. The ambulance and fire truck arrived and began their assessments.

I looked at the partially open hood and saw no reason that the accident would have caused this to open. If the latch had failed, the hood would have opened fully and the hinges would have been damaged. I saw no evidence of this. I looked under the hood and at the engine. The plug wires were missing. The driver realized my observation, and I asked, "Where are they?" He said, "They're in the field."

The field was just a vacant lot in this residential neighborhood. I shone my flashlight into the clearing, and sure enough, the plug wires were on top of the snow as if they were thrown there. I directed the driver to come a few feet away from the wreckage so that I could speak to him directly and have his full attention.

He said that he came up to the red traffic light behind a Chevy Blazer. The Blazer suddenly put its backup lights on and started backing toward them. He put his car in reverse and backed up. He expected the Blazer to stop, but it kept coming. He got scared and continued backing. The Blazer kept getting closer, so he also continued accelerating. He lost control when he got to this corner and hit the pole. That traffic light was half a mile from this accident. I could imagine now the scene of these two vehicles chasing each other down the highway. I also appreciated how lucky it was that there was no other traffic involved.

I asked about the plug wires. He said that after they crashed, the driver of the Blazer got out, opened his hood, yanked out the plug wires and threw them in the field, then lowered the hood, leaving it partially open. The explanation still puzzled me. There had to be more to the story, but he denied it. He suggested that maybe the guy in the Blazer thought that he stopped too close to him at the red light.

He described the Blazer as being black and having Connecticut plates. He couldn't tell me any of the numbers on the plate. I completed what I needed for information. Someone came to pick them up, and the on-call wrecker removed the car. The TV cable was not a hazard to traffic. Dispatch notified the power company to come check the pole and notified the TV cable company. I felt the scene was safe and could be cleared.

I went to the station to write my report. As I was getting times from the dispatcher to write my report, I mentioned my frustration about being highly unlikely that I would ever find this other car. She knew the other on-call wrecker operator. She said he had a friend from Connecticut who owns a black Blazer and often comes here to visit. So I decided to go talk with the off-duty wrecker operator.

When I turned into his driveway, I saw a black Blazer with Connecticut plates. There were several men in the garage, so I went in. They weren't surprised to see me and seemed to welcome me. I mentioned the Blazer and said that I was coincidentally investigating an accident that concerned a black Blazer from Connecticut.

The operator smiled and volunteered it was him. He told me the Chevy sedan came up behind him as he was traveling through Charlestown. Route 12 through Charlestown is a state highway with wide lanes and breakdown lanes. The sedan had its high beams on and followed him closely. He tapped his brakes a few times, but it wasn't responding. Eventually, it passed him, then suddenly stopped so quickly that he struggled to prevent running into him. He drove around the car, which then caught back up to him, again following closely with its lights on high beam. The sedan still had its high beams on at the red traffic signal. He backed up to teach him a lesson. He admitted to the high-speed rearward operation. He said that when the Chevy hit the pole, he wanted to make sure that he would not continue to harass him. He pulled the plug wires out and threw them into the field. After that, he drove peacefully to his destination.

I thought about charges. These were all violations, even though reckless operation is serious and has serious penalties, such as large fines and loss of driving privileges. Violations not in my presence would require seeking a warrant to serve them. A lot of it was out of my jurisdiction and would require involvement of the Charlestown police. Since no one was hurt, I decided that it was more effort than I really wanted to put into it. A part deep down inside me thought that a sort of vigilante justice has been served. The sedan driver withheld a major part of the story and his share of responsibility. It would be very different if someone was hurt. I am not one to write tickets just because I can. I want my efforts to make a difference. I think the original culprit had the heebe geebees scared out of him and will drive more respectfully. If not, there will be another time that will be easier to prosecute. The guy in the Blazer understood how dangerous it was. He assured me that he only continued backing up because there were no other cars and would have stopped if another car had approached.

The Randalls' Accident

Randy and Joan Randall were professionals who also contributed much to their small town north of Claremont and to the greater community. They were on the all-volunteer fire department in their town, responding to all types of emergencies. They were outstandingly respected members of the community well beyond their small town. I knew them. Like so many other first responders, they would come to emergencies throughout the area and do whatever was needed.

They were traveling home late one night after participating in a dinner to honor volunteers at the Claremont Fire Department. On their way home, they passed the community college on Route 120 and entered the S curves. The speed limit was forty miles per hour and would increase to fifty miles per hour after the curves. It was in the center of these S curves that they were struck head-on by a southbound car.

I received the call of a 10-25 with serious PI, a traffic accident with serious personal injury. It's a code 3 call, with lights and sirens and as fast as one can safely get there. I was first on the scene. Both cars were in the northbound ditch. I positioned my car to protect the involved vehicles, closing the northbound lane. I turned on the spotlights and sidelights to illuminate the scene as much as possible.

The Randalls' car was facing north. They were both still in the car with heavy front-end damage. The other car was south of theirs and facing slightly south and into the woods. The people from the other car were out and on the ground. A woman was on her hands and knees near the left rear fender. A man was lying supine on the ground on the passenger side.

I didn't recognize the Volvo as being the Randalls' car. I ran up to the driver. The window was smashed and fully open. I didn't recognize that it was Randy. He held his bloodied hand in front of his face with the seat belt holding him upright. His face was so damaged that it appeared that his eye as about to fall out. It was shocking that he was able to respond. He struggled to speak but said, "Go to her. She is worse." Already feeling shocked and overwhelmed by his injuries, I dreaded going to his passenger as he wished. I ran around to the passenger side of the passenger, dreading what I would find.

I was able to see through the window. She was slumping slightly in her seat, also held by the seat belt. I could see that I could safely open the door. As I opened the door, she looked at me but didn't speak. I didn't see any obvious injuries. However, she was obviously hurt as she seemed to be trying to assess the extent of her own injuries and her concern for Randy.

The fire truck and ambulance arrived. I called them to the Volvo as I felt that they were most seriously hurt. The ambulance EMTs tended to them. I went to assess the two from the other car. It was a large old Pontiac. The other two were also seriously hurt. Fortunately, the firefighters were able to provide immediate assistance. The ambulance crew had already called for a second ambulance. It was a private ambulance service. We are very fortunate that they are in the center of the city and are well-run and staffed by highly qualified and dedicated people. The second ambulance arrived in less than four minutes. This was only possible because the backup crew listens to their radio and automatically come in when there is a serious emergency. The second backup crew would also be headed in once the backup crew were dispatched.

My backup officers arrived and helped me control traffic around the scene. As the injured were receiving the best care possible, I was now free to begin trying to reconstruct the accident. The only skid marks I saw were from Randy's car. They showed a full skid for twelve feet in the center of his northbound lane that suddenly changed direction at an angle to the side of the road, like a large double set of check marks on the road. Undoubtedly, the other car crossed the center line and collided head-on. Being a larger car and having likely greater speed, the momentum at collision was enough to overcome the Randalls' car, knocking them backward, and both ended up in the northbound ditch. The Pontiac pushed the Volvo out of its way and continued after the collision to its final position.

The injured people were all transported to the hospital. I measured the vehicle positions and the skid marks. It was difficult finding a reference point from which to take measurements. I carried nails and a hatchet in my case and drove a nail into the edge of the pavement corresponding to the initial contact of the vehicles. Since this wouldn't stand out over time, I marked a large pine tree and drove a nail into that mark so that I could reconstruct the scene with reasonable confidence.

Now that I had all the measurements, I allowed the cars to be towed away. My fellow police officers remained so that I could go to the hospital to further assess the injuries and, if possible, get statements. The Pontiac was registered to Andy Washburn, a person who was frequently in trouble with the police. His license was suspended. If he was driving, it would be a very good arrest. I wanted so much to prove it was he driving that car. His position at the scene and his injuries did not support it. Julie, his girlfriend, had the classic steering wheel injury to her chin and lower abdomen. Both refused to talk to me. The driver is required to cooperate with police or risk administrative suspension of her license, but this was not a good time to take such an aggressive stance. I could follow up later.

The Randalls were still being assessed. The plan was to make sure that they were stable enough; then they would be transported to Mary Hitchcock Memorial Hospital's trauma center. Randy was looking a little better and spoke with me briefly. I assured him that the evidence was clear that the other car came into his lane. He remarked about how surprised he was. He said, "It just came out of the woods and was airborne straight at me. All I could do was slam on the brakes."

I was thinking that it was a simple center line crossing. With Randy's description, I decided to return to the scene. It wasn't immediately obvious in the dark, but when I light it up, there were indications in the shrubs and wetlands of the car being off the road. I went to the north side of the S curves and saw how the southbound Pontiac seemed to have no steering correction from the short straight way into the curves. It went straight off the road and then tried to get back onto the road. It traveled through shrubs in the wetlands several feet off the road. The path continued up the embankment onto the highway. The tire markings faded away, verifying Randy's description of it being airborne.

I prepared my initial report with this evidence. I still wanted to get Julie's statement of what happened. I went to her house after she was discharged from the hospital. Her mother met me at the door and said that Julie would not speak with me and said that she had a lawyer. I told her that she was required to make a statement, or her license would be suspended. I told her that I would give her one week and assured her that she could speak with me with her lawyer. If she didn't, I would send the letter to the commissioner of the Department of Motor Vehicles that would revoke her license.

After the week passed, Julie's mother called and asked to speak with me. I met with her at her house. She said that her daughter was in great emotional distress. She was still in emotional trauma from the accident. She had broken up with Andrew and didn't want to take all the blame for the accident. She then told me how the accident happened.

Andy and his brother, John, had left their home together with their girlfriends. Their home was at the far end of the straightway north of the S curves. Julie and Andrew left first. John and his girlfriend were behind them in John's pickup. John pulled out to pass them. Always competing, Andy did not want John to pass. He urged Julie to accelerate, preventing John from passing. Julie accelerated but not enough to block the pass. Andy then placed his foot on top of Julie's. She protested greatly, tried to remove her foot, and screamed at him to stop, but Andy persisted. The car accelerated so much that Julie lost control and went off the road. She tried unsuccessfully to control the vehicle and get it back on the highway.

I prepared a supplemental report with this additional information. I referred it to our detectives with a recommendation for prosecution by the county attorney. It bothers me that John drove away from the scene as his brother and three others were seriously hurt. The county attorney did bring reckless conduct charges against Andrew, but in district court. He paid a fine.

Hit-and-Run with the Clerk of Court

Liam Lamont was one of the teenagers I got to know. He and his younger brother were often truant. They have been caught shoplifting in several stores. They were always quiet and respectful whenever I dealt with them.

I felt sorry for them. They lived in very substandard housing in my neighborhood when I lived in the city limits. Their mother was only available when she had to be. Their father was absent. Their clothes were dirty, tattered, and torn. Their shoes were worn-out with holes in them. They seldom bathed. Their long hair was greasy and unkempt. I thought that they might thrive if they had a better environment.

I got a call of an accident at School and Walnut streets, by the Junior Sports League and very close to my house. I found two cars involved in the accident. One was heading west, down School Street, and was stopped just beyond the intersection with Walnut Street. The door to the car on School Street was open. I saw a woman inside. There appeared to be no one around the other car, that had just cleared the intersection, heading south on Walnut Street. Walnut Street has stop signs while School Street has none.

I walked up to the car on School Street. The woman was bleeding from her face. I called to announce that there was personal injury. The ambulance was automatically dispatched. My notice would assure they were needed. It also brings the fire department. They will bring the jaws of life and check for any fire hazards, such as leaking fuel and electrical hazards that might start a fire.

As the ambulance arrived, I noticed a familiarity in the woman. When she spoke, I recognized that she was the clerk of court, Marsha. Her injuries were painful, but not serious. She told me that Liam Lamont was the driver of the other car, and he ran away. She pointed in the direction of his house. She was also confident that he recognized her. Liam had been to court several times. I saw no urgency in pursuing him. He would be easy to find later.

While I was talking with Marsha, dispatch called the other patrol officer to take a report of a stolen car. It was stolen from the front of Ben's Market just around the corner from where we were. It was my beat, but I was committed to this accident, and such a call shouldn't wait.

Marsha was on her way from work to pick up her daughter from the babysitter. Marsha gave to me the babysitter's phone number. I asked dispatch to make the notification and to assure her that Marsha was okay and just needed to be checked further at the hospital.

I checked through the abandoned car. I knew Liam didn't have a driver's license. I radioed the registration number to dispatch and the other officer. It was the car being reported stolen. Apparently, the car owner left the car running while she ran in to quickly pick up something from the store. Liam, who was walking by, saw the running car with no one in it. The temptation was too great to resist. He had no driving experience and couldn't resist this opportunity. He decided to jump in it and go for a joy ride. He took the first turn, which was Walnut Street. His plans ended abruptly when he blew through the stop sign at School Street and hit the clerk of court. He then left the scene of the accident when someone was hurt. Liam was on a roll of a series of bad decisions.

I finished processing the scene. Wreckers hauled the broken cars away. I went to Liam's house. No one answered the door. It was near the end of my shift. I decided to circle the neighborhood, looking for Liam, on my way in to write my report. I didn't expect to find him. The next shift could look for Liam.

In circling the neighborhood, I drove past Ben's Market. I noticed someone in the phone booth outside the store. I looked closely as I got nearer. It was almost unbelievable. It was Liam. He returned to the scene of his crime. I signed off, "10-17 in front of Ben's Market." 10-17 is the code for arrest.

I parked to obstruct any attempt to run from the both and got out. Liam held his head down in a futile attempt to hide his face. He glanced up and recognized me. I heard him say, "I got to go now. I am going to jail."

Liam cooperated fully with me. I handcuffed him and brought him in. I processed him. He had just turned eighteen a few days ago. He knew that he was in serious trouble. He surprised me when he asked about Marsha. He knew she was hurt and hoped that it wasn't serious. He wanted me to tell her that he was sorry.

Though I hadn't read Liam his *Miranda* warning, his statements were voluntary. The warning is only if I was intending to ask incriminating questions. I had no intention of interrogating him. Marsha was all the evidence I needed to convict him. I didn't even need to ask Liam his basic information such as name and address because I knew it. I only needed his birth date, which is not an incriminating question.

I charged Liam with leaving the scene of an accident involving property damage and personal injury. If it was just property damage, this would be a misdemeanor punishable with fines and no more than a year in county jail. Since there was personal injury, it was a felony that involved fines and up to seven years in state prison. Driving without a license and failing to stop for the stop sign seem so minor in comparison, just violations with only fines.

The bail commissioner set bail at five thousand dollars, cash only. Liam probably couldn't come up with fifty dollars. He had no money on him. I brought him to the county jail. It was already well past my shift, and I still had to write my report. The prosecutor would need it for Liam's arraignment in court in the morning.

Liam wanted to plead guilty to everything. The district court couldn't accept a guilty plea for the felony, so the judge entered not guilty pleas on all charges and set a date for a probable cause hearing. The judge lowered his bail to five hundred dollars, which Liam didn't even try to raise. The court appointed an attorney.

Liam was indicted by the grand jury before his probable cause hearing, making the hearing unnecessary. Liam plead guilty in superior court. He was fined five hundred dollars, ordered to pay restitution for the damages and injuries, suspended his license for one year, and sentenced him to jail for six months, with credit for the sixty-eight days served. He could get out in four months with good behavior.

When I started in law enforcement, I thought that it was strange to suspend someone's license when they didn't have one. It does change the game considerably if he drives again under suspension. Driving under suspension is a misdemeanor and very likely to receive jail time given the circumstances of the suspension. Also, the director of motor vehicles would not reinstate his privilege to get a license until all restitution was paid. This makes an impossible barrier for most people in Liam's way of life. Some never get their license because of this. However, it doesn't prevent many from driving.

Couldn't He Have Just Waited?

Dispatch informed me of a 10-25 with PI in front of Kmart. This was a motor vehicle accident with personal injury, demanding a code 3 call with lights and sirens. The ambulance and fire department are automatically dispatched to all accidents with confirmed personal injury. Since I was already on Washington Street when I got the call, I knew that I would be ahead of the ambulance and fire truck.

It was almost five o'clock in the afternoon. Washington Street is the busiest, most commercial area of the city. Everyone is trying to get something for dinner and get home. It is four lanes wide, two in each direction. There is a traffic control signal at the plaza entrance where Kmart is. No one wants the inconvenience of a police siren, so they are reluctant to move out of my way. They suspect I am only after a traffic violator. I know more than to get some speed up; then I must brake sharply to avoid hitting one of these cars too reluctant to get out of the way, and some were even pulling out in front of me. I occasionally glanced in the mirror to see if there were any other responders or my backup was behind me. I knew that the drivers would respect the second, third, and fourth vehicle with lights and sirens, which makes it possible for them to catch up with me. I saw no one and arrived at the scene alone.

I made my preliminary assessment before I had the car fully stopped. Traffic was stopped. I saw a midsized tan Dodge opposite Kmart and on the distant side of the intersection, toward Newport. It was facing diagonally toward the city with its front right tire against the curb. It had a large dent in the driver's side. The window was broken, and I could see an elderly man slumping forward in the driver's seat. I could see at least one other person inside. This is not good as most people get out of their cars if they can.

There was a larger maroon Chrysler on the other side of the plaza entrance, facing out of the city, toward Newport. It straddled the both lanes. It had front-end damage. I couldn't see anyone in the Chrysler yet. Since no one was standing by, I assumed that there would be significant injuries to whoever was in it. Both vehicles had significant damage. I expected the injuries would be serious.

A police officer's primary responsibility at an accident is to keep the scene from getting worse. There is a very valid reason for this. One accident has already occurred, so there is a hazardous condition present even before the accident; otherwise, it wouldn't have happened. Now on this very busy and four-lane wide street, I had two significantly damaged vehicles on both sides of the street. Where I park the police car will add much to keeping the scene safe or make it worse. The police car seemed much too small to adequately protect this scene. I made a split-second decision to park a little closer to the car with the serious dent in the driver's side, assuming that would be the car with the most serious injuries and the greatest obstruction to traffic. I got out of the car to see what more I could do to make the scene safe.

I was surprised that the fire truck was right behind me. Later, I asked this firefighter how he got there so quickly. He chuckled and said, "I just put it in the middle of the road and floor it. They get out of the way." He parked with equal strategy, blocking traffic behind the large Chrysler facing out of the city. His preliminary assessment was the Chrysler posed a more serious fire hazard with the damaged engine compartment. The first thing the firefighters do is to chock the tires on their truck. Again, it is to make certain that their truck doesn't contribute to the harm. Next, they check to make sure that the broken vehicles are safe, free of hazards such as a fire. They check for fuel leaks and electrical hazards that might start a fire as the scene is processed. With this done to their satisfaction, they will render assistance to the injured. They were very thorough and efficient, accomplishing their safety checks in a few seconds.

Immediately behind the fire apparatus was the ambulance. They took advantage of the traffic that moved out of the way of the fire truck. They parked beside the fire truck. These responders immediately tend to the injured but scan for hazards to be sure they can accomplish their mission.

I could see the blue lights of my supervisor coming. I desperately needed his help to control the traffic. In many busy accident scenes, there are often bystanders who are eager to help. I was fortunate to have some come forward. Often, they are the ones who were trying to tend to the injured and now have to get out of the EMTs' way. Two were happy to help me to direct traffic into the plazas on each side of the road. Traffic could go into one entrance and out another farther down the road. My supervisor arrived at this time and assisted me with traffic control.

Now I made a quick survey and was reasonably satisfied that the scene would not get worse. It was terribly inconvenient for many drivers, but they cooperated, and things were moving again. There is always the problem of what we call the gawk effect. People look to try and figure out what happened, then if they knew who was involved. When we see terrible things, our hope is to know how it happened for assurance that it couldn't happen to us. Unfortunately, when they gawk, they don't watch what is in front of them and can crash into the car ahead.

With the scene reasonably safe, I now checked to make sure the EMTs and firefighters were sufficient to care for the injured. There were two injured in the Dodge and one in the Chrysler that needed medical attention. Only two EMTs are on the ambulance. Since most firefighters are well trained in tending to the injured—some are also EMTs—there were enough people. However, there were not enough ambulances. They had already asked for the backup crew to respond.

With things reasonably progressing, I could now start the next priority, gathering and preserving evidence to analyze the accident. I quickly determined the point of contact. When vehicles collide hard, dirt and material drop from the undercarriage. It can also show some direction of the dominant force. I saw the debris in the first lane outside the plaza entrance. With the side damage to the Dodge across the street and the front damage to the Chrysler that passed through the intersection, it was certain that the Dodge was entering the highway and the Chrysler was passing through. I looked again at the debris. Its scatterings supported the force of impact consistent with this quick analysis. I also found a pair of glasses on the ground. It puzzled me a little; then I began to formulate how they got there. The Dodge entered the intersection, intending to turn toward the city. The Chrysler struck it, adding lateral velocity, that is, knocking it sideways. After the impact, the Dodge had forward and side-way motion, coming to rest on the opposite side of the intersection from where it was headed. The Chrysler continued mostly straight through the intersect but acquired some left, lateral velocity from the Dodge, causing it to come to rest, straddling both lanes.

I now knew about the physical evidence at the scene with one quick walk-through. I needed to know the types and extent of the injuries. With so much damage to the driver's side, I suspected that the Dodge would have the most serious injuries.

The backup ambulance arrived. For a moment, my mind went to how great it is to have such competent, professional, and caring people so available in an emergency. Everyone knew their roles well and performed in perfect coordination. This is why I decided to live in Claremont when I returned from the army. The surrounding towns have volunteer services. Volunteers mean well, but response times are sometimes forty minutes. In less than two minutes, we had two police officers, four firefighters, four EMTs, and three good Samaritans working this scene. Everyone knew their roles well. The coordination was automatic.

In the Dodge across the street was an elderly couple; the husband was the driver. Looking at his head injury, it appeared that his head had hit the door window. I don't think his head alone broke the window. The force of the impact from the other car was the likely force to shatter the window. Regardless of how the window broke, his head was sufficiently jolted to cause his glasses to fall off and into the road. Both occupants of the Dodge were wearing their seat belts. It helped the passenger considerably. Since the car caved in upon the driver, the seat belt wasn't much value for him during the initial impact. It did keep him from bouncing around the cabin after impact. Their injuries appeared significant. They were in good care. It was not a good time to interview them. I would catch up to them at the hospital later.

Now who had the green light? Again, luck was with me. Bystanders were stopped for the traffic light at this intersection at the time of the accident. They all told me the elderly couple in the Dodge had the green light, and it was green well in advance of their entry into the intersection.

I went to the Chrysler. They were removing an elderly large woman from the car. She too was wearing her seat belt. She was telling them her injuries and a long list of other medical conditions. I continued listening to the lady in the Chrysler, who I now know caused the accident. She was telling the EMTs that she was in town to see her doctor. She lives in New London and was eager to get home. She saw the light turn red but didn't want to stop, even though she could. She explained that she wanted side traffic to let her through the intersection so that she could get home. She blamed the man for driving into the intersection even though he had the green light. I remember her words very vividly: "Why couldn't he have just waited one more minute? I didn't want to stop and just wanted to get through the light so that I could get home." It's one of those statements that I just can't believe I was hearing. I took a deep breath and resolved to put that quote into my report.

The ambulance folks efficiently treated, prepared, and transported the injured. The firefighters checked again and determined the vehicles were safe. They helped me make the measurements for my report, then returned to their station. I called for the wreckers to remove the cars. We could now allow traffic to use the middle two lanes so it moved better than through the parking lots. I thanked and dismissed my volunteers. The wreckers arrived, and the roadway was returned to normal.

I went to the hospital emergency room to better determine the injuries and interview the drivers. The man had suffered a concussion and several broken bones in his arm and hip. They were preparing to transfer him to Dartmouth Hitchcock Memorial Hospital (DHMC). I didn't think he was in a condition to be interviewed. I spoke to his wife, who was being treated for minor injuries. The emergency room folks had called her son who was on his way to get her. They would drive up to DHMC when they were ready to transport her husband. She seemed to be such a nice lady. She had no negative thoughts about the driver that had so disrupted her life and caused such serious injuries to her husband. She maintained focus on her husband's well-being and helping him. I told her that I had to ask the question even though I knew the answer. She assured me that she wanted to help me. She confirmed that the light was green, allowing them to enter the intersection. They saw the Chrysler but expected her to stop. When they realized that she wasn't going to stop, they were already in the intersection and couldn't avoid the collision.

The other driver was in a separate room. She was waiting for the doctor to tell her about the X-ray results. She was impatient. She wanted him finish with her so she could go home. I asked about her injuries. She pulled her hospital gown down and showed a developing large bruise caused by the seat belt, saying, "Look at this. See how ugly it is. I am never going to wear a seat belt again." I tried to explain to her what her injuries would be without the seat belt. She said, "I don't care. This is ugly. I'm never going to wear a seat belt again." My thoughts were more along the line that I hoped she never drive again. The doctor appeared with the news that she would be required to remain overnight for observation. She was not happy. I had no sympathy. Had she stopped and delayed her ride by two minutes, she and the other couple would be safely home now.

I had all that I needed for my report. Most of us in my department didn't write summons following an accident. I read the law literally. If it didn't happen in my presence, I would need to get a warrant to serve the summons. My chief had said that it was a "summons in lieu of arrest" and I could write the ticket. I didn't see where the law allowed it, so I didn't. My purpose would be to establish fault in the accident, which my report does very well. It will support well any civil action.

I was particularly concerned for the gentleman. I stopped by their house the next week. They were surprised but happy to see me. He would be using a walker for the next six weeks and have physical therapy for several more weeks, but he was expected to fully recover. They never uttered a single negative word about the other driver. They were truly nice people.

Karl the Car Walker

Karl was one of those regular nuisance people. He was tall, well over six feet tall. His dark hair and beard were long, scraggly, and dirty. His clothes were always dark, disheveled, torn, and dirty. He didn't work regularly. He occasionally got short-term employment when local contractors needed an extra person for roofing or painting. They didn't keep him long. His work ethic was poor, and he showed up late, if at all. The quality of his work was also poor. He got fired from every job soon after beginning it.

Karl was often arrested. He did a lot of shoplifting. His method was bold. He just walked in, picked up what he wanted, and walked out. Most of the time, it was beer. If anyone tried to stop him, he usually just pushed by but wouldn't hesitate to strike someone who tried to restrain him. When the store clerk called, we knew it was Karl right away by his description. Sometimes we caught him. When we did, he always resisted arrest.

Karl would get drunk, probably from stolen beer, and walked around town. He liked spreading terror to anyone he passed. He demanded money or cigarettes from them. If he didn't get what he wanted, he threatened and even assaulted them. He selected victims by their likelihood not to contact the police. These were people who had their own legal troubles, and the police were the last people they wanted in their lives. Karl got away with a lot.

There were times Karl would get severely intoxicated to the point he staggered excessively and crashed into people and objects. He also staggered into traffic. One of his favorite things to do was to stagger into the road and block traffic. His dark clothes, size, and appearance were intimidating to drivers. If they sounded the horn, he would block their path. He would peer into the windshield at the driver. Then he would step on the front bumper and walk onto the hood, roof, trunk, and back onto the street. He would then just walk away.

Karl caused scratches and dents in these cars. They called us, but none could pick out Karl from a photo lineup. We knew it was him because we sometimes found him staggering in the area. Even if we were able to prove it was him, he had no means to repay the damage he caused. As with so many others, he wasn't afraid of going to jail. He got free regular meals and a nice place to sleep. The only disadvantage for him was going without his beer for a few days.

We all suspected that Karl would eventually meet his demise when he got accidentally run over by one of these drivers. Our greatest regret would be for the driver, so we remained motivated to bring charges when possible. We did what we could to spare the grief from undeserving drivers.

As with most things, a day of reckoning for Karl finally came. Fortunately, it didn't involve an innocent person as we feared. Karl was partying with his buddies in Moody Park one warm summer night. They all got drunk and decided to go for a ride around the park through the trees and open areas. Two decided to ride on the front fenders. Karl was on one fender. They enjoyed a wild ride, with a beer in hand, sliding around on the fenders and hood.

Fate caught up with Karl when the driver tried to make a donut in reverse. The driver, already impaired with alcohol and marijuana, didn't notice Karl fell off the fender. The front tire ran over him. As usual, they didn't want to call the police. They tried to bring him to the hospital themselves. They realized that they were too drunk, and Karl was unconscious and too big to move him into the car. They finally decided to call the ambulance.

The ambulance responders called the police as usual when responding to an incident when someone is seriously hurt and especially since this was on city-owned property. They knew only that someone was injured and not responding. They had no idea at this point that a car was involved. I wasn't assigned to that beat, so I remained closer to town to be available for other possible emergencies. I learned the details from the beat officer.

Karl was seriously injured, far beyond the ability of our local hospital's resources. They stabilized him for transport to Dartmouth Hitchcock Memorial Hospital. His prognosis was bleak. We expected he would die.

Weeks later, we learned that Karl survived but has severe physical handicaps. He couldn't walk and could barely move one arm. One officer joked that he would be fine because all he ever wanted to do was to sit and drink beer. He had enough movement in one arm to do this.

Karl spent many months in rehabilitation. He progressed slowly but managed to gain considerably more motion. Eventually, he was able to walk, using a walker. He was set up in an apartment with home-based services. Karl no longer had access to beer and mari-juana. He had an income through disability and services paid by Medicare. He continued to progress in his recovery and was able to take walks around town. He was no longer the intimidating former self. He now lives a much more respectable lifestyle. He seems happy.

From menace to decency through tragedy, Karl has achieved a lifestyle I would have never expected from him. He will never be truly independent, which is perhaps how he will maintain this better lifestyle. Someone will always be watching and assisting so that he cannot return to the alcohol and drugs that were so much in control of his earlier life.

Fatal Backyard Mechanic

Early one evening, the dispatcher announced an accident with serious personal injury in the yard of a nursery and landscaping com-pany on the far edge of the city, near Vermont. So far out of the center of the city, I knew that I would be there far ahead of the other emergency services. From the dispatcher's information, it involved a vehicle, but it didn't sound like a typical crash. I wasn't sure what I would find. Being a code 3 run, I focused on driving. If I asked for more information, it would take from the dispatcher's efforts to dispatch the ambulance and fire department. With the siren running over my head, it's also very difficult to understand the dispatcher. Whenever I run the siren, I must turn the volume up full on the radio. The sound level inside the car is intense.

I headed toward Vermont with my foot holding the accelerator to the floor or on the brake. Traffic was light, and the drivers all pulled over as they should. I backed off on the throttle as I traveled through the rural residential area and into the agricultural area. I turned onto Route 12A North and through the S curves. I used the driving skills that I learned at the police academy through the curves and onto the straight, flat farmland, across the straights, and I arrived at my destination. I saw an elderly lady standing in front of the business. I brought the police car to a stop, turning off the siren but leaving the blue lights running. I knew the other responders knew the location as well as I did but not where to go once there. She was directing me to behind the house. I left the car pointing in that direction so it could be a reference for the other responders.

Mr. and Mrs. Jewell were well respected in the community. They operated this business for many years. It was a good place to buy trees and shrubs and plant them oneself or hire them to do it for you. Mrs. Jewell directed me through the yard of young trees and shrubs to the back of the business. I had never been back here.

I ran, holding my service weapon and radio as they bounced. As I made it through the little forestlike area, it opened into a work area. I saw a car in front of a small barn. It was suspended with four bumper jacks, facing the garage. A younger man was standing behind this car, looking sad and helpless. He pointed to the driver's side of the car. I saw a man's legs protruding from under the driver's door. He was mostly on his back, turning slightly to his right with his left arm across his chest.

I reported my location with directions to the dispatcher. She didn't need to know this, but I knew the ambulance and fire department would be monitoring my transmission. It would help guide them to my location quicker. It would also help them to decide what equipment to bring with them from their vehicles.

I approached the man under the car. I first saw his feet, dressed in brown work boots, and he was wearing dark green pants protruding from under the driver's door. I looked under the car. He was wearing a matching long-sleeve shirt and a brown belt, his typical work clothes that I knew Mr. Jewell always wore when he worked. I checked the security of the suspended car and found it to be extremely dangerous. It wiggled back and forth with a light push. It could easily fall over and onto anyone under the vehicle. I cautiously approached Mr. Jewell, reaching to him without placing more than my arm and shoulder under the car. He was not responding. I noticed the driveshaft of the vehicle still connected to the rear differential but disconnected from the transmission near his head. I very much wanted the help of the other responders, but I still couldn't even hear their sirens.

As I tried to assess the man's condition and what happened, I asked the man now standing beside me. He explained. When his father didn't come in for dinner at five o'clock, his mother called for his father. She went to look for him and found him under the car with his feet protruding. She went back into the house and called him. He lived a mile away, in Cornish. He rushed to help his father. When he didn't respond, the younger Jewell tried pulling him out from under the car but couldn't. He got the four bumper jacks and jacked the car up off him. When his father still wouldn't respond, he and his mother went back into the house to call for assistance. It was now six twenty. Mr. Jewell had been under this car for well over an hour.

The younger Mr. Jewell explained that his father was attempting to replace the transmission. He had driven the car onto wheel ramps that I could see in front of the car. Mr. Jewell did not set the brake, nor did he block the wheels. When he disconnected the drive-shaft from the transmission, the car rolled off the ramps and onto him. It appeared to me that the car had enough clearance so that Mr. Jewell was not crushed by its weight. I expected that it placed sufficient pressure on his chest to suffocate him.

The EMTs arrived. They ran with their resuscitation gear. I warned them not to touch the car. I knew the team well, having been on several calls together. I spoke with Kyle as he crouched down to assess Mr. Jewell. We agreed that it was too dangerous to go under this car and we would cause Mr. Jewell no further harm if we pulled him out from under the car. I tried as quietly and nonjudgmentally as I could to explain that Mr. Jewell had been under the car for a considerable amount of time before he was even found and the amount of time for his son to respond and jack up the vehicle. Without having to say it, we knew that our efforts would be futile. Nonetheless, the EMTs did their best.

The fire department arrived soon after we pulled Mr. Jewell out. The EMTs were performing CPR (cardiopulmonary resuscitation). The firefighters assisted in preparing Mr. Jewell for transport, loading him onto a backboard while continuing with the CPR. One firefighter drove the ambulance to the hospital while the EMTs continued their efforts.

I had given enough information to the EMTs about the delay for medical care that they could share with the emergency room doctor. They continued the CPR for a short while in the hospital before calling off the heroic attempts to revive Mr. Jewell. It's sad to lose such a respected member of the community for something so simple. Perhaps he had set the brake, and it didn't hold. If only he was extra cautious and block the wheels too.

CHAPTER 6

Driving while Intoxicated

Maxum's Directional Signal

I had worked the night shift and got stuck working over because my relief called in sick. It's practice that if there is overtime, the most senior officer has first dibs. If he or she turns it down, it's offered to the next senior. If no one else wants it, it trickles down to the junior officer being required. It fell to me, not that I didn't mind. It was a Sunday morning and should be very quiet. My relief would be determined similarly. The evening shift people scheduled would be offered the overtime in the same way. I expected to be relieved at noon.

It had been a busy night. I looked forward to the quiet morning and decided to patrol the outer roads and enjoy some views. It was ten thirty and I was counting on being relieved at noon. One of my favorite views is from East Mountain Road, and I was headed that way. I was driving up the Old Newport Road and nearing East Mountain Road when I saw a car stopped in the middle of the road. A man was standing behind it. He had his hand on the back of his neck, his head bent forward and looking at the back of the car. It was one of those big old cars, so I expected that it broke down. I didn't expect that this would spoil my intentions to enjoy this one last view and only delay it. I was wrong.

I radioed to dispatch that I was with a 10-13, disabled vehicle, and gave its plate number and my location. I walked up to the man and asked, "What's wrong?" He took his hand from the back of his neck and waved toward the back of the car and said, "Blinkers don't work." This puzzled me why he would stop here, directly in the middle of the road and no turn in sight. I noticed an eight-year-old boy looking out the back window of the car. He was the only occupant in the car.

Maxum was tall and thin with long wavy brown hair. His clothes were ruffled and dirty. I asked him why he stopped here. Still looking at the back of his car, he said, "I can't be driving around with blinkers that don't work." I, like many other people, have had a turning directional signal that stopped working, but I notice it when I take a turn. I fix it when I get home. Others may go to a mechanic. It made no sense for him to stop in the middle of the road far away from a turn. I looked a little closer, trying to get a sense of his mental status. I asked him where he was headed. He said that he was headed to a company party at Sunapee. He added it was for the Holson Company and was supposed to start at two o'clock in the afternoon. He expressed concern about getting there on time. It was about twenty minutes from our location. As he spoke, I noticed that he was drunk. Oh, I so much didn't want to deal with this now, but I had to.

Every officer has their preferred things to enforce. I have always felt that people who drive drunk risk their lives. I'm OK with people doing stupid things that places only themselves in danger, but they have no right to place others in danger. That includes other people on the highway and that little boy in the back seat, who I learned was his son. I arrested him. It is department policy to apply handcuffs to every arrest, and I fully intended to do this even with his son watching. As I placed the handcuffs on his father, the boy broke out in tears. I placed both in the back seat of the police car and seat belted them. I called dispatch and said that I was 10-17, DWI arrest. I requested 10-28, a wrecker. When the wrecker arrived, I remained for traffic control, though it was very light.

I processed Maxum for DWI. I asked if he had someone who could come get him as we never release intoxicated parents without a responsible person to care for them. He called a coworker. I released Maxum and his son to this coworker when he arrived a few minutes later. They still intended to attend the company party together.

Maxum plead guilty to the charge and paid a significant fine. It's sad that he had to pay so much money. The Holson Company paid better than other manufacturers but still not that well. Though it saddens me to have money taken away from this family, I know full well how much money goes to alcohol that should go to caring for children. I have hope that Maxim and others would find the strength to stop spending money on his addiction, seek help if he needed it, and spend his money on his son.

Byron's DWI

One Saturday evening, we noticed a party being sponsored by an affluent local businessman's son, Byron. He was in his early twenties but still strongly influenced by his parents. It appeared that his parents were out of town. Like an unruly teenager, he took the opportunity to have this large party. We expected problems. The party went on well into the evening.

This group liked large motorcycles. Eventually, they started making forays into the neighborhood, and we got the complaint we were expecting. My friend, Peter, was assigned to that beat, but we remained poised to back him up.

Peter stopped Byron on his motorcycle and arrested him for DWI. Since the breathalyzer was down for routine recertification, Peter brought Byron to the hospital for blood to be drawn. Byron's friends assembled at the hospital to protest. We went to keep the peace.

Few people realize that the hospital is private property. You are admitted to the hospital when you meet their operating policies. They have some complicated obligation to care for the sick and injured. Byron was neither. The hospital provided this service to the police department, not to Byron.

Byron's friends have no right to enter the hospital's private property. They even have no right to be in the parking lot. The hospital supervisor was growing concerned about their disruption of the medical staff inside. The friends complied with our order to leave the building. They remained in the parking lot, yelling at law enforcement. Tensions were building but were quickly abated when the blood was drawn and Peter brought his prisoner to the police station for processing. The crowd dispersed from the hospital but reassembled in front of the police station.

Once organized, the group entered and filled the police station lobby. Though it's a publicly owned property, they were interfering with government operations, preventing others from entering and interfering with the dispatcher. The supervisor commanded most to leave and allowed Byron's closest friends to remain seated in the lobby. They could remain so long as they were reasonable. The unruliest ones were in the alley outside the front of the station. They became increasingly loud and disruptive in the downtown area. Their behavior was such that it would intimidate any other citizen desiring to enter the police station. The supervisor decided to warn them to move farther from the station, far enough to allow easy egress and ingress for the public. They refused and escalated their behavior.

Disorderly conduct is a relatively minor charge and sometimes difficult to prove. Noise or language that disturbs another reasonable person in a public place or private place that can be disturbing to the public or another private space qualifies. Unfortunately, this usually requires a neutral citizen complaint, which we haven't had here, though we had it at the hospital. What we clearly had was that they were blocking the entrance to the police station and refused to move, which is also a violation of the disorderly conduct statute.

We were outnumbered but not short of courage. We were emboldened because we were sober, in good physical shape, and armed with pepper spray. The supervisor told us to disperse them. I selected the loudest, most boisterous person. I approached him and ordered him to leave the alleyway. He leaned toward me, shouted several profanities, and refused to move. I said, "You're under arrest."

We refer to the "magic words." A police officer must communicate clearly and in a way the defendant understands that he is under arrest. "You're under arrest" spoken directly to someone is considered the magic words. If he doesn't submit to arrest, it is considered resistance by most. However, our judge wanted a little more than just a verbal refusal or a gentle pull back when an officer grabbed the arm. None of this became an issue with this guy, who I identified later as

153

Darren. When I reached to grab him, he turned and ran, undoubtedly refusing to submit to arrest.

I enjoyed foot pursuits. They were far less hazardous than vehicle pursuits. I was also in really good shape from my army conditioning, and I routinely ran for physical conditioning. I didn't try to outsprint my adversary. I simply stayed close until they tired, typically within one hundred yards. At this point, they are so exhausted that they have little fight left in them. Being drunk, they think they have an inflated idea about their ability to fight, but I found no challenge.

Like my other foot pursuits, Darren ran down and around the corner and was out of steam. I grabbed his shoulder and the shirt in the middle of his back. There was a fence handy, so I pushed him up against the fence. I was surprised when the fence bent under his weight. There was a ten-foot drop on the other side of the fence. I started to regret this decision instead of throwing Darren to the ground. The fence swayed to about forty-five degrees, slowed, and came back, much to my relief. I pulled Darren off the fence and put him on the ground. He resisted but, as the many others in his poor physical and intoxicated condition, he wasn't much of a match. I handcuffed him, stood him up, and walked him back to the police station.

Peter was in the processing room with Byron. I didn't intend to process Darren right away. I wanted to go back and arrest another if they hadn't dispersed. I placed Darren in a cell and returned to the front of the police station. The group had scattered. A few stood separately in the area, but the disorderly conduct had ended. I returned to patrolling but stayed close to town. I instructed the dispatcher to let me know when the processing room was available.

Peter was a very competent and thorough officer. He and I shared a 100 percent conviction record for our DWI arrests. We were both very meticulous in gathering information to present in court. A typical DWI requires at least two hours to process and write the report. The time is usually equally divided, an hour processing and an hour writing. After an hour, Peter had finished processing, and Byron was bailed by a sober uncle. The processing room was available for me to process Darren. Mike backed up Peter during his processing of Byron and continued as my backup.

I brought Darren from the jail cell to the processing room. He sat beside me as I asked the identifying questions, address, etc. These are important questions when it comes to the bail commissioner's decision about bail. If he refuses, he shows no ties to the area and would likely get a high bail. Darren was much more reasonable now and answered all these questions. During this entire time, we are being recorded on video. In addition, I learned later that his friends were in the lobby and could hear our conversation over the intercom monitored by the dispatcher.

I proceeded to the fingerprinting task. Darren cooperated fine and allowed me to guide his fingers to make the prints. Questions were all completed, which allowed normal conversation. Darren expressed his feeling that we were assholes. I didn't deny it, and I reflected that he was a bit of an asshole too. He agreed. There were a few more exchanges of this nature, and we settled into the difference between us is that I got paid to be an asshole, and he did it naturally.

There was no physical reason to be concerned. My partner, Mike, was justifiable in staying close as we continued this discussion. He then decided to join in, and we all were assholes, but Mike was more bothered than I was about it. He got a little closer and started to call Darren names such as "dirtbag" and "loser." Mike continued to close the distance between him and Darren as this conversation regressed. All the while, Darren was entirely cooperative with the fingerprinting.

Darren returned an insult to Mike, "Why don't you just suck it?" That infuriated Mike, and he got very close, face-to-face, noses about an inch apart. Mike was yelling his insults loudly at Darren. Darren instinctively raised his free hand and placed it on Mike's chest. It was a move any ordinary person might do when feeling threatened. Most notably is that I had Darren's other hand, and he offered no resistance to me. If Darren tried anything, I could easily pull him to the floor and handcuff him. Mike pointed at Darren's hand on his chest and said, "Do you know what you just did? You just assaulted me." I thought he was joking, and things calmed down enough as I finished the fingerprinting. The bail commissioner set personal recognizance, and I released Darren to his mother. We went back on patrol. Things were quiet now. A few people standing around the police station slowly dispersed.

After about an hour of the quiet, I felt it safe to go write my report. I brought charges of disorderly conduct and resisting arrest. At the arraignment, Darren pleaded not guilty, and a trial was scheduled six weeks away.

On the day of court, the police prosecutor told me that Mike had to testify in superior court, and I would be testifying for his charge. It is a perfectly acceptable practice. An officer could testify to another's charge if he or she was there. A good example would be the police airplane transmitting the speed of a car to the trooper on the ground who writes the ticket. What surprised me was that Mike had a charge. Much to my surprise, he charged Darren with simple assault, unprivileged physical contact.

Darren's lawyer was a seasoned defense attorney. One that I respected very much. I answered the questions from the prosecutor, establishing the evidence for the three charges. I described the assault just as it happened, Darren placing his hand on Mike's chest as I fingerprinted him. The prosecution rested.

The defense attorney didn't challenge the charges I brought. They occurred outside the police station, in public. They were obvious, disorderly conduct and resisting arrest. The attorney focused on our conversation. I could tell that he was trying to establish that Darren was provoked into the minor assault. I couldn't say that I agreed with him. I could only answer his questions.

Again and again, the attorney asked about the name-calling, specifically "asshole." I answered we did call each other assholes. I denied that it provoked Darren. He asked in many ways. I responded that the difference was we were paid assholes and Darren was just an asshole. I said that this was a friendly argument. Still, he continued and even warned me that Darren's friends could hear what we said from the lobby over the intercom and would testify. Still, I said, "It wasn't that." I repeated my response with the lawyer's two subsequent questions, but I placed increasing emphasis on "that." I was growing very frustrated that he wasn't asking a question that allowed me to get to the whole truth. Finally, the attorney caught on. He said, "Oh, what was it?"

Finally, I felt relief. I could now explain. I said, "Darren told Officer [Mike], 'Why don't you just suck it?'" I described the extreme proximity Mike placed his face to Darren's and the loudness of his language. I added that I felt Darren placed his hand on Mike's chest in a way that I thought was defensive act, to try and maintain some distance between them.

The defense eventually rested, and the judge rendered his verdict. Guilty for my charges, disorderly conduct and resisting arrest. He fined Darren fifty dollars and suspended him for thirty days. He found Darren not guilty of simple assault, further ruling that it was a justifiable nondeadly force. I was very pleased with the ruling. It seemed strange to hear a judge rule justifiable nondeadly force to a defendant. That expression is often used to justify police use of force.

Now I feared the prosecutor would bring this back to the other officers and they would retaliate against me in subtle ways. As best as I could determine, he never told anyone. Perhaps he shared my feelings. Regardless, I wasn't going to misrepresent the facts or even stretch them on behalf of a fellow officer, even one with whom I worked well. In the end, I maintained my personal integrity.

Unexpected Driving while Intoxicated

Each officer has his or her favorite thing to enforce. Some seek motor vehicle driving violations, especially traffic control devices. Some chose to enforce vehicle equipment violations. Due to my childhood experiences, I wanted to find people who drive while intoxicated. During my first few months, I sought them with great intensity but couldn't seem to find any. It's when I backed off upon my efforts that they seem to find me.

Late one Friday winter evening, I was driving through our commercially intense Washington Street. I was hoping to stay busy with moving violations, especially speeders. I also intended to be vigilant about any property crimes, such as stealing form cars, vandalism, and mischief with shopping carts. I typically drive slowly out to the far end of the businesses, then work my way back, checking around and behind the buildings.

On my way out, I noticed that snow was knocked into the road from the snowbank. I could see the tire marks of a vehicle that drove up, onto the bank, then back into the proper lane. I thought that it might have been done purposefully, which is what I like to find and enforce. A few feet farther, I noticed it again, then again. This is not what I would expect from someone's purposeful actions. They tend to do different things. This looked like someone struggling to keep it on the road. Most innocently, it would be someone with poor night vision. It could also be someone quite intoxicated, who is struggling to keep it on the road. I increased my speed, hoping to catch up to it. I didn't expect to catch it. It was likely to already be out of town.

The road curved to the left as it approached the largest shopping plaza. I noticed a Chevy Blazer traveling slowly as it approached the traffic signal at the entrance to this plaza. I saw it bump into the snowbank and scatter snow into the road like to other places along the road.

I caught up to it easily and turned on the blue lights. It slowed down so that it was barely moving but did not stop. I radioed in the plate number and that it was not stopping but was continuing at a slow speed. When it approached the entrance into the plaza, it turned into the plaza. Still traveling about five miles per hour, it drove diagonally into the parking lot. Finally, it stopped in the middle of the lot.

I walked up to the driver. He was middle-aged and dressed casually. I told him that I stopped him for his erratic driving and asked for his license and registration. He slowly, with uncoordinated difficulty, removed his driver's license from his wallet. He retrieved his registration from the glove box. I did not know him, but I recognized the business to which the Blazer was registered. It was a wholesale distributing business in the adjacent town, Newport, the direction he was traveling.

I asked Norman to step out of his vehicle. He responded very respectfully and agreed to participate in a field sobriety test. I asked him to place his heels together, hands to his side, close his eyes, and tip his head back. He wobbled significantly so that I was afraid that he might fall. I stopped that test and decided to skip the finger-to-nose test. I demonstrated how I want him to walk heel-to-toe along the side of his vehicle. He very willingly started this test. He wobbled a lot and occasionally reached to the Blazer to steady himself. He curved to his left as he passed the back of the Blazer, turned around the back of it, wobbled, and reached to the ground with his hand to regain his balance. I stopped the test and told him that I was arresting him for DWI. Norman made no admission to his condition as he surrendered to the arrest. He was very polite and respectful.

I asked him if he was OK with me locking his vehicle and leaving it in the parking lot. The other option would be to have it towed. He gave me permission to lock it.

Norman was very respectful and cooperative through the processing. His blood alcohol level was almost twice the legal limit. I recommended personal recognizance to the bail commissioner, who agreed. He knew Norman as the business owner. Norman called a friend who arrived within minutes.

Norman challenged his DWI charge in court. He had a well-known attorney. The attorney tried to negotiate with the prosecutor who directed him to me. Attorney Patnode said that my case was weak and asked for me to reduce the charge to reckless operation. When I expressed my unwillingness, he tried to argue that Norman would lose his license for even a longer period than with the first-offense DWI. I told him that I would not agree to the reckless operation charge. Norman was drunk, and he knows it. I wanted nothing other than the first-offense DWI charge. I explained that I felt that it would be a deterrent to a subsequent DWI. We could argue that he had the right to risk his own life, but he had no right to risk the life of another person. DWI second offense carried one-year loss of license, a significantly larger fine but, more importantly, mandatory ten consecutive days in jail. It's this deterrent I wanted most. Attorney Patnode said, "I guess we'll have a trial." I prepared myself for the rigors of an intensely challenging trial.

I have testified and won attorney-defended trials. I recorded my evidence in a very detailed report. My mentor for DWI arrests said,

"Don't write too much in your report. The more you write, the more lawyers have to argue." He showed to me one of his reports that was a small paragraph. I did not follow the advice of my mentor. I wrote very detailed reports using my scientific observation skills developed in college. My reports were always three to five pages long. My mentor had a 50 percent conviction rate, which he felt was better than most. Mine was 100 percent so far.

Norman's case was called. He stood with his attorney. Much to my surprise, Attorney Patnode told the court that his client wished to change his plea to guilty. Outside the courtroom, Norman came to me and shook my hand. He thanked me for being a good police officer. He felt deeply sorry for presenting a risk to other people, and this was a wake-up call for him. He assured me that he hadn't driven when drinking since I arrested him and never will again drive after drinking. He added that he had entered therapy and quit drinking entirely. I thanked him for his intentions. Whether sober or intoxicated, Norman was a person who earned respect.

Albert was a very different kind of a drunk. I was driving through a neighborhood in the downtown area. I approached the Mulberry and Myrtle streets traffic light that was red. This is a complex intersection. The two streets cross this intersection plus Tyler Street, which had a separate stop sign. An old brown pickup approached from the opposite side of the light from me on Myrtle Street, which was also red. It was moving toward the center of the city and a little fast for my comfort, then drove through the red light. It moved side to side and occasionally came into my lane. I could see that the driver was the only occupant as it drove by me. I turned around to stop it. I turned on the blue lights, and it kept going. I expected that he would pull over right away since he had to see me, especially when he was partially in my lane. I sounded the horn, hoping to get his attention. He continued driving. I was concerned that he would soon be in the center of the city, driving through the next red light and maybe hurt someone. I turned on the siren, and he continued.

I called the dispatcher to report that I had a vehicle that wasn't stopping. It's a real attention-getter for the dispatcher, other officers on patrol and scanner land. The siren transmits over the radio like an alarm. Their quiet radios would suddenly erupt with the sound of the siren, followed with my voice. We approached the next set of traffic lights, which was also red. He slowed for the corner but appeared to prepare to drive through that light. I decided to gamble and maneuvered the police car around and in the front of him, blocking his way. Fortunately, he stopped.

Albert immediately expressed his annoyance with my intrusion. He reluctantly provided his license and registration after fumbling for several minutes. I asked him to step out of his truck. Again, he was reluctant but complied. I directed to walk between our vehicles. He walked with his shoulders crouched forward. He looked around the area as he walked. He moved his shoulders in odd directions, inconsistent with his walk and head movements. His gaze, too, was inconsistent and unsteady. When we were safely between the vehicles, I asked him to perform some field sobriety tests. He refused, saying that he hadn't been drinking. He then started to scold me for stopping him especially with the siren blaring and driving around his truck.

I told Albert that he was under arrest for driving while intoxicated. At first, he refused to submit for arrest, insisting again that he hadn't been drinking, then scolding me yet again for the way I stopped him. I warned Albert that he was under arrest, and if he continued his refusal, I would also charge him with resisting arrest. He looked at me and said, "You're serious, aren't you?" I assured him that I was serious and that I was arresting him for DWI, and I fully intended to take him into custody. I said it firmly to get him to realize that I was very willing to use force if he didn't submit. He reluctantly submitted. I locked his pickup on the side of the street.

On the ride to the police station, he continued scolding me for the way I stopped him, "Whoop, whoop, like Starsky and Hutch." He asked why I stopped him. I decided to keep it as simple as possible. I was well experienced with intoxicated drivers. They always deny any weaving. I told him that he drove through a red light and came into my lane. He told me that I was wrong. He added, "You don't go through that intersection a dummy." He explained the five-way intersection as crisscrossing road with another one coming into it.

I drove into the sally port and walked Albert into the processing room. I asked him if he had anything in his pockets. He looked at me, momentarily speechless. I explained that I needed to empty his pockets before I removed the handcuffs. He seemed to think for a bit, then told me what he had in his pockets, and allowed me to remove his wallet, a jackknife, and some change. After removing the handcuffs, I asked him to sit in a chair. He resumed his scolding me for how and why I stopped him. Throughout the entire processing time, he frequently repeated that I stopped him like Starsky and Hutch and that "You don't go through that intersection a dummy." He also repeated his description of the intersection.

We didn't have dash or body cameras, but the processing room was recorded. The camera recorded Albert's numerous objections to the Starsky and Hutch stop and description of the intersection and not going through it a dummy.

Albert refused to take a breathalyzer test. I explained that the director of motor vehicles would automatically suspend his license for ninety days. Albert argued that the director didn't have any such authority. Fully aware that this is being recorded, I very patiently read the implied consent law. He interrupted me many times, "You don't go through that intersection a dummy" and "Whoop, whoop, Starsky and Hutch." I finally got through it, though I didn't believe he paid any attention to what I was reading, nor did I think he could understand it.

I completed the booking forms and took a photograph. DWI is a violation. Fingerprinting is expected for crimes, not violations. I asked Albert if he wanted to call someone to come get him. He replied, "No, I want you to bring me back to my truck." I felt it necessary to be less patient and more assertive. I explained that if he didn't have someone sober to come get him, I would place him in a jail cell until he was sober.

Albert thought about what I said. He seemed to be gaining some understanding of my intentions. He wanted to argue to be brought back to his truck. I stopped him abruptly. I pointed to the telephone on the wall, then the corridor to the jail cells. I gave him the choice. He decided to call someone.

I didn't have the classic evidence for DWI convictions. He refused the field sobriety and breathalyzers tests. What I did have were my observations and this processing room video. I don't dial numbers for people I arrest. I let the camera record their attempt. Albert took the wall-mounted phone off the hook and dropped it. He picked it back up, fumbling as he brought it to the side of his neck, below his ear. He reached toward the phone and struggled to align his fingers with the numbers. He pressed several numbers then said, "Cancel that." I told him to press the receiver button, but he only appeared confused. I showed to him how to press it to disconnect his connection.

With this call canceled, Albert clumsily slid the phone up his neck to his ear, then back down again. He seemed to be checking for a dial tone. He tried again to press numbers on the phone. It resembled an overacting comedian as he extended his finger, circled it around, then suddenly advanced it and pressed a number. He pressed several buttons, then said, "Cancel that." I gave up expecting him to disconnect the call and pressed it for him. It took several more tries before he got through to a friend to come get him. I was happy to release him. I certainly will never go through that intersection a dummy, thanks to Albert's sound advice.

I was somewhat surprised that he hired a lawyer. Attorney Knight did the typical before trial dealing to plead guilty to reckless operation. He argued that Albert had already lost his license for the implied consent and would lose it even longer for a reckless charge. I steadfastly refused any deal.

This lawyer was one who I know doesn't do his homework. Attorney Knight appeared to be reading my multipage report for the first time while I testified. The prosecutor played the videotape from the processing room while I remained on the stand. The lawyer could have reviewed it and even demanded a copy. He did neither. This was the first time Attorney Knight had seen it. His most significant challenge was to my reading of the implied consent law. He asked if I thought Albert had understood it. I said no. He thought he was gaining some ground with a follow-up question about how I could be certain that he didn't understand his rights. I replied, "I believe that he was too drunk to understand what I read to him." The lawyer abandoned this line of questioning.

The very experienced judge listened to my testimony, and we watched the video. I was surprised of myself by how much patience I demonstrated with the numerous repetitions, "You don't go through that intersection a dummy" and the other protests. As it became painfully redundant, the judge looked out of the corner of his eye toward me, then winked. I knew my case was won, and the lawyer did too. The lawyer only made some minor hopeless complaints about my presentation. I knew it was to appear to earn his fee. Albert was found guilty.

Another that stands out to me was when I was reluctantly stuck working late, past my normal four-o'clock-to-midnight shift. It was two o'clock in the morning. It wasn't such a bad deal. I was driving a spanking new cruiser with less than two hundred miles on it. It was a quiet night, and I would be relieved in two more hours. The overtime pay would be helpful.

As I drove toward the traffic circle in the center of the city, a car drove toward me from this circle. The car came completely into my lane. I pulled as far to the right as possible, into the parking spaces, stopped, and prepared for the crash. It was driving very slowly, so I didn't expect to get hurt when he hit me. My worries were from my peers for damage to the new cruiser. For some odd reason, the driver corrected his course at the last moment before impact and returned to the proper lane. It was a midsized sedan and appeared to have only the operator in it. I turned around to go stop it.

The three- and four-story buildings lined the street. Stopping cars in this area usually brings an audience out. The flashing blue lights bounce all around off the windows and get lots of attention. However, the car didn't stop. It continued at less than twenty miles per hour. I called in that I was attempting to stop a vehicle on Pleasant Street, read the plate number, and described the car. I didn't want to announce that I had a vehicle that wasn't stopping. That signals a high-speed pursuit. I could ride my bike faster than we were driving. I didn't want to turn on the siren to respect the people who were asleep in these buildings. I had hoped the car would stop soon.

It kept moving in and out of its lane. His slow speed was some relief that any collision would not likely be serious.

We drove to the first intersection with traffic lights. He turned right and continued at slow speed. I reported to dispatch the new location and that it was still not stopping. I reluctantly turned on the siren. The car continued, still driving slowly. The sound of the siren was echoing off the smaller buildings on this street. I was feeling guilty about the blaring siren moving so slowly by their homes, waking them and their kids.

The car turned right at the next two intersections. Now I am beginning to wonder why I had no backup. It didn't appear that this person had any intention of stopping. He drove around like I wasn't even there. We now made a full circle, back to where we started. The siren echoed intensely among these taller buildings. I felt confident that if I drove around him to block his path, he would drive into me. I could imagine my peers complaining the damage to the new car. I was more worried about it than confronting this person who might be trying to get away.

I slipped around him and stopped the car diagonally in front of him. I took a deep breath and tensed my body, preparing for the crash. I was very relieved when he stopped. I ran around my car and cautiously walked up to the driver. I worried that he might try to go around my car or back up. Fortunately, he remained staring forward as I opened the door. I guarded myself with one hand as I reached in with the other to shift the car into park. I then turned off the engine and removed the keys.

I told Lenny to get out of the car. He continued staring forward, oblivious to my presence. I grabbed him and pulled him from the car. Jacked up on adrenalin, I easily lifted him and stood him next to the rear door of his car. My intention was to have him lean against the car while I searched and handcuffed him. When I released my grip, Lenny fell, straight down, toward the ground. I caught him and stood him back up. I tried releasing him slowly, but he could not stand. I mostly carried him to my car and placed him in the back seat. He passed out, still breathing. I could get him to respond but could not get him to fully awaken.

I reported 10-17 (DWI arrest) to the dispatcher, adding that I was to bring him to the hospital. The dispatcher automatically notifies the emergency room. The hospital was also having a quiet night when I got there. I got the wheelchair from just inside the door. I lifted Lenny from the car and placed him in the wheelchair. A nurse came out. Lenny was slumped in the wheelchair with his head hanging to one side. I told the nurse that I needed him to be examined before I brought him to jail. She said that the doctor was sleeping, and she didn't want to wake him for someone who was drunk.

She and I were standing next to the wheelchair with Lenny. I showed her that he was mostly unresponsive, and it was our standing procedure to have him medically evaluated before placing him in a cell. She said he's drunk, and she didn't need to wake the doctor. I said, "Okay, you are doing the medical assessment." I took out my notepad, looked at her name tag, and read her name aloud as I wrote it down. I said, "I will put your name in my report." She decided to get the doctor.

She returned with Dr. Spears, who I knew as a very competent emergency room physician. I expected that he would do a thorough assessment and a blood alcohol level. Dr. Spears looked at Lenny, then said, "He's drunk." He turned to walk away, so I asked, "Is he okay to spend the night in a jail cell?" Dr. Spears replied, "Yes."

I called my supervisor by radio with the results of Lenny's medical examination. He advised me to bring him to the county jail where they were better able to monitor him. We can only monitor by camera from dispatch. The jail supervisor was unhappy about Lenny's barely responsive condition, but he was obligated to take him. We met our duty to have him examined by qualified medical providers. I returned to the station to write my report and prepare charges.

Once in county custody, the sheriff is responsible for transporting inmates to court. They brought Lenny the next morning. He tried to plead guilty. The judge refused to take his plea because he was still intoxicated and set bail. Lenny couldn't locate a sober person to take him, so he was returned to jail. The judge accepted his guilty plea the next day. The judge revoked Lenny's license, fined him, and gave him thirty days in jail with credit for the two days served and twenty-eight suspended during good behavior.

Edna was another DWI that found me. I was driving in traffic heading toward Vermont on a Sunday afternoon. An old yellow Chevy El Camino was ahead of me in a line of traffic. I never saw much use for the Chevy El Camino nor the Ford Ranchero. They were basically station wagons with a pickup back. Why not just buy a pickup? It suddenly sped up, drove onto the shoulder, quickly corrected left and across the double center line. Oncoming traffic swerved to avoid a head-on collision. I sped up to the Camino and turned on the blue lights. It immediately pulled over.

Edna was an elderly lady and the only occupant in the car. She struggled to find the license and registration that I requested. She managed to find her license in her purse but was unable to find her vehicle registration. I noticed that Edna was intoxicated. I could smell the fruity odor of someone drunk with wine. I accepted only her license and asked her to step out of her car. Though her movements were quick and effective, she reached toward the ground as she exited the car. She stood up straight and paused before walking along the side of the car to the space between our cars as I indicated to her. Though Edna performed my field sobriety tests better than most of my DWI arrests, she still performed poorly. I arrested her and drove her to the police station.

I processed Edna. She was seventy-two years old, retired, and lived along the edge of the Connecticut River. She was very cooperative and respectful. Her blood alcohol level was nearly three times the legal limit. I charged her with DWI, first offense. I didn't ask for any bail and released her to her son with a court summons to appear in two weeks. She pleaded guilty and received the standard fine and license revocation.

My colleagues gave me a lot of harassment for arresting an old lady. I remained firm in my conviction. Had there been someone walking on the road, which there often is, she would have killed him or her. She narrowly missed a head-on collision that would have seriously hurt herself and others or killed them. She exceeded the speed limit. She was not wearing a seat belt. These real dangers are not lessened by someone's age or frailness.

I remained dedicated to my conviction to do my part to reduce the death and hardship caused by drunken drivers. I had seen a lot of it in my youth and as a police officer. I never negotiated down any of my DWI charges. I was challenged in court many times by experienced DWI lawyers. I retained a 100 percent conviction rate, for which I am proud. I am not sure that Norman remained sober. At least my efforts persuaded him to seek help for his addiction. I hope that he is doing well. I suppose that it is good news that I have never heard anything more about him. The ones like Albert will never change. Lenny is young enough. I doubt that Edna gave up her wine. From what her son told me, I don't think that she ever tried to get her license back. He intended to drive her wherever she needed and would enlist other family members to meet her needs. I am reasonably satisfied for having impacted people in a way that likely saved their and others' lives.

DWI Firefighter

My quiet winter night of patrol was interrupted with an urgent transmission from Bob, who was patrolling the southern beat. He was in pursuit of a pickup heading south on Broad Street, in the center of the city, at a high rate of speed. He then announced that it had turned onto Chestnut Street, which goes to Unity. I was not far away but in no position to help him intercept. I headed in his direction to assist in backing him up. He then announced that the vehicle had crashed at South Street, the first curve on Chestnut Street.

When I arrived, the truck was suspended on the snowbank. Bob had the driver's door open and was trying to pull the driver from the truck. The driver was leaning inward, wrapping his arms firmly in the steering wheel, and pressing his left foot against the inside of the doorframe. Bob was struggling his best, but the driver was much larger and stronger than him. The two of us were able to pry loose his left hand and drag him from the vehicle. He didn't fall onto the ground as we wished and was trying to stand. As with one brain, Bob and I changed direction and pushed him forward into the side of his truck. He held his hand in front of him, resisting the application of handcuffs. I pressed him hard into the truck with my right shoulder while firmly grabbing the collar of his jacket with my right hand. I took my flashlight from my left leg pocket and shone the thirty-thousand-candlepower light into his eyes. This light is so bright that it would cause some night blindness, making it harder for him to fight us.

As I shone the light into his eyes, I brought my face close to his and whispered my "sweet nothings" to convince him that resistance is futile and would only result in his being hurt. He seemed to tire more than cooperate. Bob was able to apply his handcuffs.

I should have recognized Martin Jackson. When people you know are far outside the realm on how you know them and in a condition that you wouldn't expect, they look entirely different. Martin was a firefighter. I had worked with him at numerous accident scenes and chatted with him in the fire station. Tonight, he was drunk and being a real jerk. He kept swearing at Bob and refused to cooperate during processing. Refusing to take the breathalyzer test would automatically suspend his license for ninety days. We prepared him for the jail cell as we often do for uncooperative, intoxicated persons. Once they sober up a bit, they will participate better.

After placing Martin in the cell, we inventoried his belongings and found his driver's license. This was when I recognized who he was. We called the fire station and spoke with the lieutenant on duty to let him know. He didn't offer, nor did we want his influence. It was just a courtesy call. We didn't know how this might affect their staffing. Even if he beat the DWI charge, his license was still suspended for ninety days and the fire chief should know. Our firefighters are well respected and true professionals. One incident like this not only hurts the relationship between our departments, it has a negative impact with the public.

Two hours later, Martin was ready to cooperate enough to process him. He was still being a jerk. Being a city employee, we didn't ask for bail. A fellow firefighter came to get him.

He fought the DWI, failure to obey a police officer (the pursuit), and resisting arrest. He was found guilty on all charges. Since it was his first DWI conviction within the past seven years, he lost his license for only six months. It could be reduced to ninety days if he completed an approved course, which he did.

We expected Martin would be fired from the fire department. We expected it from his actions with us and his loss of license. The fire chief decided to follow previous policy. He could remain employed on full shifts where they would have others to drive the fire apparatus.

It was hard for me to work with him as a professional after seeing him in this very criminal state of mind. I must wonder, did we see his true colors that night? Is he a competent professional with a problem with alcohol? Had he sought professional help for his alcoholism, I would have respected him more.

CHAPTER 7

Car Chases

Airborne Pursuit

On a Friday evening, my partner, Pete, patrolling the north side of the city, announced that he was in pursuit of a black Datsun pickup. He was at the intersection of Washington and North streets, turning onto North Street. I turned to join him. It was impossible to get into position to help with the pursuit. I would be able to back him up if he managed to stop it.

Pete announced that the car had turned south onto Fremont Street. It now appeared that it may be heading into my beat, so I changed my response route to try and head him off. Just as I turned onto Main Street and thinking I might have a chance of intercepting him, Pete announced that it was off the road on Spring Street. I was there in seconds. Pete was out of his car and heading over the rail onto the steep riverbank. I was right behind him. The truck was on a very steep bank, facing the river. I wondered why it hadn't continued into the river.

Pete descended the bank, sliding along the driver's side of the small pickup. I went down the passenger side, slipping and sliding like he did. I could see two people inside the truck; neither was moving. Pete tried the driver's door, but it wouldn't open. The windows were down, so we could see the two young men inside. The driver was leaning on the steering wheel. He was wiggling a little but didn't seem to be aware of his surroundings. The passenger was lying face-first onto the dash and completely unresponsive. I tried the passenger door, but it wouldn't open either. Pete called for an ambulance, fire department, and a wrecker. The truck was precariously on the riverbank, and it appeared that a gentle push could send it into the fast-flowing river. We hoped that the wrecker could stabilize it.

The ambulance arrived first. They were closer and nimbler than the fire truck. The EMTs slid down the bank just as we did while trying to carry their emergency equipment. Pete tried the driver's door again. He tugged several times with no avail. I cautiously walked around the front of the truck. With the two of us, we managed to open the jammed driver's door. The EMTs attended to him, checking vital signs, then preparing him for transport. The fire department arrived. They did a quick assessment of the danger then joined me on the passenger side. Together, we were able to open the passenger door. The firefighters began first aid. The second ambulance arrived. Pete and I no longer needed to attend to the injured. Pete would follow up with them at the hospital.

I joined Pete in discussing the pursuit and how this vehicle was able to be on the other side of a relatively thin metal rail that looked more like a handrail. Pete explained. When the truck turned onto Fremont Street from North Street, it accelerated. Pete, an excellent driver who performs well at high speeds, soon recognized that this truck was not going to back off on its acceleration as it approached the junction with Maple Street. Fremont Street ends on Maple Street. Pete back off his pursuit, expecting the truck to crash into the garage and trees of the Maple Street residence at the end of Fremont Street. As the driver's luck would have it, good or bad, he found a thin spot in the trees where he passed straight through. He emerged on the other side. There is a significant drop over a retaining wall as the old riverbank descended onto Spring Street. The truck went airborne. It never touched Spring Street, flying over it and the rail. With his luck still on his side, the truck was stopped by the large rocks placed to stabilize the riverbank. He was very fortunate that his truck remained upright and did not go into the river.

The two young men were transported to the hospital. They were responsive at the hospital with only minor injuries. Pete and I felt that they were faking their injuries at the scene.

Walt was a good wrecker operator, and we liked working with him when he was on call. He responded much quicker than others. He attributed it to listening to the scanner. We also realized he exceeded the speed limit. We never complained because we liked his response times. His joke was, "Just make sure your radar is pointing in the other direction."

Walt was talented but also a bit reckless in his recovery of vehicles. He managed to pull this truck up that steep bank and leverage it over the rail. Any other wrecker operator would have crushed the rail.

Walt impressed me later with a different accident. A mechanic from the Ford garage rear-ended a car stopped at the traffic light on Washington Street. The mechanic was driving an old, very rusty Toyota. He ran into the back of a Ford pickup. No one was injured. The accident was simple. So my investigation was brief. The Ford pickup was damaged but roadworthy. The front part of the Toyota was demolished, mostly due to its rusty condition.

Walt connected to the Toyota and pulled. It would not separate from the Ford, dragging it. Walt tried several times without success. We looked closer and saw the reason. The mechanic had welded angle iron along the inside of each front fender to hold them on. These two pieces of iron acted like harpoons to the Ford pickup. They were wedged deeply into its body.

Walt came up with a new plan. He dragged both vehicles into the adjacent restaurant parking lot. He stopped with the Ford next to a streetlight in the center of the parking lot. He chained the front of the Ford to the streetlight and reset his wrecker to winch the Toyota free. Still, it would not budge. Walt turned up the wrecker's engine and pulled again. The streetlight began to bend back and forth. I worried that he would either break it or pull the light out of the ground. I left, telling him that he was on private property and no longer my concern. If he caused damage, I didn't want to be a part of it. Naturally, Walt managed to separate the vehicles without damaging the light pole.

It's nice to have dependable wrecker operators. We had three that rotated call. Sometimes they had difficulties getting paid. The wrecker operators had impoundment yards, but since they were well-known, many people knew where these yards were. The wrecker operators also charged for storage. They were willing to negotiate these fees or accept payments. Now and then, someone would just remove their car from it. When this happened, we would threaten theft of services charges. This was usually enough to persuade them to pay for the tow.

Trooper Motorcycle Chase

It was a busy Saturday summer night and we were fully staffed. So there were two officers in each car and one on the street. The Claremont police cars do not monitor state police, but the dispatcher does. She informed us that there was a trooper pursuing a motorcycle from Newport to Claremont. He was requesting assistance.

To completely block a highway is deadly force. Deadly force doesn't have to be with a gun. Using the police car as force, baton strikes to the head, slamming someone headfirst into a walk or ground, and similar acts can be deadly force. To completely block a vehicle at high speed without an escape route is forcing it to crash, so it's deadly force. A police roadblock is designed to slow the vehicle down enough to make subsequent blocking it nondeadly.

We drove toward the Newport town line. Before we could get there, the dispatcher said that they had just crossed the town line. We set up the cars on the four-lane wide Washington Street diagonally and staggered. We then took positions behind our cars. Fortunately, the drivers of the other cars recognized the odd setup and all the blue lights. Traffic cooperated nicely, stopping in the right lane on both sides, which channeled the motorcycle into the middle two lanes and our semi roadblock.

Just one set of blue lights make dancing shadows. Two sets or more make it very confusing to someone who is not accustomed to them. We learn to focus on the object of interest and ignore the bouncing shadows. It then becomes an object that is rapidly and alternately lighted, but in a stable view. We left our headlights on high beam and illuminated the takedown lights intended to light the inside of a stopped car. To a motorcyclist traveling at high speed and pumped full of adrenaline, it is very difficult to see our police cars and the opening we left between them. The lights also confused his depth perception.

Pete and I worked together well and almost always rode together when we were fully staffed, like this night. Peter was driving and stopped the car at a perfect angle. We could see the trooper's blue light and hear his siren coming at high speed. We immediately got out of our car and took positions behind it. This is a safer place in case the motorcycle crashed into the car, and it allowed us to respond quickly if we got a chance to grab the motorcyclist. One plan was to bump him by hand if he were to pass through our cars.

Luck was with us as the motorcyclist didn't fully downshift as he slowed rapidly and couldn't accelerate. He was just in front of our car, on Peter's side. Almost as though we practiced such things, Peter ran to the motorcyclist's right side and grabbed his right wrist. In less than a second later, I had his left wrist, then reached up, and grabbed the back of his helmet. We both lowered our center of gravity and extended a leg toward the front of the motorcycle. I was confident that if the motorcyclist tried to speed away, the motorcycle would go, but the operator would stay with us.

It seemed like the motorcyclist was accepting his fate at this point. Peter calmly and respectfully spoke to him, telling him that it was in his best interest to do as he said. Peter then reached with his left hand and turned the motorcycle engine off.

Jack and Tom arrived at this time in another police vehicle, the transport van. Tom got out of the right ride and Jack from the driver's side. Both ran toward Pete and me who had a firm grasp and full control of the motorcyclist. I expected them to stand by while Pete and I continued taking our captive into custody, but they ran right up to us. Jack drew his service revolver and pressed the muzzle into the motorcyclist's forehead. He continued to push, forcing the motorcyclist's head back. Jack started shouting obscenities and calling him such names as "dirtbag," "puke," and "scumbag." Jack seemed to be extremely irrational, so much so I thought it was very likely that he would fire his service revolver. We carried .357 Magnums back then. I squinted my eyes and turned my face away and down while maintaining my grip. I expected that if Jack fired, there would be blood and bone sprays that would cover me.

Peter maintained his calm composure. He told Jack, "It's okay, we got him." Jack shouted some threats about how he would regret a recurrence of this action in "my town."

The trooper was out of his car and approaching now. I was pulling the motorcyclist's left arm behind his back. I started reaching for my handcuffs when the trooper said, "Here, use mine." It made sense. It was the trooper's arrest, and he would be taking him. Getting my handcuffs back would be awkward, and I might need them soon on this busy Saturday evening.

Pete and I maintained our contact as the trooper applied his handcuffs. Pete held the motorcycle as the motorcyclist dismounted it. Pete respectfully supported the motorcycle and set it onto its kickstand. I started to walk the prisoner with the trooper back to the state police car when Jack pushed past me and said, "I'll go with him." The trooper brought him back to the Claremont Police Station. Troopers were welcome in our facility to process prisoners and write their reports. It's also a good place to meet the bail commissioner.

Pete asked the dispatcher to call for a wrecker to remove the motorcycle. We pushed the motorcycle to the edge of the road, freed traffic, and waited for the wrecker. I never heard anything more about this case.

I privately called Jack "Wack-em Jack-em." He and Tom both thought that they were supercops. Both lacked physical fitness and openly expressed hatred of running. Both quickly resorted to baton strikes and head punches to subdue a prisoner. I always thought that police collect a good salary for their little education and at least owed the community enough to at least remain in condition to protect it. Instead, they relied on their brutality. I was glad to see that they went to other departments, where they could be the "real cops" they wanted to be.

Fatal Motorcycle Pursuit

It was my day off. The dispatcher called me because the supervisor wanted my assistance with an accident in which the police were involved. Usually, the state police are called whenever our department is involved with an accident. None was available, and a timely investigation was urgent.

The reason I was called is that I was additionally trained in accident investigations and photography. I either led or assisted in the fatal accidents. So I wasn't surprised that my assistance was requested. Since time was of the essence, I didn't bother to change. I grabbed my badge and placed it on my belt and reported wearing shorts, T-shirt, sneakers, and my camera.

The accident was in West Claremont, just past Goulet's Curve, a thirty-five-miles-per-hour zone. Traffic was being diverted around the scene. I met the supervisor in the parking lot of the nearby business. I then learned that he wanted me to be the lead investigator. The motorcycle operator was at the hospital.

The Claremont Speedway is on this side of the city. Races were usually on Saturday evening. Because it rained, they rescheduled it for Sunday afternoon. The races had just ended, so traffic was heavy. Officer Bradbury attempted to stop a motorcyclist in the downtown area. The operator quickly increased speed and went down Main Street toward Vermont. He lost control on Goulet's Curve. There was another car involved. It was parked at the stop sign on Bowker Street, on the right side of Main Street, where traffic typically leaves the racetrack when headed west, toward Vermont. I took it from there.

I started from where motorcyclist first lost control of the motorcycle and walked the scene. I noticed yaw marks, skid marks left as a vehicle turns too sharply, when the motorcycle wobbled back as the operator attempted to regain control. I found the mark where the metal parts of the motorcycle made first contact. I was still about four hundred feet from the car parked on Bowker Street. In the interest of time, I didn't walk the whole distance and returned to my vehicle to get my camera and bag.

I returned to the beginning. I use black-and-white film since it is considerably cheaper and easier to develop. Often, it is easier to make measurements off black-and-white prints as the image borders are more distinct. I take pictures about every forty feet when the accident covers as much distance as this one has. I take close-ups on special things like the yaw marks, first metal contact, pieces broken off, etc. I have a six-inch ruler in my bag to include in pictures for scale.

The operator separated from the motorcycle when it went down. I photographed the path of the motorcycle because it was easier. Hard objects leave more distinguishable markings than soft human bodies. The motorcycle left deep gouges and scrape marks in the pavement as it tumbled and slid until it came to rest against the guardrail on the left side of the road. I photographed the motorcycle in great detail. I not only wanted to show damage caused by the accident, I also want to call out any mechanical defects that I observe. This was an old large Harley Davidson. It was in overall poor condition. The rear tire was bald with belts showing but was still inflated. Tire failure was not a contributor to this accident. I asked the other officers to make the measurements for me so I could expedite this investigation.

I returned to the point where I estimated the operator and motorcycle separated. Officer Bradbury was a lot of help describing the operator's separate path as he left no discernable marks with his body. Bradbury explained that the motorcyclist started tumbling, struck the car stopped on Bowker Street, passed across the front of that car, and came to rest, on the right side of the travel lane, about fifty feet beyond the car he struck. I could see the spot with the asphalt darkened by blood. I continued with the pictures. I had already taken three rolls of thirty-six pictures.

I got close to the family parked in the car. I saw the parents in the front and three preteenagers in the back seat. The dad was the driver. He greeted me with his window rolled down, explaining that he was told to wait. As I returned his greeting, I noticed the dent in the front left of his car and pieces of body tissue sprayed down the left side of the car.

I was chosen to be a specialized traffic accident investigator and photographer because of my math and physics education and interests. I also have a degree in biology. When I looked closely at the tissue on the side of the car, I recognized the somewhat-granular tissue found in kidneys. I knew then that this was a very violent crash. To damage the torso so badly that kidneys were found against the spinal column and the organs between the spine and abdominal wall were either smashed free or at least split open. I knew then that I was investigating a fatal accident. It would not be possible to survive regardless of skilled medical care.

I told the dad that I agreed that he should stand by and remain in their car. I switched to color film, which does better when photographing bodies, blood, and body tissue. I took pictures of the kidney tissue as close as my camera was capable. When I was satisfied that I had gotten what I could, I confirmed that Officer Bradbury had all their information for the report. I then recommended that they not get out of the car and that he should go through the car wash. He saw how serious I was and followed my recommendation. What I didn't realize until years later, when I was the water and sewer superintendent, that car washes recycle their water. Had I known then, I would have gone to and recommended that the car wash dump the water before washing other cars. How disgusting it seems that this man's microscopic pieces of body tissue was spread to other cars.

I was satisfied that I and the others had all that I needed from the scene. I now had to go photograph the body. Though I hadn't heard, I knew that I would be photographing a body and not the injuries off someone still living. I was greeted by Nurse Amy when I arrived. I knew Amy from other cases. She was the emergency room nurse. She and my wife, a nursing supervisor, often worked together. Amy brought me into the room where the door was closed.

The man had long black unkempt hair and beard. His chest was exposed. They were many road abrasions all over his body. Massive bandages were wrapped around his abdomen. Amy explained that the ambulance crew knew that he was injured badly and wanted to transport him as soon as possible. They placed large pieces of gauze on the injury, soaked it with saline, then just wrapped him.

With a new roll of color film, I started photographing. Amy was a great assistant, turning the body for me. It's nice when the person handling the body wears the gloves so I don't have to keep taking them off and on to prevent contamination to my camera. I then asked her if we could remove the bandages. She cut through the wrap and pulled it aside. She then started pulling the large pieces of gauze from his left side of his abdomen. She pulled several out, exposing a large cavity. Still, there were more to be removed. I am always very careful not to include my helper in the photographs. Only Amy's gloved hands will appear in any of my pictures.

Amy said, "I didn't realize that there was this much damage." I said, "I knew because I saw kidney tissue on the side of the car he hit."

She didn't know that he hit a car. As she pulled the remaining pieces of gauze, she said, "I wished that I knew that there was this much damage. We wouldn't have worked so hard to revive him." I said, "I wished that I could have told you sooner. I saw kidney tissue on the side of the car." I explained how I thought he had separated from his motorcycle and was traveling backward when he hit the car, his left lower back striking the bumper of the car.

I finished taking the pictures that I needed. Amy covered the body with the sheet. They were waiting for the family. The family would have to decide on the funeral home. Since they lived in Windsor, Vermont, we expected they would select one over there. It would be a little while longer. It wasn't of any of my concern regarding my investigation.

I returned to the department. It was getting late, so I secured my film in the photography room and resupplied my camera bag. I was due for my normal shift in the morning. They had sufficient personnel. My supervisor agreed that I could complete the report then.

It took most of that shift to write the report, draw the diagrams, and develop the film. From the yaw marks, I was able to estimate his minimum speed before losing control at one hundred five miles per hour, more than three times the thirty-five miles per hour speed limit and more than twice Officer Bradbury's top speed. I developed and filed the film but didn't make any prints, which are expensive. I would make prints if requested. No one ever requested prints. I had no further involvement with this case. My report may have been viewed as many have been. I rarely had to testify, which I attribute to reports that presented the accident with enough detail to answer any questions.

A man died. A family is grieving a loss. True, he crashed during a police chase. He probably wouldn't have died if he wasn't chased. Back the events up one notch and he wouldn't have been wanted by the police if he hadn't violated the law. He died by his own actions. There was no contact with the police car or any other car to cause his loss of control. His life was entirely in his hands. The family in the car that his body struck is also a victim. They must have felt a significant jolt from the impact of his body against their car. They likely suffered some emotional trauma from this man's unfortunate decision.

Persistent Pursuit

Maple Avenue is a nice long wide street through a residential area. There are a few quiet businesses and a large wooded city park, but it is mostly residential. On this early summer evening, families and children are playing in the yards and along the street.

I was driving into town when I noticed a car heading toward me. It caught my attention because I thought that it was going faster than it should. The radar confirmed that it was traveling forty-six miles per hour in this thirty-miles-per-hour zone. I turned around and stopped it.

I recognized Stan right away. He handed me his license and registration and apologized for his speed. I knew Stan from my substitute teaching and that he worked in his uncle's business. I told Stan that I appreciated his apology and accepting responsibility. I returned his license and registration and asked him to drive a little slower especially when there are kids playing outside.

I got back into the car. I usually left the blue lights on until the other driver gets back into traffic. As I was sitting in the car, I saw a car approaching at high speed. The radar indicated sixty miles per hour and increasing to sixty-eight as it passed by me. I turned around to stop it. It continued accelerating. I suspected this guy saw me in a traffic stop and was taking advantage, thinking that I would not leave one for another. I would have, but I was done with Stan. He wisely remained stopped while this high-risk car approached.

I was trying to keep my speed down, given the kids playing in the front yards. The car was not slowing and likely still accelerating. I called into dispatch that I was trying to catch up to a car traveling toward town on Maple Avenue at high speed. I was now traveling eighty miles per hour and still not gaining on him. My lights and sirens were encouraging kids to run out to the edge of the road to see what was happening. This concerned me greatly. I called openly for a backup to prevent this car from getting to the even more compact part of the city. Everyone was just a little too far away.

Suddenly, the car braked hard and turned quickly into Claremont Manor, a multifamily complex. A short man with short hair, dressed in a light-green T-shirt and worn jeans, got out of the driver's seat and ran into the building. Each building has twenty-four apartments, so I needed to be quick to keep him in sight. He ran through the front door, down a half flight of stairs, and into the first apartment on the left, closing the door behind him. I burst through the door and into the apartment. The living room is the first room with the kitchen to the left. I heard an interior door close but couldn't tell which one. An older lady was startled. She turned her gaze from the bedroom area to me. I asked, "Where is he?" She was still speechless. I said, "Who just ran in here? Where is he?" I knew that I was on good legal grounds to have crashed through her door. It was a fresh pursuit by anyone's definition, which gives me the right to enter any premise or property.

My concern was that it is possible to climb out a bedroom window. I would be happy to continue the foot chase outside but needed to know if he climbed out. The lady called, "Eddie." Eddie reluctantly came out of the bedroom. He was an experienced prisoner and didn't present himself for immediate handcuffing. I notified dispatch and my backup that I had "one in custody."

Eddie said, "My accelerator got stuck." I expressed my skepticism, noting that he was able to control the vehicle to stop where he did and that he made no attempt to apply the brakes before that.

Being a little vindictive, I called for a wrecker. It was my intention to have the car impounded to be examined by a mechanic.

I brought Eddie to sit in the rear of the police car until the wrecker arrived. The car was a technical evidence, for which I needed a continuous chain of custody. The wrecker operator arrived quickly. I was glad that it was Walt, who is always quick to respond. I explained that I wanted the vehicle taken to be examined for a sticking throttle. He examined the car and assured me that the throttle was free and was not sticking. I was disappointed that he didn't tow it to add an additional cost to Eddie's recklessness.

I processed Eddie at the police station. He had a criminal record for assaults and burglaries. I charged him with reckless operation and resisting arrest. I felt that I didn't get close enough to justify a charge of failing to obey a police officer, the charge used for pursuits. The short foot pursuit justified the resisting arrest charge. The bail commissioner set bail as personal recognizance. He had never missed a court date. Motor vehicle reckless operation wasn't enough to present a level of danger to the public that a bail commissioner would consider.

Eddie was on parole. I reported the incident to his parole officer who petitioned the court that Monday for a violation of the conditions of his parole. He was returned to jail that day on the violation of parole. He would not be eligible for parole again until these charges were resolved. I felt satisfied that justice was done.

Motorbike Foot Chase

A neighborhood on a dead-end street had feuding neighbors. They frequently called the police to complain about trivial things. One of these was the fifteen-year-old Terry who rode his dirt bike on his own property most of the time. The limits of his family's lot grew boring, so he sometimes ventured onto neighbors' property and into the street. Though technically illegal, the dead-end street with fewer than a dozen homes didn't present much danger. The angry neighbor would call, but by the time we got there, he was nowhere to be found.

One day was a little different. Having responded to this nuisance dirt bike call, I found only one neighbor working in his yard. I stopped to talk with him. Officer Pedro was with me. The neighbor affirmed that he found it annoying. His annoyance seemed to be based more on it being illegal rather than being a real hazard. As we spoke, the boy drove by on his dirt bike. I went to stop him, and he accelerated.

It was a short pursuit. He turned into an old driveway, then up a steep hill into the woods. I could see that he struggled getting the bike to climb the steep hill. I stopped the car and ran after him. I caught up to him on the hill and grabbed the back of his collar, then his left wrist. I told him to turn off the bike, and he complied. Terry expressed concern about his bike falling and getting damaged. Pedro was along the right side of the bike now and assured Terry that he had it. Terry would still not step off the bike as I instructed. I then lifted and pulled him from the bike as Pedro held it.

Terry continued to struggle. He was tall but very thin, and I could easily restrain him. I placed him facedown on the ground as I applied the handcuffs. He continued to squirm, turning his head side to side. Each time he turned, he rubbed his chin on a tree root. It left an abrasion on his chin.

Terry was concerned about his bike that Pedro was holding. By this time, Pedro had the bike turned around and facing downhill. Pedro said, "Oh, are you worried about this?" Terry said yes, in a pleading tone. Pedro then said, "Let me take care of it for you," and released it to roll and tumble down the hill. This, of course, upset Terry immensely. He struggled against me some but was too thin to offer any significant resistance. I guided him carefully down the steep hill and into the police car.

We brought Terry to the station. Juvenile processing is brief; only a little information is required. It's a referral to the juvenile officer with a description of the laws that would have been violated had he had been an adult. I was only interested in pursuing the unlicensed, unregistered, and failure to stop for a police officer. Resisting arrest would not look good because he was so frail. Judges want resisting charges to be significant. Sadly, had he not run off, I wouldn't have brought any charges. When an officer uses force, there must be some justification. Charges can be dropped later.

His parents came quickly. They immediately complained about police brutality that caused the abrasion on his chin. They were convinced that we beat him. This went on for several weeks. I was the evilest person in their eyes. It all changed one day when I arrested the neighbor they hated even more than me. Suddenly, I was the greatest guy in the whole world who taught their son a lesson.

There was another similar incident involving a minibike in the wintertime. Minibikes were small motorized cycles that did not go very fast. They had one speed with a friction gear. Unlike some dirt bikes, they could never be roadworthy. One winter evening, Pete was driving the cruiser and I was riding with him. It's Pete's beat and his decision on how to handle the events. We encountered Henry, who we knew well. Henry lived off the grid beyond the city maintain road that turned into a wooded trail. Finding Henry on a minibike in the center of the city was surprising.

Henry was driving a black minibike down the Summer Street sidewalk with a friend on the back. Minibikes could barely carry one person, and they had two. It was struggling to carry its load, so it was moving slowly. Pete drove the car along the side of Henry, who stopped immediately. Pete reminded Henry that he cannot drive that on the sidewalk. Henry agreed and apologized. Henry explained that they were headed just a few houses away. Pete told him that he could walk alongside it now, which he did. Pete added that if he saw him again, he would arrest him. Henry agreed, and we thought this would be the end of it.

Two hours later and on the other side of town by the airport, we saw Henry and friend on the minibike coming at us in the other lane. Pete expressed surprise and determination to hold true to his word. He turned around to stop them. We're in a high-performance police car. Henry's driving a minibike that can barely handle its load, on a snowy street, with snowbanks on each side. Pete easily caught up to it, but Henry kept going. Henry then turned off the road, through the snowbank, and behind a factory. His passenger fell off. I chased after the minibike on foot. It lost a lot of traction, so I was gaining on it. I slipped on some ice, fell to one knee, and managed to slide back onto my feet. I grabbed Henry's shoulder. He stopped the bike and surrendered. Pete called to check on me. I told him that I had one in custody. He affirmed that he had the other. He drove around the factory where I could best meet him. Pete called for a wrecker to retrieve the minibike.

On the ride to the police station, Henry seemed nervous. He asked, "Am I going to jail?" Pete assured him that he would not be going to jail. Henry surprised me with his disappointment: "I thought that I would be going to jail so I can take a shower." I thought how sad it is for someone living off the grid, without running water and with very little education. After processing, Henry was released with a date to appear in court. He would have benefitted from taking a shower.

Fred's Chase

I was patrolling on what we call Chestnut Flats. It's past the urban compact but well within the residential zone. The speed limit was thirty-five miles per hour. I saw a red car speeding toward me from the urban compact. The radar showed sixty-eight miles per hour. As it went by, I noticed that it was a red Ford Mustang, there were at least two people in the front seat, and had New York plates that I didn't have time to read. I turned on the blue lights and turned around. At first, it started to slow down and pull over but suddenly sped up.

I called to dispatch that I had a car that was not stopping. We typically do not announce that it is a pursuit, for whatever reason— legal, ethical, for the media monitoring, etc. We also seldom directly report speeds. We may describe it in general. I mentioned that he was traveling over the speed limit. Soon, we were traveling over eighty miles per hour.

I kept dispatch informed of our location. Almost immediately, my fellow officers announce their availability to assist me. All were behind me. Dispatch called out to the state police and the Unity part-timers. None was available. My supervisor would be my backup.

I was driving an old Ford Crown Victoria. They had a larger engine than the public could buy. They also had a stiffer suspension, making them ride a little higher. Both these features helped immensely on accelerating through the corners. I was at a great disadvantage to the Mustang's ability to accelerate much greater than mine. So the chase went such that I caught up to him on the corners, but he accelerated away from me out of the corner. We quickly crossed into the town of Unity. I can legally pursue anyone across the state if the pursuit started in my jurisdiction. He got a considerable lead on me going up Unity Mountain.

It was a rough ride on the other side of the mountain. The road had many bumps. At eighty to ninety miles per hour, the car tended to float off the road. The police car seat belt was one that could be pulled tight at the waist. To control a car under these conditions, one's butt needs to be stable. Each time, the car went airborne, and I felt that I was floating in the car. My head hit the ceiling. I pulled the strap a little tighter.

I often lost sight of the Mustang as it entered a corner. I would close the distance and regain sight coming out of the corner. Finally, I didn't regain sight, but I should have. As I went by it, I noticed the Mica Mine Road on my left was dusty. There were no other cars on it, so I gambled that this was where my quarry went. The Mica Mines are a popular picnic and party spot. The road narrowed through the trees. It opened to an area where a group could assemble. There is a deep pit from where they mined mica that was used for the aircraft instrument panels during World War II. The pit had water, and party debris was scattered everywhere. Only trail machines can go beyond this point.

Unfortunately, the road forks about a quarter mile before this party spot. No longer did I have the dust trail to guide me. The fork to the right eventually deteriorates into trails like the Mica Mine side. I stopped at this point, knowing my quarry was trapped. I described my location and waited for my supervisor to arrive. Surprisingly, the part-time Unity officer showed up, though not in uniform. As we were developing plans to pursue both routes, the Mustang came down from the Mica Mine side.

Two men occupied the front seats of this shiny new Mustang. The one in the passenger seat seemed younger. He also seemed frightened. He held himself rigidly against the seat and stared forward with his eyes and mouth wide open. I focused on the driver. He was tall, blond, in excellent physical condition, well-dressed, and fully cooperative. Nonetheless, the situation required that he be arrested and brought in for processing. He agreed that his passenger could drive his car, adding that it was his brother. This saved him a tow charge.

Fred was quiet during our ride to the police station. He cooperated fully with the processing. He provided all the identifying information required. I photographed and fingerprinted him. When presenting an identification, he gave to me his military license. He was an airman, grade 5. We sat beside each other when I told him that I just finished my time in the army artillery and was a captain in the reserves. He seemed embarrassed and was worried how this would affect his military career. He was expecting to be promoted soon. His charges of failing to obey a police officer (a misdemeanor), reckless operation, and speeding (violations) would delay any promotion for a long time. He intended to make the air force a career.

I called the bail commissioner and recommended personal recognizance due to his military standing. The bail commissioner agreed. Since he was on one week's leave and would have to travel back for a later date, we set a court date that was three days from now. I released him to his brother who was waiting in the lobby.

Fred came to court with a lawyer. Usually, lawyers deal with the prosecutor and seldom directly with the arresting officer. When I saw the lawyer approach the prosecutor with Fred by his side, I walked over. The lawyer tried his typical trying to reduce charges, pleading to a lesser one. He offered to plead to the reckless operation if I dropped the failure to obey, the most serious charge. I stood next to Fred and told him how I very much understood his promotion dilemma in the air force. Even the reckless charge would have a negative impact on his promotion and his career. He was very remorseful and disappointed in himself for the impulsive behavior. I offered to Fred to drop both the failure to obey and reckless operation if he pleaded guilty to the sixty-eight miles per hour that got my attention in the first place. He and his attorney gladly agreed. The prosecutor was surprised, but they were my charges and ultimately my choice.

Years later, my wife was working with Fred's brother, Corey. I didn't remember him, but he remembered me. Corey talked about Fred. He did well in the air force and always appreciated that break I gave to him. He added that Fred never did anything so stupid again.

Chasing Casper

I was on patrol on Route 120 early one Friday winter evening near the community college. As I drove into town, I saw a small vehicle coming toward me too fast. The radar indicated fifty-eight miles per hour in this forty-miles-per-hour zone. It didn't slow down at all when it saw me and sped on by. I turned around to stop it. When I caught up to it, it became clear that it did not intend to stop. I called dispatch to inform them that I had a vehicle that was not stopping.

As usual, the other patrol cars announced their locations. Since we were headed north and out of the city, it was obvious that I was on my own. The supervisor would head in my direction, but his assistance would only be a backup should the vehicle stop. Dispatch called for assistance to the small towns north of us to see if any part-time officers were on duty. There was no response from them. Dispatch called the state police. There were also no state troopers in the area. I felt very alone but confident about my safety.

I caught up close enough to transmit the plate number and a description. It was a Datsun B210, a small average sedan. It was driving quite irradicably, on the wrong side of the road then on the right shoulder as it went around corners, now traveling about eighty miles per hour in the fifty-miles-per-hour zone. My supervisor asked, "How are the speeds?" I told him that they were fast but not too bad, expressing my concern about being on the wrong side of the road. He told me to "stay with him." We never transmit the actual speeds. It would thrill scanner land but might open the department to some criticism.

I couldn't see the driver. When I chased someone at night, I turned my headlights on high beam, hoping to add intimidation to the already-bright blue lights. It didn't seem to have its intended effect.

Dispatch came back on to tell me the owner of that car was in the police station, reporting it stolen. I expressed disbelief about it being stolen because such reports were often a cover, a way to avoid liability if something happened. Dispatch assured me that it was truthful. The owner had stopped to pick up a pizza and left it running. When she came out, the car was gone. This upped the ante a bit. It's now a felony.

Speeds were getting closer to ninety miles per hour now, and the driving was even more erratic. I had horrible visions of a head-on collision with a family in a van coming the opposite direction. Though I never wish serious harm to anyone, I couldn't see this ending without a crash, so I hoped he would leave the road on the right and crash into the woods.

I reported the speeds were starting to get unreasonable. My supervisor asked for my location. The radio was breaking badly as we were getting out of range. The blaring siren added to the difficulties in hearing transmissions. Dispatch told me to switch to the county frequency. It's a good idea, but I had to take my eyes off the road to find the button on the radio. The county radio had more power, increasing its range, and is monitored by all county police agencies and the local state police troop. Once I establish contact on the county frequency, I reported my position. We were already coming up the hill out of Cornish Flat.

I was surprised and a bit disappointed that this little Datsun could perform this well. Once over the hill, it accelerated to ninety-five miles per hour. I called to my supervisor that speeds were becoming more unreasonable. There was still no response from the local part-time police agencies. Dispatch called Lebanon to BOL (be on the lookout). I was not looking forward to chasing this thing to Lebanon. I certainly didn't want responsibility for chasing this thing at ninety-five miles per hour into a busy city. I asked to break it off. My supervisor said, "No, stay with him." The tone of his voice seemed to be an attempt to encourage me, expressing confidence to assure me, like a cheerleader.

We continued a few more miles. Radio contact even on the county frequency was intermittent. I retransmitted my request to break it off. This time, the supervisor agreed. I braked and started my three-point turn. I gave one more look over my shoulder. I could still see the taillights. At that speed, the Datsun should have been gone. I radioed that there appears to be something wrong with the vehicle and I was going to check it out. I don't know if dispatch heard me. I didn't hear any reply.

I caught right up to the Datsun that was going only about thirty miles per hour. I radioed that I thought that it might be giving up. I couldn't hear a reply. It continued slowing but didn't come to a full stop. It got below ten miles per hour and still slowing but not stopping. I turned on the takedown lights to better light the cabin of the car. As it slowed more, I decided to stop the cruiser and run up to it. The car was well lighted with the cruiser high beams and the bright takedown lights from the light bar.

I could see a man in his early twenties. His dark brown hair and beard were long and scraggly. I had my hand on my service revolver but did not draw it. We carried .357 Magnums back then. It could easily penetrate the car door if I saw a weapon directed at me. I was immediately surprised as I saw this man wiggling forward and backward, like a child that is trying to get a wagon to roll.

I ran up to the car and opened the door, the driver still trying to get it to roll away. I saw that it was a manual transmission, so there was no park to put it into. I reached across the man, pressing him back into the seat, and pulled up on the parking brake. The vehicle finally stopped.

As one can imagine, my adrenaline had peaked while driving. Alone, in the middle of nowhere, with no possible backup, with no idea who I had encountered, my adrenaline was beyond peaked. I grabbed this man by the front of his shirt and pulled him out the door. He was average-sized, but I felt none of his weight. I brought him quickly to the pavement, facedown, in the southbound lane. I placed the handcuffs on him. I felt no resistance. Had he tried, I wouldn't have noticed with such adrenaline and being powered up. All that anger about risking other people's lives further fueled my muscles. I picked him up from the pavement and mostly carried him to the cruiser, his feet dragging.

As I picked him up, I had a sense that I should check. There was a southbound car that came upon us as I was handcuffing him. I was too fixed on him to realize any other cars. She stopped and watched as I restrained him. She drove slowly by as I was putting him into the back of the cruiser. I apologized as she went by. She smiled and said, "Oh, no problem. No problem at all." I hope that it gave her sense of security to know that police officers can subdue criminals so quickly. I also felt irresponsible for being so vulnerable in the middle of an open lane. It restores my confidence in that good people will do what is right. She had kids in the car with her. I think about how things might have been so different, and my earlier fears were that close to being realized.

With Casper securely in the back of the police car, I tried calling dispatch. No response. We were in Plainfield now. I was thinking about my alternatives. I was making plans to push this Datsun out of the road, then driving back to Claremont. By a stroke of luck, the Cornish officer showed up. Dispatch had called him, and he came on duty right away. Still dressed in street clothes with a badge on his shirt, he had Cornish's marked cruiser. I didn't realize that we were now in Plainfield. I very much appreciated that he went that extra distance to back me up. He had radio contact with the county dispatch and called for a wrecker to remove the car. He also offered to stand by until it arrived. I thanked him and got into the car with Casper now snoring in the back seat.

I still couldn't get my dispatch on the radio as I turned the car around. After I crested the hill, I called again. I got a broken response. I reported that I was 10-11 (reporting to headquarters). Dispatch replied, "With one in custody?" I replied, "Affirmative, one in custody." My supervisor replied, "Good job." I'm not one to thrive on praise, but that simple response from my supervisor felt good.

It seemed like a long ride back. Casper was snoring the whole way. My adrenaline returned to normal levels. I looked at all the places where this pursuit could have gone very badly. I was so glad that came out well.

I was met by another officer in the processing room as I brought Casper in. It was an uneventful processing. Casper was very cooperative. He was obviously drunk and blew more than twice the legal limit on the breathalyzer. That only made me feel even more lucky that the pursuit didn't end badly. During processing, he said that he saw the car sitting there as he walked by it. He decided to jump in and take it for a ride. He didn't count on running into me around the corner.

As usual, I brought all the charges I could against Casper. I charged him with unauthorized use of the car. It's very hard to prove car theft. I would have to prove that he never intended to bring it back. It also didn't appear to be his intention. He only wanted to take it for a ride. I charged him with failure to obey a police officer, reckless operation, driving while intoxicated, and resisting arrest. I would have been very happy with dropping the resisting arrest charge. I brought it mostly because he tried to get away and didn't surrender when pursued.

Casper didn't want to call anyone to come get him. We housed him overnight. He went to court the next morning and pleaded guilty to all the charges. He was fined five hundred dollars and sentenced to serve five months in the county jail and another seven months suspended for two years. If he got into trouble again within the two years, the seven months could be brought forward.

When I wrote my report, I got the times logged by the dispatcher. The chase lasted just over five minutes. The ride back took almost fifteen minutes. On the return trip, I drove at little over the speed limit. It's a sharp contrast and shows how fast the chase was. I am amazed that Casper was able to keep the car on the road, being so intoxicated.

I later discussed the car with the wrecker operator. I wanted to know why this car broke down. He said that Casper blew the rear differential. I told him about the speeds, wondering if that was it. He said that it wasn't so much the speed as the wear. Certainly, he stressed it. It must have been just good luck that it failed at that time, before he hurt someone.

I could have brought charges of an "unattended vehicle" to the owner who left her car running outside the pizza shop. I felt that she learned the lesson in a much more effective way. Her car needs an expensive mechanical repair, and she must pay the tow charge. A fine for the unattended vehicle is trivial and would be extremely poor public relations. The natural consequences were sufficient.

CHAPTER 8

Burglaries

Arrowhead Foot Chase

Arrowhead is a city park with ski and hiking trails. It has several wooded acres. The city operates the ski and tobogganing with the effort of volunteers. The hiking trails are popular for hikers, dog owners, and people who enjoy time in more natural surroundings. I liked using the trails to Flat Rock at the top because it overlooks the downtown. It's a nice place to have a picnic with my daughters while their mother is working.

There are several small neighborhoods around Claremont that have the greater house values. These are, of course, the people with above-average incomes. A neighborhood bordering the city-owned Arrowhead Park has several professionals who often leave the area several days at a time for business or personal reasons. Dr. Marino, a rheumatologist, owned one of these houses. It was at the end of the dead-end street and the closest to the wooded area of the city park. He was often out of town on other business. He had a commercially monitored burglar alarm.

The alarm company alerted our dispatcher that Dr. Marino's alarm had been activated one Sunday afternoon. It was Adam's beat, so he was responding. Most alarms are false or accidental, but we had never received an alarm at Dr. Marino's house. I headed in that direction anyway, just in case Adam need a backup. Adam signed off, then immediately announced that he had two people climbing out a

195

window. I was at the far end of the neighborhood. When I got there, Adam had a young woman to whom he was applying handcuffs. He seemed to have good control. I asked where the other one was. He replied, "Her boyfriend ran up the hill." I was always game for a good foot chase, so I asked, "Which way?" Adam pointed in the direction, and I started to run. He said, "You'll never catch him. He has a good head start." I told him that I wanted to try.

Adam was never very assertive. He followed guidelines of waiting for backup before entering buildings. We thought he purposely neglected some things to avoid direct confrontations with any personal risk. I was a bit surprised that he even had that woman under control by himself. She must have readily surrendered. Chasing someone in the woods, like I was doing, would have never been something for him to do. So I didn't take his advice to give up the chase.

Much to my advantage was the fresh four-inch layer of snow. My adversary left a path that was easy to follow. I settled into a comfortable run. The hardest thing about running in uniform is the heavy .357 Magnum revolver and portable radio. Both bounce uncomfortably, and the radio could bounce out of the holder. I held the gun down with my right hand and pressed the radio against my hip with my left hand. I was wearing the very same combat boots that I wore in the army. We used to run five miles in these boots, so I was prepared and expected a high probability of success.

I was well into the forest in just a few minutes. I could tell by his tracks that he had stopped, then resumed his run. Perhaps he was hoping to wait for the police to leave so he could simply walk out and avoid capture. When he realized that I was in pursuit, he must has resumed his run. He had an advantage because I was carrying so much weight. My advantage was my army conditioning and determination.

Now deep into the forested area, I was beginning to worry that he might have a gun. I slowed down to be more focused. Remembering my army training, I always had a place in mind where I could duck if I had any indication he was going to shoot at me.

The trail went directly uphill for about a quarter of a mile. I was beginning to wonder if we were still on city property. I was not concerned about private property as this was a legitimate fresh pursuit. I could legally chase him all the way across the state regardless of property ownership. My concern was how to best exit the forest when I caught him.

A few more minutes of running and I was beginning to worry even more. I was a long way from any road. My backup was not as physically capable, and I wouldn't be able to tell them my exact location. The trees didn't have address numbers. I grew more cautious, occasionally stopping to listen. I could hear the downtown sounds but no noise of anyone running through the woods.

The footprints started to turn to the left, more into the city park. I radioed my vague position to the dispatcher, which would be monitored by the other officers. After a while, the trail turned back down the hill, toward the neighborhood near the middle school. My adversary emerged onto the plowed sidewalk. His footprints were less distinct, but I had a general idea of his direction. I radioed again my location, now with an address on South Street. His trail was getting more challenging to differentiate from other footprints, and I was afraid that I would lose him. He ran through parking areas, backyards, then back onto the sidewalk. There were too many footprints now for me to be certain which were his.

Officers typically hate that people monitor police on their scanners. They refer to them collectively as "scanner land." It worked very much to my advantage today. Several people stood in front of their homes. They pointed at a backyard and said, "He ran under that deck."

I ran up to the deck. There was a small opening where someone could crawl in. I was breathing hard and didn't really want to crawl in and fight with someone in that small pace. An experienced runner, I knew that I was fully capable of continuing any physical demand and a few seconds recharges my energy, but I still didn't want to tussle under that deck. I started to wait for backup.

While waiting, I was keenly aware of the growing audience. I decided to entice my quarry to come out. I said, "I am not going to come in there after you. I am going to mace the shit out of this deck if you don't come out."

I removed my can of pepper spray from its holster on my utility belt. I was trying to determine the most effective way to spray under the deck when I heard someone moving. I put away the pepper spray and placed my hand on my gun, thumb ready to release the snap that held it. I saw the top of a head with lots of curly black hair. As he emerged, crawling on hands and knees, he held his hands well forward for me to see, even though I hadn't told him to do so. I had some sense of security that he knew to do this without me telling him. It also caused me some concern as he may also have some experience or knowledge in how to effectively resist arrest.

Breathing more normally now, I could speak softly and assertively. I instructed him to keep his hands out front and to crawl toward the house. Once facing directly toward the house, I told him to lie on his stomach, keeping his hands above his head. He cooperated fully as I applied the handcuffs. I stood him up to search him. I didn't think it necessary to cause him any more discomfort in the snow. He had only cigarettes and a lighter. I expected that if he had more, he dropped it in the woods. I would search under the deck later.

It is policy and good practice to hold the arm of someone in custody and handcuff. It is not just to keep them from running away. It's to prevent injury if they fall. I scanned his person quickly and asked if he was all right. He nodded his head and said with a sigh, "I'm all right."

He was tall and thin. He was dressed better than most people I arrest. He was wearing a denim jacket, sweatshirt, well-fitting jeans, and sneakers. I didn't know him. I asked for his name. He replied, "Dino Angelo." He was being very cooperative. He was obviously unhappy with his situation but remained respectful.

I asked Dino if he was okay to walk. He said that he was fine. I was hoping for backup to arrive to transport. I wanted to get him out of this backyard and away from the growing audience. We started to walk toward the street just as backup arrived. Another officer had taken my car to the station so that I could ride with my prisoner.

When I got to the station, Adam was still processing the woman. I search Dino more thoroughly, brought him to a cell, removed the handcuffs, and locked him inside. I assured him that I would return to process him when the room was available.

Dispatch ran criminal records checks on our prisoners. Dino had recently served prison time for burglary. This explained his cooperation. They learn this routine very well in prison. Any hesitation makes a big difference in privileges.

The woman had no criminal history, so she was bailed and released. I processed Dino. It was very routine. I was charging him with burglary and resisting arrest. I called the bail commissioner who knew Dino. He set bail at fifty thousand dollars, cash only. This was based on his criminal record and that he ran from me. The primary reason for bail is to assure appearance in court. Since Dino was likely to face a much longer sentence than before and he ran from me, there was an increased likelihood that he would not appear in court. Bail can be high when there is danger to the public. The only danger Dino presented was to property.

Dino was unable to raise the fifty-thousand-dollar bail. I took him to the Sullivan County House of Corrections (SCDOC), which is better able to house him before court. I wasn't needed for his first court appearance, the arraignment. I learned that the judge maintained the fifty-thousand-dollar bail. Burglary is a felony. District courts only heard violations and misdemeanors. A person could only be fined for a violation, no jail time. Misdemeanors could involve a fine and up to one year in jail. Felonies could have fines and up to fifteen years in prison. For felonies, there is a probable cause hearing at district court. If found that there is probable cause, the district court transfers the case to superior court. There could be a grand jury indictment at any time during this process. If he is indicted before the probable cause hearing, the probable cause hearing is dismissed as no longer needed. It's part of the expedited hearing requirement. Grand juries may not meet for several months. A probable cause hearing in district court could be quicker.

Dino was indicted by the grand jury. He and his attorney negotiated a plea. He went back to prison to serve the longer sentence as expected. Often, the plea involves dropping one charge to favor the other. Our county attorney was very good at checking with the officer who brought the charges. I was very willing to drop the resisting arrest charge. Dino only ran from me. There was no struggle, and he cooperated fully once captured. I felt that resisting arrest on his record would unjustly label him for police, corrections, and parole officers. He wasn't one to physically resist or hurt an officer, which would be the assumption. The correctional system would be more willing to grant certain privileges sooner, making his time in prison a little more tolerable, and perhaps eligibility for parole sooner. I have learned that the more one is institutionalized, the more likely he or she is to return. Some begin this unfortunate life track as juveniles in residential placements or detention.

Lafayette Burglary

The discount store on Lafayette Street was a favorite target for burglars. It was just enough off the main streets and behind a dense, congested neighborhood. It was an old factory building and looked like an easy target. For those who made the bad decision to break into it, they soon learned the error of their ways. It had a very reliable, silent burglar alarm. The most challenging thing for police was to secure the outside before going in. The building was on the edge of the river. Walking on this steep riverbank with dense vegetation was difficult. Fleeing burglars had the advantage of disappearing into the neighborhood or climbing across a sewer pipe that spanned the river.

One Sunday afternoon, the alarm went off. Sundays were staffed minimally because they were mostly quiet. My fellow officer Steve and I responded. We easily found the broken window. There were no other officers on to assist us, so we decided to enter the building through the broken window, just as the burglars had.

Once inside, we could hear the burglars talking and moving things. We walked as quietly as we could toward the sounds. The floors in the old building creaked. Fortunately, the burglars were too intent on their collecting bounty to notice us. We traverse a large room of mostly furniture. We found them as we entered the next room that contained hardware and cabinets of the most expensive merchandise, electronics and hunting knives.

With our weapons drawn, Steve took the lead. He was much shorter than me, so it made sense. I could see over him. I would only block his view if I took the lead. For what Steve lacked in height, he more than made up for it in courage and dedication. As we peeked into the room, I recognized brothers Claude and Leroy. They were regulars with motor vehicle violations and shoplifting. They had broken into a large cabinet and were examining the contents of mostly large hunting knives and accessories such as leather belts and sheaths. We moved closely behind them, entirely unnoticed.

From a ready firing position, Steve yelled, "Police, freeze! Put your hands up." Both men immediately complied, extending their arms upwardly.

Claude and Leroy didn't seem very startled and complied with Steve's commands. Unfortunately, they weren't the sharpest tools in the cabinet. Claude the Clod, as his friend called him, held a large hunting knife in his right hand. Steven yelled, "Drop the knife!" Claude seemed confused, looking toward his brother, whose hands were empty. Steve yelled again, "Drop the knife!" Claude seemed even more confused. He didn't seem to realize that he held the knife Steve wanted dropped. He started to turn toward us, and Steve yelled, "Face the cabinet!" Still, Claude kept glancing toward his brother and now over his shoulder toward us while still holding the large hunting knife in his raised hand.

I began to worry that this knucklehead was going to do something even more stupid, like turn toward us. I had full confidence in Steve, but I knew he would protect himself and feel protective of me. We carried .357 Magnums. At this close range, Claude would never survive.

I knew the brothers by name, and I suspect that Steven did not. I also knew how poorly educated they were. Most people would call them stupid. Stupid is someone who cannot learn. These brothers could learn, if they wanted. They prefer the existence they have chosen rather than to gain employable skills.

I said firmly, "Claude, drop the knife in your right hand." Claude looked up at his hand and seemed surprised to see the knife. He dropped it. Steve place his weapon in his holster and took out his handcuffs. I provided cover while he handcuffed Claude. When he finished with Claude, I handed him my handcuffs, and he hand-cuffed Leroy.

We brought the brothers to Steve's car since he parked closer to the door. We placed them in the back seat and asked the dispatcher to call the key holder. The key holder lived in this neighborhood and arrived quickly. We left him to secure the building and brought our prisoners to the station for processing.

Claude and Leroy were tried separately. Because Claude had the stolen knife in his possession when we caught them, it made the burglary armed and more severely punished. Both got several years in prison due to their criminal record. Interestingly, Claude held the knife, but Leroy got a longer sentence.

Leroy stayed in the Manchester area when he got out. Claude came back to Claremont. He found a sugar mamma to support him. A sugar mamma is one who receives welfare benefits because she has a child. Anita had a girl, Maria, about two years old. Neither Anita nor Claude worked.

After a few months, Anita brought Maria to the emergency room. She had a high fever for several days. She was seriously ill. Our local hospital doesn't have a pediatric unit, so they transferred her to Dartmouth Hitchcock Memorial Hospital. They discovered that her stomach had been ruptured. The spaghetti she ate and the ensu-ing infection were distributed throughout her abdomen. Surgery was necessary even in her weakened condition. She died two days later. Anita waited much too long to seek medical assistance.

The autopsy revealed that the cause of the rupture was a severe blow to her abdomen. They ruled it homicide. Our department investigated. It soon became clear that Claude had punched her or kicked her, knocking her across the room. I remember Claude in the interview. He admitted to punching her. She was annoying him as he was trying to seduce Anita. He punched her hard enough to pur-posely knock her away from them.

Claude was charged and convicted of negligent homicide. Anita was convicted of neglect for allowing a dangerous person near her child and failing to seek medical assistance in a timely manner. This was such a sad thing and so hard to understand. Why do some people have children? Why don't they give them to people who would love to have a small child?

Claude the Clod's criminal career evolved along a path from thefts, shoplifting, burglaries, and eventually murder.

CHAPTER 9

Homicides

Unsolved Murders

Ellen's murder was never solved along with several other young women's murders. I was involved with Ellen's first as a call to check on her well-being. She was a nurse at the hospital working in the medical and surgical department. She regularly called her mother in the Midwest at a specific time after work on planned days. When she didn't call one night, her mother called us to check on her. We went to her apartment and received no response. Her car was not in the driveway. We proceeded with an unofficial be on the lookout since it was only a few hours and didn't yet meet criteria for a national report.

We found her car a few hours later. It was parked in a popular pullover on Jarvis Lane on the west side of the city. It was locked. Nothing about the car appeared out of the ordinary, just messy. There are many trails in this area with farmlands and forests. As we planned to search the area, we received word to wait for the Fish and Game tracking dog. They didn't want us to disturb the area. The dogs assigned to the police were accustomed to tracking fresh trails. We were authorized to drive a vehicle along the off-road vehicle paths if we remained in the vehicle. So I got my four-wheel drive pickup. Two of my colleagues climbed in the back with search lamps, and we slowly rode through the trails that I could safely navigate. We found nothing.

It took four hours, but the Fish and Game tracking hound arrived. It was a huge bluetick hound named Duke. He filled the back of the small Fish and Game truck. We stepped back and watched as the Fish and Game trooper brought Duke to the car. He opened the doors and let the dog smell the interior without getting into it. He then brought Duke into the woods. He tried to pick up a trail, but the dog found nothing. The trooper explained his dog's reputation of success. He was confident that Ellen was not the one that parked the car here. If she had, she must have gotten immediately into another car because Duke found nothing any distance from the car.

Several months went by before a fisherman found her body on the riverbank in Newport. It wasn't far from the home of Charles Companion. Some puzzle pieces started falling together. Charles lived with his parents who died separately and at a relatively young age. The cause of death was ruled as natural causes. There was something strange about Charles. He didn't work. He didn't have to because his parents took care of him while they were alive and left him with substantial resources when they died. The house was on the main Route 11 leading to Claremont. The parents dealt in antiques and had a sign in front of their home and a small barn for the antiques. Once they died, Charles put messages on the sign, all intending to attract a woman. He posted such things as "Woman Wanted," "Playboy Available," and "Live-in Housekeeper Wanted."

Another large part of the puzzle is that Ellen was his nurse when Charles was a patient in the hospital. She spent more time with him than her other patients, even sitting with him in the dayroom for long periods. We also discovered that she used a pay phone in these days before cell phones to call him when she was not working. There was a popular pay phone at the junction of Summer Street with Mulberry Street. It was a stand-alone phone with a cord long enough so that one could sit in the car while talking on this phone. This is the phone Ellen used to call Charles when she was not working. It's the same phone that she often used to call her mother. Despite all these suspicious connections, there was no evidence linking Charles to the crime. I wasn't involved in the detailed examinations of her car and apartment, so I can only assume that they found no physical evidence linking Charles to Ellen outside the hospital. Her relationship with him beyond normal nursing duties was professionally inappropriate for her, but not criminal for him.

A few years earlier, a woman was found murdered in Unity, which bordered Claremont, Newport, and Charlestown. Months later, another young Charlestown woman was reported missing. She was last seen walking along Route 12 heading toward Claremont. Her remains were never found. The public was growing more concerned. As years passed, several women about New England were reported missing. It was assumed that it was by the same person. All area police monitored Charles's activities, but there never was anything of substance seen to connect him to these crimes.

It bothered me that they now went back almost twenty years to the girl in my freshman class that was abducted from the bus stop. Johann was found three days later, just off the road, about a mile from the bus stop. This was devastatingly tragic news for those of us who knew her. She was a kind, polite, and well-liked young lady.

Most information about Johann we received at the time came in bits and pieces. As we assembled the information, we learned that my close friend's father found her. It was very near their farm. Like many volunteers, he went in search of her. I remember my friend being called out of class to be interviewed by state police investigators. I learned later that his father was a suspect. How hard it must have been for my friend. Police back then gave no regard for children's mental health condition. They even intimidated my friend such that he couldn't seek comfort from his friends. I also knew his father. I couldn't imagine him doing such a thing. They were a deeply religious, dedicated family who would go to great lengths to help others. It is very much in his father's character to search the woods for the three days that he did, but not to harm anyone.

Another suspect in Johann's murder was the Charlestown police chief. I heard that the family did not want the public to know if Johann had been raped. The police chief was the second one on the scene. I heard that he pulled her panties back up, thereby contaminating the scene for investigators. This chief had served more than twenty years as a state trooper and should have known better. Some say he did it on purpose to explain his identifying evidence at the scene, which was already there. He was also known to be a woman-izer, having rendezvous with married women on and off duty. I don't understand why he would force himself on Johann when he could easily seduce many others who were willing.

The circumstances of Johann's murder were very different, and I spoke up about it during my police days. I was readily dismissed. The reply was that the killer had grown and learned different tech-niques. The killer was never determined and likely has died as I now write about it.

Unattended Death

When a person dies with medical professionals present, the cause is known, and police are not needed. When a person dies unex-pectedly, it often involves the police. It was common to address the need for police presence for what was called untimely death. Many of us liked disputing the common title. It was the person's time; there-fore, it isn't untimely. His or her time had come, regardless of the cause. A more accurate description is "unattended." Police should investigate unattended deaths to rule out homicide.

I got a call to check on the well-being of a person in an apart-ment across from the police station. I was met by the neighboring apartment dwellers when I arrived. They directed me to an apart-ment on the top, the third floor. They also added that there was a smell coming from this apartment. I climbed the narrow stairway to the apartment. It was a hot summer day, and the building had no air-conditioning. I noticed the putrid smell when I crested the stairs. One neighbor followed me up the stairs. I knocked on the door. He told me that they had been knocking, and Ernest wasn't answering. I asked, and he said that they hadn't seen him for days. He quali-fied it with the explanation that Ernest kept much to himself, and it wasn't unusual to not see him for several days. He said the smell was unusual, and he was concerned.

I tried the door. It was locked. I applied more force to the dilapidated door and managed to open it. I entered a room that was intended to be a living room with the kitchen to my left. The living room had an assortment of furniture, including a sofa, chairs, bureau, and a wardrobe. I could look past the living room and into a bedroom. I saw Ernest on the bed. The smell was horrendous. It was a real struggle to be in this apartment.

The headboard of the bed was centered on the wall on the left side of the room. It was a corner room with windows overlooking the streets in front and beside the building. A fan was still running, blowing directly on Ernest. Ernest was lying on his back. His naked body was considerably bloated. All parts, I emphasize again, all the naked parts of his body were bloated. There was a large tear on the left side of his torso, split open by the swelling gases produced during decomposition. The building is overly warm in the summer, accelerating the decomposition. The apartment was disorganized and dirty. Clothes, trash, and personal items were lying about with no apparent effort to organize anything. I saw no evidence of a struggle, blood sprays, or anything that would indicate this was a homicide. I notified the dispatcher that I had a 10-54N, which is a death by natural causes. She called the medical examiner.

The ambulance arrived. The medical examiner had called them. They were going to verify the death for her and do the transport. A funeral home has agreed to take the body. I stood outside while they removed the body. I would not have been surprised if the bloated body split open more. I examined Ernest's possessions after his body was removed. I found women's clothes in one of the drawers. There didn't seem to be any other women's things, such as makeup, nail polish, or jewelry. The neighbor said that he lived alone. I suspected Ernest was a cross-dresser, not that it was important. I could better understand the presence of women's clothes if it was for his use. If it was a memento of a previous relationship, I would have expected these clothes to be in better order and find other mementos and artifacts.

I saw a doctor's bill from three weeks ago. He had prescribed some antibiotics. I found the bottle. It looked like he had only taken six of the pills, two days' prescription. I called the doctor's office. The receptionist confirmed that Ernest was there. The doctor said that he had a respiratory infection and prescribed the antibiotic. I informed her that he died. She was surprised.

Not much was known about AIDS back then. We have learned a lot since then. What it seemed like back then is that it was predominantly a homosexual male's disease. That was my suspicion. I got the coroner's report three days later. She entered the generic cause of death, "heart failure." I suppose this is true, but it seemed to me that his heart failed due to some massive infection.

I stopped by to see the ambulance crew a few days later. I wanted to let them know what I found and what I suspected as the cause of death. They started teasing me about staying outside while they moved the body. I assured them that I had my time in that apartment too before and after them. I then told them that I thought it was possible that he died from AIDS. They stopped laughing and looked very serious. We also didn't know how this disease was transmitted. Bodies that badly decomposed leaked fluids. We know now that it would not have survived the changing temperatures of this corpse. They made appointments to get tested. Their results were negative, of course.

Murder in the Family

The dispatcher referred a call to me, 10-54M at 59 Mulberry Street, apartment 2. 10-54 is a death, M means murder. I have been involved in several 10-54S, suicides, and 10-54N, natural causes. The murder call was very much unanticipated. It was ten thirty on a sunny summer Sunday morning, which made it even more unexpected.

59 Mulberry Street is one of those three-story apartment building in poor condition. It was owned by an out-of-town "slumlord." These landlords were interested in collecting rents for as long as they could until the building inspector closed in. They would make only those repairs necessary to show progress to keep the building from being condemned. They were routinely late on paying their taxes. The interest on overdue taxes was cheaper than borrowed money. These buildings frequently changed owners.

When I arrived, I found the apartment door wide open and a tenant from another apartment pacing around outside. She held her hands to her face and was crying and saying, "Alice is dead." I first looked through the open door before entering. Personal and nearby people's safety was my concern. I hadn't accepted yet that a murder had occurred. The kitchen was just inside the door. I had been to most of these apartments. I wasn't surprised by the disorder and uncleanliness. I slowly stepped through the threshold, being careful not to disrupt any evidence of a crime.

I walked past the small cluttered kitchen table on my left. There were plates with partially eaten food. Beer bottles and cans were on the table, countertops, and on the floor, among other debris. A rack of clean dishes was on the counter beside the sink to my right. The sink had a few things in it that weren't dishes, but I didn't take any special note of what it was at this time. I needed to focus on the greater details. I made my way around clothes and other things on the floor and peered into what was supposed to be the living room.

I noticed the TV and entertainment center to my right as I approached the living room. On my left was a bed. There was a person lying on this bed. She was mostly naked, wearing only a T-shirt pulled up around her shoulders. She was partially on her right side, her legs hanging off the bottom of the bed. Her right leg was nearly straightened with her right foot touching the floor. Her left knee was bent so that her foot only hung off the edge of the mattress. Her face was turned into the center of the mattress with her shoulder-length black hair covering her face. Her large belly rested on its side on the mattress. Her left arm was bent over her belly. Her right arm was under her body. The blankets, pillows, and clothes were strewn over the head of the mattress. The lower part of the mattress was covered with a sheet pulled loose from the edges. Very noticeable was the darkened area and around the body and onto the floor. I quickly assessed the large volume of blood that soaked the mattress and floor. There were no indications of life.

We had a great emergency services team working together in our community. The ambulance was automatically dispatched and remained a safe distance away until the police cleared the scene, assuring they would be safe. I called, confirming the 10-54 but not the M, murder. I wasn't yet certain.

The EMTs arrived in seconds. I met them outside and asked them to be careful of the scene. They went in; one felt for a pulse. He then used his stethoscope to listen for a heartbeat. I very much appreciated his kindness and concern for this woman but worried about protecting the crime scene. I watched closely to be an observer to record who was there and what they did. Any changes to the original scene must be explained. The other EMT stood behind me with his box of emergency equipment.

I looked around more as the EMT continued his examination. I saw a screwdriver with bloody fingerprints on the floor near the foot of the bed. A little farther away was a naked Barbie doll similarly covered with bloody fingerprints. There were bloody hand smears on the wall beside the bed and on the doorframe into the kitchen. Across the living room, I saw two doors. Across the bed, one door was closed, and I assumed that it was to a bedroom. Diagonally, to my right, the door to a bathroom was partially open. I could see part of the toilet inside.

Finally, the EMT was satisfied that she was dead. We carefully made our way out of the messy apartment, disturbing things as little as possible. As I walked past the sink, I glanced at its contents. I saw a bloody yellow flashlight and several parts to a Lincoln log set.

Once outside, I asked how the dispatcher was doing with the notifications. It's standard procedure to notify the chief, our detective division, the county attorney, the sheriff's department, the county attorney, and the medical examiner. She said that she was having little success with notifications as many were not immediately answering calls or pages. She was able to contact the state police who would be dispatching an investigation team. My supervisor arrived. He had called in other officers to cover my beat and assist with crime scene security, if necessary. I was committed to stand guard of the crime scene until I could turn it over to other investigators, minimizing the number of people involved. He covered while I returned to my car to retrieve a pad of paper to start a log of people and witnesses.

I spoke with the woman who was still very upset but better able to explain what she knew. Alice was her friend. They usually had coffee together every morning. It is their practice to walk in on each one's apartment without knocking. They were like sisters. She said that Alice lived there with her brother, Glen, and his five-year-old daughter, Destiny. She said that Glen and Destiny took the bus early this morning to visit other family in Manchester. They were expected to return on Tuesday.

A crowd gathered, but they remained very respectful of the distance that I requested for them to observe. A Claremont detective arrived. They had decided to let the state police be the lead investigators. Or course, he had to look in the apartment. I recorded his time of entry and exit. After about an hour and a half, the state police investigators arrived. I knew Detective Tom Connors well. He was always calm, meticulous, and very thorough. I was glad to see that he was in charge now. He began the slow, tedious process of collecting the evidence. I maintained security to the apartment.

The medical examiner arrived. Dr. Fortin's initial assessment was that Alice died from massive blood loss through her vagina. He would conduct a more thorough autopsy when her body could be removed from the crime scene. The eventual determination was that she died from a large laceration of her vagina caused by a Lincoln log from that child's log cabin building toy. To this day, I feel a shiver whenever Lincoln logs are mentioned.

The local TV station arrived. They were very respectful of the distance parameters that I explained. The reporter wanted to ask me questions, but I referred him to the police chief, who I thought might be at the police station by now. They asked before recording anything, even positions from across the street. The only thing that surprised me was a recording they made of me. I thought that the camera man squatting and manipulating his camera a few feet from me was preparing to use his camera. It wasn't until I saw the news the next day that I realized that he was recording me. It was a nice segment showing me with good posture, watching the scene with the building in the background.

I was eventually relieved by a sheriff deputy. I went to the station to write my report and type up the log. I worked over a half shift for extra coverage as needed. Before I left, Tom prepared an arrest warrant for Glen. With the evidence at the scene and the unnatural, perverted brother-sister relationship they learned from interviews, they were able to reconstruct the crime.

It was not unusual for Glen and Alice to have intense sex, despite being brother and sister. When he drank alcohol and smoked marijuana, he became sexually aggressive and insatiable. At some point, Alice passed out. It may never be known whether it was from alcohol and drugs or the blood loss or a combination. It is certain that when she passed out, Glen continued. When he could no longer perform sexually, he used other implements to engage Alice. These were the bloodstained objects that I observed. Tom described others that I didn't notice.

They notified Manchester Police of the warrant, but they were not able to locate Glen. We arrested him when he got off the bus. The neighbors told us his schedule, so it was easy to catch him. Glen was arrested and held without bail. His daughter Destiny was placed in foster care. Glen was convicted of negligent homicide and sentenced to eight years in prison. Destiny connected very well with her foster parents, who eventually adopted her. They described her as exceptionally cute and smart. It is amazing how children can live in such environments and still adapt so well to a lifestyle so different.

CHAPTER 10

Mentally Ill

Deinstitutionalization

When the movement to deinstitutionalize mentally ill individuals began, there were many challenges to integrating them into communities. Group homes, foster homes, and supervised independent living opportunities arose. One of the first group homes was quietly started by Gordon Wells. At that time, there were no regulations to prevent its location in the middle of a compact neighborhood. The neighbors who objected to it had only the recourse of calling the police for every unusual incident. It didn't take long for us to get to know the residents. Dealing directly with Gordon was a challenge as he was seldom around. He lived in another town.

The residents of Gordon's group home had greater challenges adjusting to their new environment. Residential programs have a routine to which they were accustomed. They felt safe there. Most had been institutionalized all their lives. A few lived with their parents until the parents grew too old to properly care for them. Gordon's home had little to no structure. They had social workers who would check in to make sure that they were getting their basic needs met, but for the most part, they were unsupervised and could freely walk about the neighborhood and the city.

Most complaints about Gordon's residents described them as suspicious persons. They were easily approachable by the police and were very attentive. The problem was that they had little understanding of how their actions caused other people to be concerned. They had little or no previous social interactions, developmental delays, a limiting mental illness, or some combination. Any training a police officer might have for dealing with the mentally ill was minimal. Even a highly educated, skilled social worker would be challenged to resolve complaints. In general, the complaints were trivial and due to the public's misconceptions of adults with abnormal but harmless behavior.

Police enforce laws. Loitering, which was later found unconstitutional, was a popular charge brought against these recently integrated individuals. A person who is at a place for no apparent reason or purpose and causing concern to others could be charged with loitering. When this law was repealed, there wasn't much police could do to remove people from a public place, regardless of their purpose. We could only charge them with a crime. Criminal trespass doesn't apply to public places. If they ventured onto private property, we could charge them. They could be charged with disorderly conduct if the behavior presented a danger or was intense enough to disrupt a business, for instance. Getting a conviction was difficult.

After a while, we got to know their names. When I got a call, I learned to park the car a short distance from them and walk up to them. Greeting them by name helped a lot. With most, it was almost like dealing with a small child. Perhaps that is where their development ended. I found that explaining to them why their behavior was causing concern helped, but they didn't always understand. When they understood, they were happy to change their behavior. When they didn't understand, the best I could do was to gain their agreement to discontinue that behavior in this place. Most of the time, the calls were what was reasonable behavior given their abilities. People just didn't want them in their neighborhood. They were known as Gordon's goonies.

Some of the mentally ill received controlled medication that had to be dispensed from the mental health agency. A popular place for police to monitor traffic was located on the route between Gordon's group home and the mental health agency. Sometimes we would watch one of these residents walk from the home to the agency. There was a noticeable change in their gate when they left the agency compared to walking there. Stan would walk normally, upright and with a bit of a bounce in his stride on the way over. On his return, he leaned to his left with his left arm mostly limp and hanging straight down. His right hand was bent across his abdomen. His head also leaned slightly left, and his stride was much shorter and slower. He almost slid his feet along the ground. The energetic gate was transformed into what appeared to be a struggle to walk. Some called this the Thorazine shuffle. I had to wonder. As I got to know Stan more, I found conversation with him enjoyable when he wasn't heavily medicated. Once medicated, he didn't seem to have the energy to engage in conversation. It still bothers me that we cannot do better at helping people like Stan in our community.

There was a woman I often saw walking around the city. She was a short, stout lady who wore a dress and shroud that covered her arms and neck. Her hair was graying and styled tight to her head. She carried a cloth bag and purse that she held close to the front of her body. The most striking thing about her is that she seemed to be engaged in an argument as she walked alone. She spoke loudly, and her face was reddened. She turned her head slightly to the right and often shook it diagonally, simultaneously up and down and side to side. She walked briskly and purposely with her short legs. She quickly gained notice from the people who passed by her, yet she paid no attention to anyone or anything. She seemed intent in an argument with herself.

I occasionally received a call about her. I would respond to confirm it was her, then radio that she was fine. Once, a caller was not satisfied with my quick assessment and wanted me to take her into custody. I had no reason as she wasn't committing any crime, nor did she present a danger to anyone, including herself. Still, this person would not listen to reason. I ended our conversation saying that she was only arguing with herself. If she was winning the argument, there was no reason for concern. If she loses the argument, I would reconsider. The unreasonable complainant was puzzled and sufficiently speechless long enough for me to leave and resume patrol.

Linnie, short for Linwood, was a very different character. He was very unpredictable. Even at his best, he was difficult to control. Our most frequent complaint was when he walked into a convenience store, picked up a bottle of his favorite cheap wine, and walked out without paying. We could be confident that it was he when we received the call. Most shopkeepers knew him. If they didn't, we could be reasonably sure by his description. He was in his midthirties with long dark scraggly hair. His eyes were wide open. He had only a few teeth, which were blackened. He always wore an open green hooded parker regardless of the weather.

When I found Linnie, he wanted no part of being arrested. He wanted to drink his wine and sleep wherever he stopped moving. Sometimes it was in the park. Other times, it could be in a wooded area or on the edge of the road. He seldom went to any residence. He lived more like a wild animal. Linnie seldom spoke. He seemed to understand, but I couldn't be certain. I hated touching him. Living like a wild animal has the consequences of being unbathed and full of parasites. It was not unusual to see body lice crawling on his neck and in his clothes. The worst arrests were when he resisted. He would kick, scratch, and bite. Fortunately, he wasn't very strong due to his horrible lifestyle. After arresting him and bringing him to jail, I had the overwhelming desire to sign off, take a shower, and treat my clothes. I also opened both rear doors of the police car and hosed it out with high-pressure water. It helped that the seats had plastic covers.

Eventually, Linnie's habit of just stopping for a nap at any point in time or place was his final demise. It came when he decided to sleep on the railroad tracks. Some people say that he might have had a seizure to explain why he was there. It really was unimportant. The saddest part was for the train operator. He saw Linnie on the tracks, but there was no way he could stop the train in time. It severed parts of Linnie's body.

Eddy brought much more pleasant experiences. He was a large person with a pronounced belly. In his late twenties, he looked like others his age. He could participate in a conversation. He spoke with what appeared to be knowledge and authority of the topic. However, if you listened well enough, it became obvious that he had no idea what he was talking about.

Eddy stayed with his mother, who took good care of him. He often went for long walks at all hours, even to surrounding towns. He walked on the side of the road and never interfered with anyone. In the winter, I would see his tracks in the snow. I knew it was him because he walked with his toes pointed outwardly. When I followed his tracks, I would recognize his special gate, with those feet widely spaced and curving around his big belly.

The most interesting call I had involving Eddy was when a homeowner who was selling her house called. She had a local real estate agent's sign on her front lawn. She said that a gentleman knocked on her door and asked to see the house, saying he was interested in buying it. She showed him around the house. He seemed to like it, and they negotiated a price. He assured her that he would return in a couple of hours with the money. When he didn't return, she called the police. I got the call.

As I took the information, I found it bizarre that she did not refer him to the real estate agent. Her exclusive contract with them was still valid. I was also concerned that she was alone when she showed this stranger throughout her house. When she described the man in sufficient detail, I recognized that it could only be Eddy. I couldn't help but to laugh. I explained to her that Eddy's intellectual functioning was deceptive, and he had no ability to buy a house. I suggested that she refer other inquirers to the agent for her safety.

Benson was a very different case. We were told that he was a Vietnam drug burnout. While serving in Vietnam, he used some powerful psychedelic drugs that permanently change his brain chemistry. He was supervised by a state social worker and lived with his brother. My early contacts with Benson was during his many walks about the city. Sometimes he would stop and go through what seemed to be some very energized karate exercises with the yelling that accompanies striking an opponent, but he was alone. His favorite places to do this was behind businesses. Never was anyone in danger. This behavior was alarming and fit the definition of disorderly conduct.

The statute requires that the potential offender be warned to stop this behavior. Only if he continues can such a charge be warranted.

There were numerous calls regarding Benson. Just his appearance was alarming to many people. He had long black curly hair and beard. He only cut it himself, with a knife or scissors, when it annoyed him, so it was very uneven. Benson seldom spoke. He stared at people and followed them along the sidewalk. I approached Benson when I got these calls; I found that he didn't realize his effect on others and gladly complied when I explained it to him.

One time, I was called for a man digging up a front lawn. When I arrived, I found Benson sitting on the lawn with his feet on the sidewalk. He had a small wooden spoon and was rapidly digging a narrow deep hole in the lawn, between his legs, next to the sidewalk. Benson paid no attention to me as I walked up to him until I greeted him, "Hello, Benson." Benson responded hi. He glanced up to me then returned to his rapidly spooning soil from the edge of the lawn and onto the sidewalk. I explained that the people in the house didn't like that he was digging a hole in their lawn. He stopped, looked over his shoulder at the house, and said, "Oh." He stood up and started to walk away. I asked that he replace the soil that he dug up, which he did with his cupped hand, packing it in place. He walked away with no further problems. Benson just didn't understand and didn't intend to cause concern.

Benson's landlord complained one time when Benson disassembled much of the plumbing in the apartment and defecated on the floor. He brought criminal charges. I wasn't involved in this but was in court for another case that day. Benson sat in the back of the courtroom as other cases were being heard. He got the judge's attention as he sat quietly but looked all around at the space immediately around him. As he looked around him, he appeared to be trying to snatch things from the air. I was familiar with this activity. Benson often tried to catch butterflies that only he was able to see. When it was time to call his case, the judge asked for the public defender and the prosecutor to come to the bench. She confirmed that Benson was the defendant. She looked at the prosecutor and asked, "What's going on with him?" The prosecutor explained, with all seriousness, that Benson was trying to catch butterflies. The judge gave a bewildered reaction, then announced that she was declaring him unfit for trial, and dismissed the case.

Darlene was another person supervised by adult services and in her own apartment. She was well-known to us and the hospital. She had many accidents, unexplained illnesses, and suicidal ideations. She always used her maximum allowable Medicaid visits to the hospital and often exceeded them. The hospital and ambulance service would not be paid for the excesses, but they still provided the quality service, even though she didn't need it.

On the previous shift, Darlene was released from the hospital for a suicide attempt. She had cut her forearm using a knife to make multiple scratches. She was released with a safety plan. I was dispatched to her apartment because she had found a knife that the social worker didn't remove. It was a wooden-handled steak knife. I asked Darlene to explain how the social worker didn't find it. She shrugged her shoulders and admitted that she had hidden it under the cabinet. She added that she was intending to harm herself but changed her mind. She was following the safety plan by calling us. I knew Darlene to be very childlike and sensed that she purposefully designed this to seek attention. I took the knife as evidence to be secured. I told her to tell her social worker so that the property can be returned to the place of safekeeping with the other knives.

Mrs. Kraft was an elderly lady living on Elm Street, near the church. She suffered from dementia. Her niece stayed with her most of the time. When her niece wasn't home, Mrs. Kraft became hypervigilant, perhaps a little paranoid. She thought that people in the neighborhood were watching her and looking for an opportunity to break into her house or steal things from her yard. When I arrived, she was always very angry at her neighbors. She would say, "They're watching from behind that tree," as she pointed to a large oak tree next to the sidewalk on the other side of the street. I looked over and didn't see anyone. She insisted that they were peeking around the edge of it. I walked over to and around the tree, trying to assure her that there was no one there. She was not satisfied, insisting that they were still there. I couldn't appease her by promising to patrol the neighborhood more frequently, so I just left with that promise.

One winter night, I was in a more jovial mood. She called to say that people were in her yard with flashlights. When I arrived, there were no footprints in the snow in her yard where she insisted people were. I walked into the dark and returned. I told her that I found them, and they apologized. They were only looking for night crawlers to use for fishing. She replied, "You better tell them not to do that here." I assured her that I would deliver the message and left.

Dusty was a Vietnam veteran suffering from posttraumatic stress disorder (PTSD). He didn't trust many police officers. I was able to gain his trust because I was also a veteran who served immediately following the end of the Vietnam War. He appreciated that I could have served with him. Dusty didn't see classic frontline combat but suffered from infiltration attacks. People near him were hurt and killed.

Dusty was being treated by the Veterans administration and receiving mental health treatment and medication. He didn't always comply with his treatment, and he suffered from alcoholism. Sometimes he didn't take his medication. Other times, he self-over-medicated. During some of these times, he would engage in arguments with people around him. His arguments were based on what he perceived as disrespect for his and fellow veterans' service and their suffering.

Dusty lived in a small house in a neighborhood close to the center of the city. He lived alone. He often helped his brother in his automotive repair business. Dusty's teenage nephew was his most frequent visitor. Dusty had three aggressive Doberman pinschers protecting his home and himself. Just knocking on the door got a violent response from the dogs. They seemed to want to come through the door to attack the intruder. The dogs responded to Dusty's commands and retreated to their designated place, but it was wise to move very little when meeting Dusty at his home.

One night, at Dunkin' Donuts, Dusty was sitting at the bar, drinking his usual black coffee and eating a pastry. Dusty had also consumed a large amount of alcohol before arriving at Dunkin'

Donuts. He soon got into an argument with two younger men next to him. Dusty had to use the restroom but intended to resume the argument when he returned. What he didn't anticipate was that these younger men followed him to the bathroom. Dusty had locked the door, but they tried to break in. Dusty had a permit for the .44 Magnum he carried. He warned them that he had a gun and would shoot. They continued trying to force the door open. Dusty fired a round through the door. He aimed downward. The bullet followed his intended path, through the door, and striking the floor in front of the young men's feet. They quickly retreated, and the Dunkin' Donuts employee called the police.

Dusty complied completely with the trusted officers who responded. He surrendered his gun immediately, first making certain that it was safely unloaded. We were compelled to charge Dusty with reckless conduct, to which he pleaded guilty and paid a fine. Dusty's pistol permit was revoked. Dusty abstained from alcohol again. Typical for our veterans and others suffering from PTSD, he suffered many relapses. Dusty was a dedicated member of Alcoholics Anonymous and sponsored many others to sobriety.

Bridge Jumper

I was called to a person threatening to jump off the Main Street Bridge. This is not a realistic place for those with serious suicide intentions. The High Bridge, the railroad bridge farther out of town, toward Vermont, is much higher and much more likely to be successful. The Main Street Bridge is still very dangerous. We often get calls of kids playing under it, climbing on its framework and the water pipe running under it.

Downstream from this bridge is a dam, so the water flows more slowly here. The dam is next to a paper mill that uses the river water to make paper. It also has a hydroelectric generator. Should someone fall into the river, they are likely to survive the fall but be in immediate danger presented by this dam.

The call was early in my evening shift, which is a busy time. Since it was a weekend, I expected to be busy throughout the evening. Trying to talk someone off the bridge while waiting and hoping for some counselor to come was not in my plans.

As I drove to the bridge, I saw someone sitting on the rail above the sidewalk on the downstream side of the bridge. He was a young man with curly black hair and a thin goatee. He was looking down at the water, leaning forward while holding on to the rail.

I parked the car near the bridge. Without saying a word, I walked briskly up to him, holding my breath and hoping he wouldn't jump or fall. When I got within reach, I quickly reached up and grabbed the back of his collar. I already felt some relief as I had a firm grip on him now. Without any pause, I pulled him off the rail. I lowered him to the sidewalk, rolled him facedown, then handcuffed him. He didn't resist in any form, physically or verbally.

I asked him what he was doing. He said, "Looking at the water."

I asked if he was planning to jump. He said, "No, just watching the water."

I directed him to walk to the police car, and he did. Especially when a prisoner is disabled in handcuffs, the officer must make certain that he doesn't fall, so I kept firm control of his arm closest to me. I was also concerned that he might jump into traffic if he intended to hurt himself.

I asked him if he knew that people were disturbed about his actions. He didn't seem to be aware. He denied any intention to alarm people. He just kept saying that he wanted the view. I was still deciding what to do with him. Primarily, I needed a charge to hold him to call a counselor to evaluate him. If he purposely caused a public disturbance, I could charge him with disorderly conduct. I could probably still get a conviction on this charge, but I wanted something more concrete. I pursued a different route.

"You know, the city owns that bridge." He agreed. I said, "You know that the bridge is for people to drive or walk across it." He agreed.

I went on to explain that the city has a small park with benches at the far end of the bridge. He could have enjoyed the view there. He said that he liked the view from the rail. I asked if he realized the rail is a physical barrier to keep people from falling in the river. It is not designed nor intended to be a place to sit. He agreed. I charged him with trespassing on the bridge rail.

Now someone with serious psychological concerns are brought to the hospital. Back then, we typically brought a charge so we could hold them in a cell until a counselor came to the police station. We ended up holding him overnight. He was certified to be safe, so we dropped the charge and released him.

Police are the front line for people with serious mental illness and the least prepared. Many people with mental illnesses are convicted and are held in our prisons when they could be better served with treatment in the community.

There are many people with mental and physical challenges living in our communities. When we learn to accept these and value their contributions, we will be a stronger community. Our strength lies in the diversity of members' ability to contribute in a meaningful way, without prejudice from other members. We all have our individual weaknesses and our strengths. We all can contribute in a way that benefits our communities.

BB Gun Suicide

The dispatch instructed me to go to 6 Sullivan Street, apartment 22, for a 10-54S, a fatal suicide. This address is apartments that are on the corner of Sullivan and Pleasant streets. It overlooks Tremont Square in the center of the city. The normally locked entrance was held open by a man who seemed to be expecting me. As I ran up the stairs, the ambulance called me, requesting instructions. I told them to stand by. When there is a shooting, ambulance people stay a safe distance away, ready to respond when needed. My backup signed off and was right behind me.

The apartment door was wide open. I walked past the kitchen and cautiously to the door of the living room. I saw a stuffed chair in the center of the room. I could see the top of a head with black hair. The right hand extended toward the floor. On the floor directly below the open hand appeared to be a .45-caliber automatic pistol.

I walked cautiously around the chair, seeing more of the young man in his late teens or early twenties. There appeared to be a bullet hole directly between his eyes. A small amount of blood was trailing down his nose and cheek. He was motionless.

Since I was the department's photographer, I looked about the room with a photographer's mind for evidence that might explain this event. One of the most important things to photograph are the blood sprays from a bullet's impact. The shape of the blood sprays is crucial in determining the direction of the bullet trajectory. They could prove that it wasn't him but someone else who fired the fatal shot. I didn't see anything that could demonstrate what I sought. Something didn't seem right.

I looked at the gun. It looked like a .45 all right. Such a weapon should have caused much more damage to his face than the simple hole I saw. It would have bulged his eyes, and there should be a large exit wound. The sprays from this exit wound would be great evidence about the angle of the gun. There were no blood sprays and no exit wound, and the damage was much too little. I looked closer at the gun. It was a BB gun. I looked closer at the person slumped in the chair. He was still breathing. I called to him. There was no response. I kicked his foot. The foot wobbled back and forth, but there was still no response. I called for the EMTs, assuring them that the scene was secure.

The EMTs examined him, then transported him to the hospital. I took the BB gun as evidence. I didn't see any value in photographing the apartment. I went to the hospital to learn about his condition.

Dr. Spears examined him. They took an X-ray and found two BBs in the hole between his eyes. I laughed about it as Dr. Spears removed the BBs and stitch the opening. Dr. Spears said that it was more serious than it appeared. If he hit it just right, where those bones come together, the BB might have penetrated through the skull.

I wrote my report. He was on probation. Seems that shooting yourself with a BB gun and causing alarm to others is a violation of probation under the expectation of being a good citizen. He went back to jail. Hopefully, he got the services he needed while he was there.

Tribal Dancer

In Claremont, there are two beats. One is the north side of the Sugar River, and the other is the south side, which is typically the busiest. The third beat is the center of the city shared by both, and calls are assigned to even the workload. I was assigned to the south side. John was assigned the northern beat. He had just cleared from one of these third beat calls. I was patrolling with no pending calls.

John was assigned a call in his beat, a naked woman walking down North Street. I knew better than to be jealous of the call. For the North Street neighborhood to complain about this, there had to be more than just a simple exposure. I suspected alcohol and/ or drugs.

John signed off. I patrolled closely, remaining in my own beat. Dispatchers call after a few minutes of silence from an officer on a call. There's no set pattern. Generally, the more dangerous the call, the shorter the time before the check-in. It didn't have to be the dispatcher to do the check-in. Any of us could call. I called John after a couple of minutes, "112, you all set?" John replied, "Yeah, for now." John and I had a good relationship, and I knew from the sound of his voice and his words that I should get closer, so I went "10-77" out of my beat. This let John know that I was heading his way and could come to his assistance if he wanted.

John said that he was "10-11 with one." Dispatch inquired, "10-17?" John replied, "Negative." 10-11 is returning to headquarters. 10-17 is an arrest, which we assumed would be indecent exposure. John asked for me to assist him in the processing room, which is standard procedure for an arrest. So I knew there was something very unusual, not that naked women walking down the street was a typical call.

I was directly behind John as he drove into the sally port and walked in as the door closed. John looked at me as he got out of the car. I saw a frustration that I have never seen in his expression. The woman in the back seat was shouting in a sort of rhythm, but I couldn't understand what she was saying. He rolled his eyes upwardly, took a deep breath, and opened the back door. A black woman of average height but somewhat obese stepped out, completely naked. She seemed to be chanting something and looking directly at John. John circled around her to retrieve the blanket we all carry in the trunk. He had tried to place it on her at the scene and was now trying to cover her. John didn't handcuff her as procedure requires before transport. I fully understood why as he again attempted to cover her with the blanket. She completely ignored his efforts, letting the blanket fall to the floor. I understood how John was so frustrated.

We tried to direct her from the sally port garage to the processing room. She fixed her attention on John, leaning toward him, jumping up and down, much of her body bouncing independently in the rhythm, her arms along her side, and chanting. It was obvious that she was not going to respond to instruction and remained fixed on John. So John led the way into the processing room; she followed, and I followed them.

I had studied several languages and was exposed to many others in my youth—high school and college education and army experience. I couldn't distinguish a single word of what she was saying. I listened to the rhythm and accent. I thought perhaps it was Jamaican, but it could have been an African tribal language. Normally proud of my education, I felt ashamed that I had not studied these cultures more.

Now in the processing room, we assumed that the dispatcher was recording, which is standard procedure. John attempted several times to place the blanket on her. It slid off with a few of her bounces. John tried to direct her into the chair where we have prisoners sit to be processed. She did not respond, remaining fixed on John, remaining within inches of him, jumping and chanting. We could now notice the intensely offensive body odor. I felt sorry for John but intensely relieved that, if she was imprinted on someone, it was him and not me.

John and I agreed that any attempts to process her were futile. We didn't want to attempt a mug shot with her nudity and continued bouncing and chanting. We decided to walk her to a jail cell. She followed John into the cell. As John exited the cell, we quickly closed the door. She didn't resist the closing of the door. She grabbed the bars with both hands and continued her bouncing and chanting. John went upstairs to call the local health agency. I returned to patrol.

We were very puzzled. Where did this lady come from? Why is this our first encounter with her? We learned later that she was a member of our community. She and her husband owned a small retail business, where she often worked. Her children attended and graduated from local schools. It was a business that I rarely went into, but I do remember her being behind the counter. She was always very polite and respectable. How did she get to this state that was so different than her normal?

The feedback we got was that she had some sort of a psychotic break. Her heritage is Jamaican though her accent was typical New England. The business continued for a while after her return to the community, but I never saw her in there again. Eventually, the family moved their business to a large New Hampshire city where I am sure it would do better.

CHAPTER 11

Internal Conflict

Newport Police Officer

I had just signed on after a lunch break at home. As I turned the corner onto the straightaway toward town from my house, I saw a yellow car coming toward me at the other end of the straight. It appeared to be going fast. The radar confirmed my observation, sixty-three miles per hour in a forty miles per hour.

I don't like writing tickets near my house. It could appear bad on two levels. It may seem I give fewer warnings or that I spend too much time around my home. In this case, all was legitimate. I was home for an approved lunch break, and this was an excessive violation.

As the car went past me, I heard the loud roar of a defective muffler. I turned on the blue lights and turned to go after it. The car promptly pulled over in the curve, not my most desired place to stop, but it will work.

It was an old Chevy Impala, a full-sized car. I approached the driver with standard caution. I could see the shoulder-length hair then clothes that matched normal women's wear. There was another woman in the front seat, no one in the back seat. I didn't need to ask for her license and registration. She had them ready in her left hand held up to the window. Very prominently on her left thigh was an open wallet with a police badge easily seen. I said, "Thank you. I will take your license and registration, and I'll take that badge."

I returned to the police car and examined the badge closely. It appeared to be a legitimate Newport Police Department badge. I still wondered if it was real. If she is indeed a Newport officer, she should know much better than to drive a defective vehicle or at high speed. I am very much aware of the unwritten code that police officers should not write each other, but this was very wrong. I wanted to check out the badge first. I switch the radio to county frequency and called, "Claremont 120 to Newport." 120 is my radio identifier.

The Newport dispatch responded promptly. I knew my dispatch would be monitoring especially since she would be listening closely since I called in this traffic stop. My dispatcher likely already knows who it is because she would have run the plate in the computer. By doing this, the system automatically reports NCIC (National Crime Information Center) outstanding warrants. She probably didn't know that the driver was a Newport officer.

I radioed, "Can you verify a Newport badge number for me?" She replied, "Affirmative." I radioed the name and number.

After a short pause, the Newport police chief came on the radio. He said, "Yes, she is one of our part-time officers." Then he gave me a supportive call, "Do with her as you wish." Coincidentally, the Newport chief lived around the corner from me. This stop was about equal distance between our homes. When I first saw her, she was in front of his father's farm. He lived a short distance down the side street.

I took out a traffic ticket and started to write it. I planned to summon her for the speed and write a "fix-it ticket" for the loud exhaust. I had them mostly filled out. I was haunted by that code but more so by the tense relationship between our police departments that I felt was mostly fueled by my chief. The Newport chief was a great guy and well respected. I decided not to issue these documents. The Newport officer would have been watching me write and must be expecting the summons. An unusual amount of time had passed. Normally, my dispatch would have called by this time to check on me. Since she knew from the radio transmissions that it involved another officer, she likely felt that I was safe. With a deep inhalation and sigh, I put down the paperwork and grabbed her badge, license, and registration and got back out of the car.

I am not one for humiliating someone in front of another. I had no idea who the passenger was or the relationship. I told the driver to step out of the car and meet me behind hers. We faced each other between the two cars.

I held her badge up in front of my chest so that she knew I wasn't ready to return it. I told her that I just spoke with her chief to verify that she was a member of the Newport Police Department. I shared what he said. In all likelihood, she monitored my transmissions on a scanner. I went on to explain that I was going to summon her, but I felt the relationship between our departments was already strained too much. I told her that I lived around the corner and pointed her badge in the direction of my house. I added that her chief lived in the neighborhood and pointed her badge in the other direction. I added, "I don't drive in your town this way and don't expect you to drive in my town like it either." I explained that I was leaving this in her chief's hands and she should speak with him. Though I had no intentions of following up on it, I wanted her to think I would. I wondered if she accelerated where she did because she knew where her chief lived because her greatest speed was at the dirt road that leads to his house. All the time, the Newport officer nodded her head affirmatively. I handed to her the badge and told her that she could leave. I added the cliché to drive the speed limit.

I got back in the car and waited for her to drive away. I turned around and called 10-1, signing back into service. As I drove by the Newport chief's house, I wondered if her behavior was a way to express anger at her chief. She should have known that he wasn't home.

Of course, this ethical issue weighed heavy on my mind and still does many years later. We arrest criminals that don't "rat" on each other. The police have "the code." I don't see any difference, yet police who honor the code won't see it. They would interpret my dilemma as being disloyal and untrustworthy.

Officer Down

Newport is the town to our east. Being smaller, it had a smaller police force. It was also generally accepted that they had more than their fair share of violent offenders. The Rock Family was large, violent, and mostly illiterate and hated the police. Their criminal activities included dealing drugs and stolen articles. The family had the prison time respect of other Newport members of the criminal community.

Administrative relationships between our departments varied with the chiefs and local leaders. In the past, we had a pact, a formal agreement to respond to police emergencies. It was like the agreement fire departments enjoy with one major exception. Police powers lie with the local governing body. They were currently reluctant to automatically grant police powers to neighboring certified officers. State law covered officers in fresh pursuit. The state gave arresting authority to police pursuing criminals across jurisdictions in the State of New Hampshire. This did not apply to an officer responding to assist other officers in neighboring jurisdictions. Once we crossed the town line, we were ordinary citizens.

One Saturday night, the Rock Family was having a party. Newport Police had numerous calls complaining about the noise and had responded, but their warnings had no effect. Eventually, one of the partiers came to their station with a bloodied face and complained about being assaulted by a person at this party. Newport prepared the warrant and went to make the arrest. In attempting the arrest, the officer was overpowered, assaulted, and unable to retreat from the apartment. Newport called in all their off-duty officers that they could find. They called for any state troopers in the area. They were not able to assemble enough officers to safely enter the apartment to retrieve their officer.

The Newport dispatcher called the Claremont dispatcher for backup, "officer down." My supervisor responded that we had no pact and could not respond. However, he instructed our dispatcher to call the chief and get permission to assist Newport. Tom and I were in a two-officer car, which is typical for these busy summer Saturdays. I was driving. The Newport dispatcher again called the Claremont dispatcher for assistance, begging "please" and obviously crying at this point.

My supervisor radioed to me to head in that direct, greater than the speed limit, but not code 3 yet. That's all we needed. I was already heading in that direction. We respected the supervisor's instruction not to go code 3, lights and siren. I always felt that a true code 3, with someone's life at risk, is driven with either full throttle or full breaking, nothing in between. The Washington Street traffic slowed when they saw my police car. It frustrated us, so Tom turned on the blue lights. Lights only is code 2, so we were obeying instructions from our supervisor. Traffic got out of my way.

I was approaching "Dump Hill" and the Newport town line. I was getting worried now. I wanted that clearance before I got to the line so I would be authorized to cross it. Tom and I discussed how we wanted to proceed. We agreed. He turned off the blue lights as I crossed the town line.

We very soon got permission from the chief. I pressed the accelerator to the floor. Tom activated the lights and siren. Eighty miles per hour climbed quickly to ninety miles per hour. Still, I kept my foot to the floor. I was now going too fast to look down at the speedometer and watch the road in front of me. The radar mounted to the dash closer to eye level so it was a little easier to view with a glance. It could display only two digits. The last time I looked at it, it showed *05, one hundred five miles per hour, in a fifty-miles-per-hour zone. I no longer looked at even the radar screen. I focused intently on the road and its hazards. Kellyville is a concentration of business and residences. The speed limit drops to thirty-five miles per hour for about a mile. It's wide and easy to see traffic. It's a well-known speed trap for the Newport and state police. I went through it at more than three times the speed limit. Someone described us as a gray streak. Our department policy allowed for only ten miles per hour over the speed limit. It's a ridiculous avoidance of administrative responsibility. The judge wouldn't fine anyone unless they were going at least ten miles per hour over the speed limit. If we followed policy, we would never catch anyone.

I knew the approximate location on Sunapee Street. That would be good enough because it would be easy to find the other officers. There were a couple of quick turns through the center of Newport. Our lights, my driving, and the many sirens before ours got plenty of notice as we arrived. Tom and I jumped out of the car and ran to assist our fallen officer. We were ready to take prisoners and question our authority later. All the combatants scattered. I suspect that they expected other Claremont officers, but we were going to be the only ones. Tom thought they ran because Claremont police have a reputation for being brutal.

The injured officer was already walking out of the apartment with assistance. He was hurt, but it didn't seem to be serious. We remained at the scene for about thirty minutes, when the Newport chief thanked us and dismissed us.

Within days, the two governing bodies reached an agreement for mutual police protection. A request for assistance from the senior officer on duty would automatically grant police powers to any responding officer from another New Hampshire community.

Officer Grant

When I started with the department, I was sworn in but not yet weapons qualified. That meant that I was assigned to an FTO (field training officer). The FTO varied with the schedule since it was an ordinary patrol officer. On my third day with the department, I was assigned to Officer Grant. I learned later than he was not in good favor with the administration.

Officer Grant stopped a lot of cars. He stopped them for expired inspections, registrations, going through traffic signals and signs, and many other trivial things. He stopped cars for rolling through stop signs even though they obviously presented no hazard. The law is the law. The sign said "stop." Grant wrote many traffic tickets. He felt a duty to write enough tickets each day to justify his salary. He was a committed traffic cop and not so focused on community relations. There were a lot of complaints about him to administration. I was not aware of this tension.

The relationship that I first developed with Officer Grant was typical. He had two very young sons. I had one daughter and expected my second child soon. He was religious and consistently attended church with his entire family. He had rigid standards and values.

The day started as usual with Officer Grant. We stopped several cars. I was getting bored, getting out of the car, standing beside the stopped car, getting back in the police car, watching Grant write the ticket, getting back out, and listening to Grant's speech about how to answer the summons. Occasionally, we got a call. Officer Grant expedited these, then returned to traffic patrol. Then we got a call of an intoxicated person on North Street.

We quickly spotted the intoxicated person as he staggered on and off the sidewalk. He was walking away from us on the same side of the street as us. His knees were bent. He walked leaning forward with most of his weight on his toes. He was wearing jeans that hung low and loose. His black T-shirt was uncentered and hanging over his jeans. He wore sneakers that were untied. His short black hair was in disarray. Grant knew him, telling me that his name was Mitch. He quickly briefed me on Mitch's criminal record, mostly burglaries. He had been to prison. Officer Grant parked the front right fender close to Mitch, who only became aware of us at that point. Apparently, Mitch knew Grant too because he stopped and faced him. I got out and stood beside Mitch. When Grant got out, Mitch said, "Leave me alone!" Grant walked around the front of the police car.

Mitch started with profanity-laced pig comments. Officer Grant grabbed Mitch's right arm and slammed him on the hood of the car. Mitch's resistance was futile. He was so drunk that he could barely stand up. Grant handcuffed him and put him in the back of the car. We got in, and Grant drove the short distance to the police station. Mitch continued his profane disdain for Grant. As I reflected on this later, he never said anything derogatory directly to me. I lacked experience to understand that he did respect cops until they had crossed him.

I had a very difficult time understanding Mitch's intentions. He was extremely intoxicated, and most of his words were incomprehensible. We drove into the sally port controlled by the dispatcher. With the door closed behind us, Grant opened the back door and told Mitch to get out. Mitch struggled with his intoxication and being handcuffed. Grant interpreted his slowness as defiance. Mitch finally got out and to his feet. Grant grabbed his right arm and pushed him toward the door into the processing room. Mitch looked over his right shoulder at Grant and resumed his profane pig dissertation.

In the processing room, there is a row of cabinets. It is at the end of these cabinets that prisoners are searched before processing. It's also the door to the evidence locker. Prisoners are faced toward this door, and handcuffs are removed. They are instructed to place the hand first freed on the door. The officer keeps a firm grip on the handcuff as it could now be a formidable weapon when fastened to only one hand. If the prisoner resists at this point, an officer can pull up on the handcuff while pushing the prisoner into the door and down to the floor to reapply the handcuffs. If the person cooperates, the handcuffs will be removed, and the prisoner will be directed to place both hands on the door. Next, the prisoner will be instructed to slide their feet back so that they are leaning on the door, giving the advantage to the officer who can now search them.

Grant directed Mitch to this spot. He decided not to remove the handcuffs due to Mitch's belligerence. Though Mitch was verbally offensive, he showed no physical resistance beyond struggling due to intoxication. Grant searched Mitch's pockets. He removed a cigarette lighter, cigarettes, a wallet with no money, and a pocketknife. He placed these on the counter until he completed his search, then placed the items in a drawer labeled cell number 1. All the while, Mitch continued his verbal barrage. Grant then told Mitch, "Go!" pointing toward the cells. Mitch did not respond to the instructions. He remained leaning his head toward Grant and continued his verbal assault upon Grant. Grant placed his hand in the middle of Mitch's back, then said, "I said go!" As he spoke, Grant pushed Mitch with domineering force.

Mitch was so drunk that he could hardly stand on his own. He was incapable of maintaining his balance against such a powerful and unanticipated push. Mitch appeared to be launched headfirst into the hallway to the jail cells. His hands were still handcuffed behind him so that he had no chance of breaking his fall. He landed face-first on the tile-covered concrete floor. His right temple was the first part to hit the floor. It knocked him out cold.

Grant immediately went to Mitch's head and assessed his condition. Mitch was mostly on his right side. He was breathing deep and hard. He did not respond to Grant's calling to him. Grant instructed the dispatcher to call an ambulance. Mitch remained unconscious until the ambulance arrived. He started to respond a little to the EMTs. Grant removed the handcuffs when they requested it. The EMTs transported Mitch to the hospital. Grant went to write his report. It was very brief. A few details about the reason for the call and that Mitch fell in the processing room.

The next day, the chief asked me to write a report on the incident. Unknown to me was that the dispatcher had already written a report. I didn't know what the chief was looking for. As my present readers can appreciate by my description so far, there is a lot of detail that can be placed in a report. A lot can be left out if it is not significant. I wrote a generic report, then decided to meet with the chief. He explained that the dispatcher had written a very detailed report, but because of our position with the camera, the dispatcher could not see the actual push. Knowing this, I now could write the concise report that the chief wanted. Grant was immediately suspended pending dismissal by the police commission. I started my police career reporting against a "bad cop." As my career progressed, I realized that there were many more problematic officers. I also began to realize that there was little guidance from the top.

I got to know Mitch over the next few years. He was poorly educated and at a disadvantage when getting a good job. He got along with a series of temporary jobs, mostly painting and other construction trades. I found him intoxicated in the street, and there were some calls about his staggering into traffic. Each time, I called him by name, asked him how he was doing, then gave him a ride home. I confirmed that there was someone sober that could manage him, then left.

I was happy doing police work but felt a draw to teach. Since I worked the evening shift now, I could be available to substitute teach. I enjoyed doing this. I felt that I was better using my college education. I worked with several cops who only graduated from high school. Some had only GEDs (general equivalency diploma). It was refreshing to work with an educated faculty and students. Mitch's sister, Kim, was in some of the classes I taught. She often took an opportunity to speak with me about herself and her brother. She had a good relationship with him. She acknowledged that Mitch did not like police and parole officers, but he respected me.

On another day, I saw Mitch walking down the sidewalk, again on North Street. He appeared to walk normally, at a brisk pace. I expected to just drive by when suddenly he raised the back of his T-shirt and pulled a gun from the back of his waistband. He then quickly jumped into the passenger side of a pickup truck. A woman was sitting at the wheel. My heart jumped. Mitch was a convicted felon and should not have a gun. The quickness with which he pulled that gun and jumped into the truck appeared to me that he was hijacking the truck. I quickly turned on the blue lights, notified dispatch that I was "out with a man with a gun on North Street," dropped the microphone, exited the car, and drew my gun as quickly as I could. Sitting in a car, a cop is a sitting duck, an easy target.

I first crouched beside my car, then moved up to the back left corner of the pickup. I yelled, "Show me the gun!" I had my .357 pointed directly at Mitch's back. I was very confident that it would penetrate the back of the truck, its bed and cabin, sever his spine, and strike his heart. Mitch looked at the woman but did not raise his hands or produce the gun. I focused my aim and yelled again, "Show me the gun!" My heart was pounding. I couldn't let this truck drive away. I was very scared now, fearing that I would have to kill Mitch. I hated being trapped in this situation. I felt my heart ponding and yelled the command again. I listened for my backup that I so desperately wanted.

Both Mitch and the woman looked back at me. I recognized his sister Kim and felt a little relief. Then Kim held the gun up by the trigger guard. Relief flowed through my whole being. I lowered my gun and walked to the driver's side of the truck. Kim held the gun for me to examine. I put mine away and took it. I first confirmed that it was not loaded. Kim explained that Mitch was collecting on a debt, and the debt was being paid with this gun. I said, "Mitch, you know that you are not allowed to possess guns." He replied, "I know, but it is the only way of getting my money. I can sell this." He explained that he kept it concealed in his back so that he wouldn't be seen. He didn't realize that I was approaching from behind. He apologized for causing me so much concern.

To do my job with some proficiency, I asked the dispatcher to check the serial number through NCIC (National Crime Information Center). It came back "no record." I returned the gun to Kim. I looked at Mitch and said, "Your sister will sell the gun for you." He smiled and agreed.

Most officers reading this now would think me a fool. Arresting Mitch for being a felon in possession of a firearm is a good arrest and a certain conviction in this situation. With his criminal history, he would return to prison for a very long time. More compassionate people will agree with my decision. Sending Mitch back to prison would do nothing for his "rehabilitation." Mitch was immersed in a way of life that was difficult, and survival often meant crossing some lines. It was a bad decision to take possession of the gun. I'm glad that he didn't take his sister into the potentially dangerous place where he got the gun. It is a crime with no victim. It is a law meant to protect people from dangerous, habitual criminals. Mitch had no intentions of committing crimes with this gun. Enforcing this law under these conditions only makes Mitch and his sister victims of the law.

Mitch left the area. He couldn't escape the chains that bound him in a difficult life. I still see Kim. She is always happy to see me and reports that Mitch is doing well working for contractors in another city. He often visits her and the rest of their family. One member of the police administration often said, "Law enforcement is not social work." He had the concept of enforcing all laws with no negotiations or alternatives. Law enforcement's intention is to change behavior and make our society safer. In that respect, law enforcement is social work.

This administrator also pledged the loyalty code, to support one another, especially when he was the beneficiary. To him and others that pledge loyalty to other officers, I point this out. I signed off with a man with a gun in a high-crime neighborhood. That should have been an all-hands alert. All available officers should have headed in my direction. It should have been a station clearing event. Every sworn officer in the police station should have headed my way. As I focused my gun in the middle of Mitch's back, I was keenly listening for my backup that I desperately wanted. I was only a half mile from the station. No one came to my assistance, not even him. If our roles were reversed, he would have certainly made a dramatic issue of no response to his call.

Benny: A Police Victim

It was a practice that officers could get a ride to and from work from the police car patrolling their neighborhood. I never took advantage of this, but many did. I started my evening shift by bringing Kent home. Before starting patrol, the policy is to test the radar instrument. It's also tested at the end of every shift and immediately after writing a violation. After conducting a successful test, we called the dispatcher to log it in the record. Since Kent was anxious to get home, I intended to delay this testing protocol until after dropping him off. It didn't mean that if you catch a speeder with an untested radar, you couldn't stop him. You were just not supposed to write a ticket based upon the radar evidence.

As we reached the edge of the urban compact toward Kent's home, I recognized a familiar large white car approaching us. The radar indicated thirty-five miles per hour. No big deal, as it was a thirty-miles-per-hour zone, and there were no noticeable hazards. However, pointing to the car, Kent said, "There he is! I have been looking for him all day. Stop him!" I replied, "OK, but this one is yours." Kent was officially off duty and should not be engaging in police actions at this time. I turned around and turned on the blue lights, and the car pulled over. Sure enough, Benny was driving.

Benny's car was poorly maintained. Some windows were stuck in a partially open position. Tires were always questionable. The exhaust system hanged precariously underneath. The engine ran roughly, and the exhaust was smoky. Inside was filled with clutter. There was a car seat with a small child in the back. The clutter filled the area around her. Benny always quickly shut off the engine so that we wouldn't hear the exhaust leaks. Any vindictive cop could easily find an equipment violation. I tried to take into consideration that writing a fine for Benny took money away from caring for his daughter. I gave many warnings for things that were not safe, such as a bald tire or leaky exhaust.

Benny had long scraggly reddish blond hair and beard. His clothes were dirty and worn. His daughter was properly cared for and dressed appropriately. Benny accepted social services that provided nutritional and clothing needs for preschool children. Though far below our standards of caring for our families, Benny was doing what he knew.

Kent and I did a practice that is discouraged—crossing between the two cars. It makes both officers simultaneously vulnerable to being crushed between the two cars. Kent crossed from the passenger side and approached the operator. I crossed to the sidewalk and provided observation and safety coverage. I never felt Benny would hurt anyone, but one must always be careful. From my position, I could hear what Kent said but nothing Ben said.

Kent said, "I got you going forty-five in a thirty," as he demanded Benny's license and registration. I was stunned. It was thirty-five miles per hour on an untested but albeit accurate radar.

Benny said something to Kent, but I couldn't understand it. Kent then said, "I got you going fifty. Now what do you have to say?" Benny apparently responded; then Kent said, "I got you going fifty-five. Still have something to say?" After a moment, Kent said, "I didn't think so." Kent walked back to the cruiser and got in on the driver's side, which I would expect to reduce the dangerous crossover.

In the car, Kent asked if I had a summons. We all carried a briefcase with such paperwork, so I gave him one. I watched in great disbelief as he wrote that ticket for fifty-five miles per hour in a thirty-miles-per-hour zone. I'm thinking, *Here we go again. I am stuck with yet another time when an officer misrepresented an event, and I will be called to testify against him.* I reminded Kent that I had not yet tested the radar. He replied, "Oh yeah." He picked up the radio microphone, seemed to think for a second, then called dispatch, "Note radar tested." He did not test the radar and caused a false record of it.

We returned to our positions beside Benny's car. Kent presented the ticket and gave the standard explanation on how he can plead guilty and pay the fine or go to trial. Benny drove away. We returned to our original positions in the car. I drove Kent home. I let Kent rant on how much Benny was a "dirtbag" and shouldn't be able to roam around. I was mostly quiet, still a bit stunned by the whole thing. I felt heavily burdened about Kent's assumption that I accept his disregard for true facts. I also knew that it was my word against his and he was much senior. I hoped for Benny to successfully challenge Kent's abuse of police authority.

As the days went by, I watched as the court paperwork was processed so I would know when the hearing would be. This caused a great deal of stress for me, thinking some lawyer was going to call me as a witness. Much to my surprise and sadness, Benny pleaded guilty and paid the fine. I am bothered to this day. Benny knew he had no chance in a court trial. Getting caught like this was an acceptable risk to him. I began to realize that this explained why Kent never drove his car to work. He was afraid that it would be recognized and eventually vandalized.

Still, I cannot understand why Kent had so much anger toward Benny. Benny wasn't the most upstanding citizen. Sure, he committed petty crimes like shoplifting, maybe even small-time burglaries. Nonetheless, he eventually got caught and paid the appropriate penalty. Kent's desire for justice is dynamically opposite mine. He took advantage of his reputation as a former army ranger. I was an artillery captain. Still, there cannot be an ethical boundary line between people on their status. Kent eventually returned to the army. I was glad to see him leave.

Automobile Lot Dispute

It was my first night back from two days off. I welcomed the foot patrol assignment on this warm summer midweek evening. Things were quiet after nine o'clock in the evening, so the sergeant told me to ride in the beat 2 cruiser. This is typical. Beat 2 tended to be a little busier beat. Should the beat officer get tied up with reports, I would take over his beat. I got in the car with Pedro.

We rode around the main streets for a while; then Pedro started checking the backs of businesses. When we drove through a car dealer's lot, we saw two men talking near the service entrance. Pedro drove up to them and asked what they were doing there. One explained that he worked in the parts department. The other was his friend who was a mechanic at another dealer. They were drinking beer, which is acceptable on private property. He told them that they needed to leave. The parts man said that it's private property and his boss doesn't care that they are there. Pedro didn't like the explanation.

Pedro, while still sitting in the car, started to put on his leather gloves. The parts man asked, "Why do you need to put on your gloves?" Pedro answered, "I put them on when I have to touch shit." The response was that he didn't need to worry because there was no shit here and that he could go do his job. Pedro seemed more offended by this challenge. I didn't understand why he didn't drive off with the first explanation. There was absolutely nothing wrong with them on private property. If the business owner had a problem with it, I'm sure that he could handle it. I spoke quietly, telling Pedro that I thought they were OK.

Pedro looked at me as he pulled his gloves on. I noticed these gloves had ridges across the knuckles that I recognized as lead lining. These were illegal sap gloves. The lead was there to add weight and cause more damage when you struck someone with a closed fist. Pedro said, "It's time for you to go back on the street." He sped out of this lot and dropped me off in the foot patrol area. A few minutes later, I heard that he was coming in with one under arrest. The sergeant told me to go in and assist with the processing.

Pedro drove into the sally port. I went from the processing room into the sally port when Pedro didn't immediately come in with his prisoner. Pedro was standing by the car's open back door. I saw the automobile parts guy in the back. His face was bloodied and bruised. Blood was coming from his mouth. He had trouble speaking but was calling Pedro an "asshole" and refused to get out of the car. He was hurt and demanding medical attention. Pedro called the sergeant and said that he was bringing his arrest to the hospital. Pedro looked at me and said he would be "all set." He clearly didn't want me involved.

Pedro brought him to the hospital. My shift ended before he returned to process his prisoner. I never heard anything more. I felt that the administration knew very well that Pedro was violent. He eventually left the department and moved to California.

Speeding Trooper

It was toward the end of my night shift. It was a slow night, so I went on Washington Street to find something to do with traffic that got progressively busier. Many people had radar detectors, so it was somewhat challenging to catch a speeder. I really wasn't interested in writing tickets to people heading to work. I just wanted to stop some vehicles to pass the remaining two hours of my shift.

There are two places on Washington Street that set off radar detectors, so people are more likely not to notice that I was there until it was too late. We believed that what set off these detectors were the alarm systems in the businesses. The music store at the far end of Washington Street sent the strongest signal, so it masked mine best. That's where I set up this morning.

At seven five in the morning, I saw a car in the twilight coming at an extremely high rate. I switched the radar from standby and immediately got a signal, sixty-five miles per hour in this thirty-miles-per-hour zone. At the same time, I noticed the car rapidly decelerating with its front depressing from the extreme braking. The radar displayed changing speeds and stabilized at thirty-five miles per hour. This was the perfect tracking history I need for accurate target identification. I went to start the car to go after this speeder when I noticed that it was a state trooper. It puzzled me a bit because sixty-five miles per hour, even with lights and siren, was too fast in this busy area. This trooper wasn't running any emergency equipment. As the car got closer, I saw the plate number, 64.

Each trooper has a plate number that matches his or her call sign. The first number identified the barracks to which they are assigned. Those beginning with 100 are assigned to troop A, the seacoast area. The plate with 100 would be the commander, a lieutenant. 101 would be the second-in-command, a sergeant. From there, the numbers did not define a hierarchy. Troop B would begin with 200. Our area is covered by troop C, based in Keene. These begin with 300. Those with only two digits worked out of headquarters in Concord. I knew 64. He is Walt Barnes and lives in Charlestown. He commutes to Concord every day. His angry or mean disposition is well-known in the community and among law enforcement. Walt is primarily assigned to an administrative position dealing with hazard materials: transport and emergency response. The only conceivable reason he was traveling at this speed was that he was running late. Even if there was a hazardous materials incident, his services were mostly follow-up and investigation of rule infractions. He would not be involved in any emergency response. Besides, if he was, he should be running his emergency equipment and would not have slowed when he saw me.

I was not going to try and stop a mark state police car, but this behavior is not just risky, it severely tarnishes community's respect for law enforcement. I decided to seek the advice on my captain, who I respected. I found him at the end of my shift. I told him what I saw, and he was elated. He said that he already had another complaint against Walt when he harassed and bullied a Claremont resident. He was going to call Walt's supervisor. He was dreading it because the Claremont resident's motives and credibility would be challenged. He welcomed this second detailed complaint. The captain naturally asked me to write it up for him, which I did gladly.

I was off the next two days. When I returned, the captain told me that Walt got a three-day suspension. That was better than writing any speeding ticket that would have seriously damaged police credibility in court. I was very satisfied with the outcome.

Fairy Gary

We had some horrible dispatchers. For example, Chance was a nice guy with a good heart. It took him a long time to get all the details from the caller, even driving directions, before he transmitted to the patrol car. His transmissions were long, and often, the address was the last thing he transmitted. I would be driving in the car with no idea if I was going toward or away from the scene. I would know that it was serious and that I needed to respond with lights and siren, but I had no idea where to go. We very rarely needed driving directions because we learned the city so well. Chance felt an obligation to understand the location himself, just in case we needed help finding it.

One of Chance's worst acts stands out to me. It's not unusual for a dispatcher to ask patrol cars for their locations. He might do this to see if we had any chance of intercepting a car. He could then decide to whom to assign the call. One night, Chance radioed such a request, "Units, what is your 10-20 [location]?" We each responded with our location. He then asked us for a 10-9 (phone call). Back then, we didn't have cell phones. We used to drive up to a pay phone and radio in the number. When I spoke with Chance on the phone, he said that someone had called him and said that he was going to shoot one of us tonight.

I couldn't believe his ignorance. I asked him why it was necessary to know our location. He said, "Because if one of you needed help, I wanted to know where you were." I explained to Chance that we were moving constantly. All he did was allow the threatening person to learn our locations by listening to his scanner. Worse yet, he then set us up to stop to make the phone call. He made us sitting ducks in a phone booth.

Gary was an excellent dispatcher. He got information quickly and transmitted to the patrol officer well. His transmissions were precise, short, and with the important information first. Once we acknowledged the call, he would add the extra details as we drove to the address. I appreciated his style very much. I immediately knew where and how serious it was. It's my decision to whether run the lights, siren, or go with normal traffic; but I had the information I needed in seconds. Gary had a skill to first extract these most important details from the caller, then dispatched police, fire, ambulance as needed. With everything rolling, he then continued the conversation for the extra details. He provided the extra details like descriptions, direction of travel, and injuries as we drove to the scene.

Gary was not only a good dispatcher, he volunteered at the community center, refereeing basketball and soccer games. He often volunteered at other community events and his church. Gary didn't have much of a social life outside of his service to the community. He was gay and remained single. Now and then, an officer would jokingly call him "Fairy Gary," which he didn't seemed to mind as he laughed about it.

We often got loud noise complaints to parties. Sometimes these parties involved school-aged kids when their parents were out of town. I started to grow suspicious when I noticed Gary at many of these. He was at least ten years older than these kids. My suspicion culminated one night.

I had just patrolled down the long Maple Avenue through an average neighborhood. I turned up Industrial Boulevard along the back of the airport. It's a dead-end street with only industrial facilities that were all closed on this weekend evening. A car approached me. The radar first showed thirty-eight miles per hour in this thirty-miles-per-hour zone. It accelerated to sixty-one miles per hour as it approached me. After it passed me, I turned and stopped it.

I immediately recognized Sam, who was driving this car alone. I went to school with Sam's mother. We shared only grades 5, 6, and 7. She dropped out of school when she became pregnant with him. I met Sam when I substituted for his class in school. His mother was very ill with cancer at that time. She had died. Sam was living with her sister, his aunt, now. He was a good kid from poor and sad experiences.

Sam was sixteen years old but didn't have a license. He didn't know where the registration was but added it belonged to Gary. I asked for clarification that it was our dispatcher Gary. He said, "Yes." I feared that my impression of Sam would suddenly change with my next question, "How did you get Gary's car?" He must have sensed my concern and said, "Gary let me drive it." I knew that Gary sometimes did some driving instruction for kids, but I never knew of him letting a kid take his car alone.

I asked Sam, "Where's Gary?" Sam explained that he was at a party with Gary on one of the side streets off Maple Avenue. I told Sam to lock up Gary's car, and I brought him to the party. The party was mild, with only a few attending. I asked him to get Gary. Gary came to the door. I explained that I caught Sam driving his car and that the car was locked on Industrial Boulevard. Gary accepted my offer to drive him to his car.

I was deeply troubled with Gary's actions, which made the ride difficult. I managed to keep the conversation on how I knew Sam. I was glad that it was short. I didn't see any alcohol, nor did I have any complaints, so I avoided discussion of the party. I could charge Sam for driving without a license and Gary with allowing an improper person to operate a motor vehicle. I felt that Sam had learned a good lesson and how it would impact his driving record. I didn't want to charge a coworker, someone with whom I worked almost daily. I dropped Gary off at his car and resumed patrol.

The next morning, I decided to take my concerns to the police chief. I explained that other officers and I were growing concerned about the number of times we have seen Gary at these teenage parties. I also told him how he let one child drive his car without a license. The chief replied, "What he does on his own time is his business." He added that if I was concerned, I could charge him. I thanked him and left his office. So much for the take command and lead, to which I was accustomed and did in the army. The chief often boasted about having served in all branches, though some were short. He didn't complete any enlistment, finally leaving with a neck injury.

Gary started doing part-time police work as a special officer with the department. Special officers are trained solely by the department, not the police academy. They work directly with a certified officer or direct traffic. Gary occasionally took a beat assignment for a half shift, filling in when the assigned officer was out.

Gary then started working as a part-time officer for the town of Unity. Eventually, he became the chief in Unity. Several years passed when a story hit the headlines. Chief Gary had been arrested after a state police investigation. A sixteen-year-old boy had accused him of sexual assault. Gary had diverted this kid's burglary arrest to community service. The community service was for the Unity Police Department. It's during this time that he groomed and eventually sexually assaulted him.

Gary went to prison for several years. When he was released, he lived out of the immediate area. I crossed paths with him in the town where he lived. His health was poor. He died shortly after.

I can't help feeling that, if the chief took the responsibility I sought and worked with us, we could have redirected Gary. He had so much to contribute to the community. If he was willing to participate in counseling, the outcome could have been very different. I also met his victim since I knew his father. The victim never received any therapy and eventually went to prison himself.

Things are not always clear when humans are involved. It's not as simple as we see on TV and the movies. Bad guys are not always bad. People who commit a criminal act may also do great service to the community. Gary didn't get the intervention that might have made a difference. I must hope that many with whom I have been involved have been able to be redirected. I can be sure of only one thing. I will never stop trying. I will always continue to ask myself and others these questions.

Masters Motorcycle Club Party

Some say the Masters Motorcycle Club members were Hells Angels wannabes. They drove loud Harleys and often road through the city together. There were a few who beat other people. I encountered some members following bar fights. Most of the officers with whom I worked were very concerned about their potential for violence. I didn't see anything that distinguished them from nonmembers. Even the bars fights broke up before we got there, and they cooperated for the most part. With all that involved me, it was the reaction of a master who was assaulted by another bar patron. True, he may have used more force to defend himself than necessary, but it was likely to be mutual combat, a minor charge. In my cases, the other guy was quite intoxicated and spent time in the lockup to sober up or get someone to take him home. Intoxicated witness lack credibility.

There were reputable members in this club too. Some owned a small business. Others were professionals and skilled laborers. One was a photographer who sometimes showed up to traffic accidents to take pictures for the newspaper. He was particularly respectful and cooperative with my investigation. The masters participated in some community events. I remember their involvement in Toys for Tots and food drives for the soup kitchen. I knew only two that served prison time. These were the ones that didn't work and were involved in these bar fights. Still, there seemed to be a fear of this club for several in the department.

When an individual or organization wishes to use city-owned facilities, it goes through a review process. The police chief's part is to decide whether security is required and how much. For a family using a meeting room for a birthday party, there wouldn't be a security requirement. For a school dance, one or two police officers would be required. These extra duties were choice assignments for officers because they were easy and were paid as overtime. For the organization, this was a significant expense that often took much of the funds raised during the event.

The masters applied to us the city gymnasium for a Christmas party. I understand that the city administration was concerned but felt the members were tax-paying residents and should have the right to rent it. The chief, who I am confident is one who was most scared of the masters, decided that there would be three officers instead of the typical one or two. I have never known any organization to be required to have three officers for security. The masters were understandably angry. I believe the chief had hoped that this requirement would compel them to seek another place, but they stood their ground and rented it.

The party was scheduled from six o'clock in the evening to twelve o'clock midnight. For me, it was a lucrative six hours of overtime. I signed up along with Martin and Jacob. I am one of those people who is compulsively early to all my obligations. I reported to the gymnasium around five fifty in the afternoon. Several club members greeted me as they arrived and carried things into the party. I remained at the entrance, standing just outside the door. I didn't anticipate any problems. The chief, who was somewhat sensational sometimes, expected trouble.

Six o'clock in the evening passed. Marty and Jake had not yet arrived. I was a little uneasy, given the chief's confidence that there would be some arrests to be made. I noticed neither had arrived when it was six twenty, then six thirty. I was beginning to wonder if they were coming at all. Finally, a police car stopped in front of the building, and Jake and Marty got out. I thought it odd that they needed a ride. The police station was practically across the street. I lived in town at that time. I always walked to work, where I kept my equipment. We could bring our equipment, including the service revolver home. I didn't want it around my young daughters, so I secured it at the police station. I walked from home to the station then from the station to the gymnasium.

The evening progressed without incident. I spent most of my time outside the entrance. I occasionally walked a short distance into the gym. Everything seemed very peaceful, and there was just a group of mature friends enjoying their time together. Midnight came, and they had completely picked up the gym and left. I walked to the station to put my equipment away, then walked home. Marty and Jake called for a police car to take them home.

I didn't think much of Jake and Marty's being late. I just let it go as typical of some of the antics officers do. I stayed true to my own values and was satisfied. When I arrived for my next regular shift, the dispatcher asked me if Marty and Jake were late to the masters' detail. I said yes. She asked if I noticed how late. I replied that I wasn't sure, but it was more than one-half hour. I thought that she was just curious.

The next day, the chief intercepted me as I reported to work, early as usual. He brought me into his office and closed the door. No one likes it when this happens. It's never good when the boss closes the door. He sat at his desk and asked me about Jake and Marty being late to the masters' detail. I confirmed that they were. He asked, and I responded again that it was more than one-half hour. He then shared with me that they put in for the whole time, even the time that they were not there. He added that the masters' club had lodged a complaint. They didn't want to pay for officers who were not there.

The chief came to me a few days later. He told me that he had spoken to the other officers and I should know how they responded. Jake freely admitted that he was late and apologized for putting in for the time. The chief deducted it from his pay. Marty emphatically denied it, but all the chief did was to deduct his pay. The chief said that he would be sending a corrected bill to the club.

I wasn't surprised with the officers' responses. Jake was a good cop. He was honorable and trustworthy. He told me the only reason he put the time down was because Marty pressured him into it.

Marty was a jerk with whom I had other problems. He was a bully to everyone, citizens and fellow officers alike. He came to our department from Springfield. I suspect that they were glad to get rid of him. I refused to submit to his attempts to bully me. He resorted to passive-aggressive tactics. After this, I started finding magazine cutout pictures of rats and cheese in my mailbox. In his eyes, I violated that code to not report misconduct of fellow officers. Since I didn't initiate the report to the chief, I wondered how it became a priority for him. The chief usually didn't follow through on citizen complaints. I discussed this one night with a very trusted fellow officer. He told me that the dispatcher was dating a masters' club member who was one of the party organizers. She was the one who encouraged the club to complain and not pay the full price.

Marty continued with his passive-aggressive tactics. I neither reported it nor confronted him until one shift change. I was coming off shift, and he was coming on. He also had a dog, a medium-sized German shepherd. It wasn't as disciplined as the dogs used by other officers, but it did lie at his feet during shift change.

Canine officers use alert signals to get their dogs to respond and appear ready to take down a suspect. I heard Marty quietly say his signal word "dirtbag" as I walked by. The dog sprung up and cued on me. I turned to Marty, who was still sitting in his chair and trying to pretend that I was the cause of the dog's response. I replied, "I heard your signal. If your dog bites me, I assure you that it will never bite another person." I added, "I won't shoot him, but he will lose all his will to attack anyone ever again." My intention was to defend myself with my baton or flashlight. I also have experience working with other canine officers and know the dog's most vulnerable part is its feet. I have trained dogs not to bite or jump on people by grabbing and gently squeezing a front foot. A police dog is trained to maintain its bite on its target but would respond to a very strong grip on its foot.

Marty and my relationship remained tenuous throughout my remaining time with the police department. Jake and I remained good friends. He admitted that he was wrong. I knew that he was very much out of character to submit a misleading time sheet.

Boredom

Everyone likes to talk about the exciting things police do. The reality is that there are many boring hours. We fill these times by patrolling. We look for crimes in progress, which is exciting but rare. We look for evidence that a crime has been committed and follow up on it. We also keep a "police presence" to discourage crime. Still, there are times that are extremely boring. As sapient human beings, we need intellectual stimulation.

Since we must respond "code 3" sometimes, it's good to be familiar with the changing street conditions and how fast we feel we can drive the various routes. Some of us would practice taking corners at increasing speeds. My colleague, Mike, told me how he used to practice "bootlegger turns." For those who don't know what a bootlegger turn is, it's applying the parking brake to lock the rear wheels. Just as you lock the rear wheels, you initiate a turn, causing the car to spin around. If you are skillful at it, you can spin the car around and go in the opposite direction quickly. Bootleggers used this technique to escape a pursuing sheriff, who would take more time to turn around. What is a bootlegger? During the days of prohibition, when alcohol was illegal, people used to carry their illegal whiskey in a flask that they hid in their bootleg. Bootleggers provided the illegal moonshine for their flasks.

Though the bootlegger times are passed, the technique remains exciting especially for movies. I felt that they were much too dangerous and could take more time in turning around. Mike still liked to practice them. His favorite place to do it was in West Claremont, near the Vermont State Line, under the High Bridge, a railroad trestle. He described one that didn't go so well. He went backward into the guardrail, hitting it hard.

When we do something stupid like that, we worry about who might have seen it. So Mike pretended to be responding to an emergency. He turned on the blue lights and got out of there. Clear of the area, he turned off the blue lights. Turning off the lights isn't unusual as we sometimes begin to respond then get called off. Mike drove to a lighted area to check for damage to the car. He was lucky. Since he went directly into the guardrail, the bumper absorbed the impact, leaving no noticeable damage. Mike added another detail when he told me about it. The High Bridge wasn't his beat that night. If someone saw it and complained, the other officer would have been the chief's first suspect.

I was riding with Mike one night when he suggested another risky stunt. It started from causally patrolling some of the less traveled roads. He drove up Bible Hill and was starting to head down Piper Hill Road on the other side of the hill. We were looking at the dairy farm on the top of the hill as he drove slowly. Then he stopped the car and said, "I have wondered how fast the car would go if we just coasted down the hill." I thought that it was harmless enough and agreed. He put the car in neutral and took his foot off the brake. As the speed increased, we were both amazed when the car reached sixty-five miles per hour in this thirty-five-miles-per-hour zone.

We had reached the lowest point and coming up the grade to the Charlestown Road. I expected that he would have to apply the brakes for the intersection with Charlestown Road. To the contrary, Mike said, "I bet that, if I dropped this in drive and punched it, we could jump clean over Charlestown Road and onto Grissom Lane," which is opposite Piper Hill Road. That was too much for me, and I expressed my disapproval. He seemed like he wanted to try it. I jokingly reminded him that I didn't think it was a good idea and reminded him that I was carrying a gun. I suggested that, if he seriously wanted to do it, he could leave me by the roadside and I would watch traffic for him. I was much relieved when he decided not to try to vault the car. I expected that he could have vaulted completely over Charlestown Road, but he probably wouldn't be able to keep it on Grissom Lane because it connected with Charlestown Road at an angle.

We also found some entertainment in turning off streetlights using our spotlight. Shining the light on the light sensor on top of the light would turn it off, just as the sun does in the morning. It was a distorted target practice activity. Aiming the spotlight and having it hit the targeted sensor was somewhat challenging. We developed a rationale to explain the benefit of doing this. If we wanted to enter an area and not be exposed by the streetlight, we could turn it off. It would give us five or ten minutes before it would come back on. When it comes back, it takes it a while to come to full light.

I was particularly bored one night and challenged myself to turn off all the streetlights on Charlestown Road. I drove down the street, perfectly targeting the lights on both sides of the road. I turned around at the end of the street to drive down to admire my skill. As I drove down the dark street, it struck me that maybe this wasn't a good idea. If someone had an accident, I must report the conditions. Whether or not the streetlight was working is one of the data points we collect. Of course, I wouldn't report a light as working when it wasn't. The dilemma is that it automatically generates a repair order to the electric company. I decided not to turn off a whole street again.

These spotlight-aiming skills were useful in a game we called laser tag. The object of the game was to target the other patrol car when he didn't expect it. A successful hit made the other guy "it" just like the childhood tag game. Just like the children's game, you were it until you tagged the other guy. Similarly, you had to give a chance for the escape.

Typically, one would sneak into the other guy's beat and ambush him. We often hid behind a building we knew he would likely check or drive by. We practiced our covert maneuvering skills with lights off and using the parking brake so as not to light the brake lights. Using the parking brake was another skill. It worked best by holding the release so it wouldn't lock. Care was required because using just the rear brakes requires extra stopping distance.

My best tag was as I was just driving aimlessly around my beat. I was on the south side of the Sugar River where I could see the back of the Washington Street commercial buildings on the north side of the river. I noticed Mike dutifully checking the doors and equipment behind these buildings. I stopped in the road, just before a house. I turned off the car lights and took careful aim. With a quick flip on and off with the spotlight, I hit my target perfectly. I carefully moved the car with the lights off and used the parking brake to hide behind the house.

I imagined Mike looking around the corners of the buildings for his laser assailant. It took a few seconds for him to figure it out. He realized the light came from across the river, but he still had to determine my location. Soon I heard his voice on the radio, "Right behind that house." I knew I had been discovered. Now I had to make my escape. With the lights still off, I accelerated and snapped one more shot as I cleared the edge of the building. I earned a compliment from Mike, "Nice."

Later that night, when we met for coffee in the station, we asked the dispatcher what she thought about our radio transmissions. She burst my bubble when she replied, "I gave up trying to figure you guys out."

I heard about a trooper that was assigned to interstate duty for discipline. Trooper Laramie had little patience with the people he arrested and sometimes used excessive force. His commander was growing tired of the complaints. When Trooper Laramie moved just over the line of his assigned area, the commander temporarily transferred him to interstate highway duty for disciplinary reasons. Trooper Laramie took his boredom relief to a whole new level. He shot at crows. He took on great distance challenges, leaning across the hood of the car to take steady aim. He was a good shot, killing crows at distances remarkable for a handgun. Like us, they carried .357 Magnums. It was very effective on a crow.

The closest foolish gun activity that I heard about from my fellow Claremont officers involved two who were off duty. They used to ride around in their car, shooting street signs on the back roads. They were quite drunk one night, and the shooter fumbled his nine-millimeter automatic. It accidentally discharged through the dash, firewall, and into the engine, killing it. The bullet struck the computer component required for the engine to run. The car owner's response was "He shot my car in the brain."

Boo-boo Boutin

Jack Boutin was hired shortly after I was. He was from Massachusetts, and we were told he had experience. I learned later that he was a security guard in Massachusetts and former military police. He seemed impressive at first, as he spoke about his experience. Our regard eroded over time.

One of Jack's earliest alarms was that his former girlfriend's new boyfriend was hunting for him. Personally, I don't have a lot of concerns for people who got into relationships that got that far out of hand. Nonetheless, I kept an extra vigil on his behalf.

A while later, Jack had "intel" (intelligence) on a bank robbery that was supposed to occur in Claremont. He got this information from his contacts in Massachusetts. He had us on edge for a few days. There were no bank robberies, and this seemed to just fade away.

A police force's strength is how well they work together. Especially for a beat officer, we care about whether he will be there to back us up. Jack was there, but usually the last one to arrive. It also seemed that for every physical encounter, he got hurt.

It was informally expected for us to arrive to work ten minutes early. It was unpaid but showed courtesy and respect for the officers we were relieving. Those ten minutes were used for shift-change briefing so we were ready to take over and our colleagues could go home to their families.

Jack was one of those who was habitually late to work. He didn't think much of being ten minutes late. The difficulty was that one of us had to stay until he arrived. Overtime pay didn't start until after fifteen minutes. When Jack came in, he was still strapping on his gear. He presented with energy and ready-to-go attitude, but he missed shift-change briefing. The person stuck behind to cover for him was expected to brief him before we could leave, without any extra pay. When we started mentioning this to Jack, his response was "f—— the city." After a while, I pointed out to him that it wasn't the city that was getting screwed by his tardiness. It was us who were covering for him. He never changed his ways.

When an officer calls out sick, overtime is offered to cover for it. The most senior has first choice or refusal. When it trickles down to the least senior, it is no longer a choice. It is mandatory. Similarly, someone must come in early to cover the other half of the shift. The same procedure applies.

Some officers got quite creative about avoiding coming in early. There's no creative way to getting out of staying over. Obviously, you are already at work. Even court wasn't an excuse because they can call you when the case is ready and the supervisor can cover your beat while you testify.

As a member of the police force, you were expected to answer your phone when off duty. The reason is more for emergencies requiring extra personnel. I think no one would try to get out of such an emergency, but many did not want to come in early. A sure way to get out of it was to say, "I can't. I just had a beer."

One time, Jack was called. He was sleeping and claimed to have been startled by the phone and reached for it quickly. When he made the reach, he strained a muscle in his neck. Personally, I felt that this was no excuse and he should have come in. Much to my dismay, he not only got out of coming in, he turned it into three days of workmen's compensation. I couldn't believe it.

With his propensity to getting injured during arrests and especially his neck injury, we gave Jack the title of Boo-boo Boutin. It seemed to flow naturally. He accepted it, knowing that he was the most injured. He took it as a badge of honor. He believed he was so courageous that he willingly risked personal harm. Those of us with him when he got hurt and unable to see how he got hurt had little respect for his injuries and felt the opposite. I felt he lacked courage and regularly sought ways to collect pay without working.

There were other reasons to have low regard for Jack. I was riding with him one snowy evening. He parked in the bank parking lot opposite the IGA (International Grocers Association) store one snowy night. It was just before it closed at ten o'clock in the evening. He took out some binoculars and was looking into the storefront. I grew uncomfortable and asked what he was looking at. He said that he had some intel that this store was going to be robbed. His intel had never produced any results, so I was not concerned. I also felt that he didn't have any intel. He was just trying to impress me. I was just very uncomfortable sitting next to this guy with binoculars.

The store finally closed, and the employees started coming out. I thought Jack would drive away at this point, but his observations seemed to be more intense. Suddenly, he put down the binoculars, put the car in drive, and zoomed into the IGA parking lot. He drove directly to the front, something that one never does if there is a possibility of a robber with a gun. This put me on an alert. I asked, "What did you see?" He did not reply but just maneuvered the car to the store entrance, then around to the side where the employees were parked. This area was not plowed, and there was about six inches of snow on it. I cautioned him not to get stuck and suggested that we get out to check what he wanted. Again, he ignored me.

Jack drove up to a young woman who was brushing snow off her car. He rolled his window down and started speaking to her. It very quickly became obvious to me that he was hitting on her, trying to impress her with the police car. Now I was thoroughly embarrassed and tried to melt into the seat. He was stalking her this whole time, with me beside him.

Jack was interested in martial arts weapons. He even spoke about being interested in ninja tactics. Oddly, we were aware of several prowler complaints in the surrounding small towns. They described someone dressed in a black ninja outfit.

Boo-boo had another obsession that was frustrating to many of us. He was a sort of an anti-Cupid, but it seemed more like a perverted addiction to me. On Friday and Saturday nights, at the beginning of the midnight shift, he went immediately to the outer areas of the city. These are busy nights with many calls in the center of town. The problem grew in my awareness when every time we needed to concentrate forces for a call with violence, he was always "travel time from" one of these outer areas.

What Boo-boo was doing is seeking out the people having back-seat sex in these private areas. Naturally, we would come across these now and then while routinely patrolling. The only concern was to assure that the encounter was mutually consenting and of legal age. Once this is established, we usually backed off and let them continue. Boo-boo energetically sought them and intruded completely. When he was finally and repeatedly confronted on this, he only stopped calling in these encounters. It only worsened the problem because he turned off his portable radio as he sneaked up on them so he didn't hear the calls to which he needed to respond.

We thought that Jack was able to survive in the department because he spent a lot of time hanging out with the administration. It must have paid off because he was promoted. He was still there after I left. I heard later that he returned to a security job in Massachusetts.

Suspended

I first met Joey when he was eleven years old. I served a juvenile petition on him for being a runaway. I was confused as I found him with his mother, Charlene. They were at home in their lower-class apartment. He was small for his age, standing tightly against his mother's side. He had dark brown hair and eyes. His eyes were wide open; his expression was blank. He alternated his gaze between his mother and me.

I explained to his mother that I had a petition for Joey being a runaway youth. I expressed my bewilderment as I had been involved with many runaways and never found them with their parent. She explained that Joey was supposed to be living with his father. His father was such a jerk that Joey often couldn't take it anymore and would come to her. His father was fully aware of Joey's location.

Though it sounded like a civil parenting matter to me, I did my duty and served the juvenile petition on Charlene.

A few minutes later, the dispatcher sent me to Joey's father's home. Reginald wanted to ask about the serving of the juvenile petition. Veronica, Reginald's mother, met me at the door of their well-kept mobile home. She led me down the long hallway to the bedroom on the end. Reggie was sitting in bed, propped up by pillows. It's obvious that he was significantly paralyzed. He had only limited motion in his neck and right arm. The fingers of this hand were mostly fixed and flexed awkwardly. Reggie invited me to sit in a nearby wooden chair. Normally, I don't sit when speaking with people in their home. Since I towered over Reggie, I thought it would be better to compromise so we could speak at equal eye levels.

Reggie wanted confirmation that the petition was served, which I did. He was the official petitioner, though he could not sign his name. He barely could make an X on a document that another person moved to assist in signing. He asked for the court date. Since he required an ambulance to move him to court, he would not be attending until the adjudicatory hearing. He retained a lawyer, Andrew Hudson, who would handle most of the details.

It was legally none of my concern, but Reggie felt compelled to explain to me. He broke his neck while on vacation with his brother, Randy. They jumped off a pier. Reggie broke his neck when he hit the ocean floor. Randy and others saved his life. He sued the hotel that owned the pier because they did not post the low-tide schedule. He was awarded four hundred thousand dollars, his possible earnings for the remainder of his life. With the money, he bought this mobile home, a sports car, and an apartment building. He decided that Charlene wasn't properly supervising Joey and filed for full custody. They settled with Reggie being the primary custodian with visits to Charlene.

Reggie went on to describe Joey as a very defiant child, prone to temper tantrums. He predicted that he would soon end up in the Youth Development Center (YDC), the state's juvenile detention center. Reggie and Randy both went there as teenagers. Their crimes were vandalism and burglaries. Joey needed to go there too. Later, they both went to the New Hampshire State Prison for burglaries and forgery.

I told Reggie that I have hope that Joey could avoid this path and perhaps the court can find some interventions. I felt that I should return to patrol and left. I heard nothing about the outcome from court. I met Joey again later that summer. When I found Joey and his cousin, Jerry, walking along a sidewalk, carrying rakes, they were knocking on doors, offering to rake lawns for ten dollars. They were proud to be earning money and that people were glad to hire them. They were still in that young and cute phase. Joey particularly had a broad and engaging smile. He told me that he still lives with his father but spends many overnights with his mother.

It wasn't much longer and Joey was reported a runaway again by his father. I went to his mother's apartment and learned that she had moved. The new occupants explained to me how to find her. I was a little frustrated that they couldn't give a precise address. They described the street and the building well enough so that I found it.

Joey wasn't with his mother either. She hadn't seen him for several days. She said that he sometimes stays at Arthur's apartment. Again, she couldn't give me a precise address but described it well enough for me to find it. I found Joey there and brought him to his father, with whom I spoke. Reggie reiterated his point from our first conversation. Joey needed to go the YDC, and the juvenile officer wasn't doing his job.

This went on for several months. I would learn during the shift-change briefing that Joey was a runaway again. It was a low priority since it was so common and never was Joey in any real danger. As time permitted, I knocked on doors and got some suggestions, but there were still no concrete addresses. I learned a lot about Joey's world and developed a knack for finding him.

Now fourteen years old, Joey considered himself equal to the adults in his world. We talked about his rationale for his behavior. He was correct in that he was able to make better decisions that the adults around him, but they were still flawed decisions. Joey and his cousin Jerry were quite adept at survival in their world. They were welcome in several places. They could find someone willing to share food and a place to sleep most of the time. They also found someone willing to share marijuana with them.

One afternoon, I was called from patrol to meet the juvenile officer in front of the police station. I announced when I was there. Sergeant Darby James walked out with Joey. He placed Joey in the back seat, and he got in the front. He told me that we were transporting Joey to the residential group home in Claremont. Joey was silent, looking down toward the floor of the car and occasionally glancing up at Damien. I knew Joey well enough to understand how much he hated Damien.

Damien was a small man. He came to Claremont from a department on the more populated side of the state. He started as a sergeant, supervising the night shift. He made it clear that he did not like working the night shift and spent most nights in the sergeants' office. He eventually became the juvenile officer, a day job.

I rarely saw him out of his office. I found him to be very inconsistent in performing his duties. Many cases worthy of prosecution were ignored. Other minor things that could have easily been resolved with a little diversion went to court.

We brought Joey into the building where he was met by the staff member on duty. I listened as she described the rules. I read Joey's defiant body language. Damien and I left. Once in the police car, I said to Damien that Joey wouldn't stay there. I knew he was too experienced at surviving on the street. Damien replied, "Good; then I can lock him up."

This comment deeply disturbed me. I remembered Reggie's desire to have his son locked up, like he was at this age. It seemed that Damien was being manipulated by Reggie. Damien also seemed to have a personal score to settle against Joey. Joey didn't show the respect he demanded. Joey had learned not to trust adults, but Damien didn't understand how to gain trust from adolescents.

I too had little respect for Damien. I had numerous reasons not to respect him, but wise enough not to show it. Damien had a GED (General Equivalency Diploma). He did not graduate from high school and had no other formal education. He knew nothing about child development. I had a master's degree. He never served in the military. I had been a captain in the artillery, a highly demanding job supervising ninety soldiers. If you carefully listen to someone as they describe their credentials, it's possible to learn more than what is spoken. If their only credentials are the years of experience and various impossible-to-fail certifications from only their professional assignment, I value their credentials very narrow in the scope of our complex society. For instance, Damien was "certified" in conflict resolution. He completed a five-hour "training" in Massachusetts taught by "certified trainers." I had graduate credits in conflict resolution—a forty-hour course taught by someone with a doctoral degree in personnel management and who was a professional arbitrator. Those supervisors with certification in an area where I had extensive education quickly dismissed my education and experience as not being certified. This is a major reason why it is so hard to challenge police authority. That certification is a significant barrier to professional progress in their respective institutions. They emphatically exclude any other qualifying education.

Three days after we dropped off Joey at the group home, he was reported missing. I learned about it during my morning shift-change briefing. I went on patrol at eight o'clock in the morning. I knew that it wasn't a good time to be knocking on doors looking for Joey. If anyone answered, they would be less likely to cooperate. I started looking at ten o'clock in the morning. I found him within twenty minutes. I radioed to dispatch that I had the missing juvenile. Damien came on the radio and told me to bring him directly to court.

Joey described how he hated the group home. I understood how he had a great deal of difficulty following instructions from adults. Adults in his life were inconsistent and often unreliable. I interpreted Joey's explanation of his actions based on my knowledge of him and the group home staff.

Joey was a regular marijuana user. There was a lot of denial about its addictive properties. I could usually convince people of the emotional dependence, though most denied physical dependence. I suspected Joey very much needed some marijuana from having gone a period without it and particularly to alleviate the stresses in the group home. He left the group home at three o'clock in the afternoon with a two-hour pass. He didn't return until after six o'clock in the evening. Dinner was completed, and he was not allowed to have dinner. They offered him Skittles to alleviate his hunger. Joey was suffering from his marijuana munchies, and Skittles would not suffice, so he left. He could find more substantial nourishment from his contacts.

We waited outside the court until our case was called. Judge Stone was seated at the bench as we came in. Joey was directed to the defendant's table. The judge had recruited a public defender from a previous hearing. Neither of Joey's parents were present. She listened to Damien recount how Joey was an uncontrollable child. The New Hampshire Division for Children and Youth Services social worker gave her brief history. Damien reported that the group home was not willing to accept Joey back. So this was an emergency placement hearing. Damien recommend ACD (Awaiting Court Disposition), a secure facility that is a branch of YDC where kids awaited adjudication by the court.

The judge was obviously troubled by the recommendation of a secure facility. Joey had not been charged with any violent crimes and presented no danger to anyone but himself. She asked an open question to everyone in the court, "Is there anyone willing to accept this child?" She gazed around the room and stopped, looking directly at me. All the others in the courtroom were social workers, police, and lawyers. None would even consider taking a child. As Judge Stone looked directly at me, I agreed to take him. She looked at the DCYS worker and asked if this was possible. The social worker supervisor agreed that they could issue an emergency foster care license to me. The judge placed Joey with me.

I brought Joey to an office downstairs. I called my wife and told her what had happened. She agreed, and I brought Joey home. I showed to him the spare bedroom and left him to get acquainted with Kay while I finished my shift.

Joey taught us a lot about how to parent difficult children. We also learned about stigmas and expectations from community members. Joey is in a good home now, so his behaviors should be immediately corrected. The assumption is that, if his behaviors didn't improve, we must be bad parents. Indeed, his behaviors seemed to worsen as we pressed greater structure and accountability. The difference was that we were much better at supervising and reporting his behaviors.

Lieutenant Perry Allen caught me on my way into work one day and brought me into his office. He made it perfectly clear that he did not approve of me taking Joey in as a foster child. He knew that he could not order me to not do it, but he insinuated that my job could be affected. Perry supervised the juvenile officer but not me. I told him that I would not give up on Joey. He wasn't happy. I went to the shift-change briefing.

Joey brought friends with marijuana into our home. He felt that we had marijuana too. From his perspective, everyone used it. He searched everywhere in our home when we weren't home. He never found any marijuana because there was none. He did find the hidden spare car keys. He decided to take the car from the hospital parking lot while Kay was working. He waited until I got off duty. He didn't count on my relief taking advantage of Burger King's 50 percent discount to police, where my relief drove up behind him in the drive-through. We brought all these charges in a juvenile petition.

While this case was proceeding through the court system, Joey's aunt Beverly, cousin Jerry's mother, specifically requested me to come to her home. When I got there, she reported that her gun was stolen. I took the information for the report. She showed me the padlock on her bedroom door. She didn't allow her two sons to go in there. I could see that the bracket screws could be easily removed and replaced with a screwdriver. She blamed Joey. I immediately told her that I had to refer this case to another officer. She didn't want to make an official report. She wanted me to get her gun back. I told her that I could not be involved with this report. I returned to the station and dispatched the patrol officer for that beat.

The officer described the gun as a .25-caliber gun. It's one that is small enough to fit in the palm of an adult's hand. Joey was listed as the primary suspect in the report. I felt that Jerry was likely the leader on this but had no doubt that Joey was a participant. Most of their mischief was together or Jerry with his younger brother.

After about a week, just as I was leaving for the day, eighteen-year-old James walked into the police lobby and asked specifically for me. I knew James distantly as one who knew Joey. I never spoke directly with him. As I approached him in the lobby, he reached into his pocket, removed something wrapped in a bandana, and handed it to me. He said, "It's a gun." I carefully unwrapped it and saw that it was a .25-caliber handgun. James went on to explain that he had learned that it was stolen. He said that he got it from Liam, who got it from Jerry.

I had the worst luck for trying to remain out of this case. I couldn't undo the gun being in my possession now. I tagged it as evidence and locked it in the evidence locker. I decided to write the report the next day and went home.

When I put my jacket on to go to work the next day, I checked my pockets as I usually do when putting on a jacket. I found the bandana in my pocket. It was a minor "oh shit" moment. I felt that the chain of custody was intact, and I could account for its authenticity. When I got to work, I placed it in an evidence bag, labeled it accurately, then proceeded with writing my report. I documented all the events accurately, including having the bandana overnight.

I continued with my usual cases that I was working on. I was a bit puzzled when Sergeant Walt Bean asked me, "What's happening with Beverly's stolen gun case?" I told him that I was not working on the case. I explained that Dotty was trying to blame Joey when it was her own son Jerry who likely stole it. With Joey being accused, I had to stay out of the case. He just said, "OK, just wondering."

I had two days off. When I returned to work, Walt asked me to come with him to the chief's office. When I entered, I saw the chief at his desk and the detective supervisor, Perry Allen, sitting in a chair. The chief told me that I was suspended pending an investigation. He told me to surrender my badge and gun. He said that it was with pay and that he would let me know within two weeks.

Of course, this bothered me. I was certain that it was about this gun case. Not being one to sit around, I made myself more available to do substitute teaching. After three weeks passed, the chief's secretary called to tell me that I was now suspended without pay pending dismissal. Only the police commission had the authority to hire and fire, which would happen at their next meeting. I went to a lawyer, and we demanded a public hearing before the police commission.

My lawyer was given a date for me to report for a lie detector test. I never believed in lie detector tests, knowing human psychology and physiology too well. I also felt that the "certified" operator was similar inadequate like other police certifications. I had seen criminals who I felt were guilty pass these tests, even to the criminal's surprise. Nonetheless, it would be grounds to fire me if I didn't submit. I took the test at the Keene State Police Barracks. The examiner concluded that I was truthful.

The police administrators were not happy with the results and demanded another test. It was in Concord. That examiner concluded that I was being deceptive.

Four months had passed. When they moved to fire me, I demanded a public hearing before the commission. I alerted the press. I knew that I had nothing to hide but didn't trust the chief or Perry. The public's presence would keep them more accountable. Because so many people showed up for the public hearing, it was held in the courtroom. The regular meeting room wasn't large enough.

Perry Allen, Chief of Detectives, presented their case. Perry had a high school diploma, but you wouldn't know it if you ever read a report that he wrote, which he rarely did. One of his reports was once circulated for us to see. It was about three sentences long. Every third word was misspelled, and often, it was the wrong word, a homonym. Most particularly were the "there" and "their" errors. After reading the report, I still didn't understand what he was trying to record. If you listened to his flamboyant speech, he spoke the same way. He was just so animated and flamboyant that the average listener is impressed with the presentation of his speech and doesn't notice the misused words. He lacked content, real meaning.

The hearing progressed through two days. From my perspective, it was a show that gave me a unique perspective on how they treated everyone they investigated. My lawyer was very aware of their techniques. He condescendingly referred to them as the Claremont Police Department Brain Truss. It seemed sad to me. Only the chief had education beyond high school. It was from a college that failed to gain accreditation, survived barely due to the GI Bill, and went defunct. It was in sharp contrast to my attorney's and my education from well-established, very reputable colleges.

Perry presented my reports: the first call, receiving the gun, the delayed report, and placing the bandana into evidence. He implied that I had a motive in delaying the bandana because it implicated Joey. He offered nothing as to how he made this determination. I never saw Joey with any bandana and certainly not with this one. Perry never made a link beyond this unqualified suggestion.

A star witness for the offense was Beverly, the gun owner and Joey's aunt. She said that Joey took it, and Jerry was a follower. She said that they brought the gun to my house and fired it in the backyard. They had her describe my kitchen. There's a cabinet between the refrigerator and stove that had every drug imaginable in it. All the way to the left, the cupboard had large bags filled with cocaine.

I whispered to my attorney that she had never been to my house. The cabinet between the refrigerator and stove had Tylenol, Motrin, aspirin, cough drops, and similar medicine. The place described as containing cocaine held confectioners' sugar. He told me that he wanted to allow this testimony because it would destroy her credibility and theirs.

When Perry rested with this witness, my lawyer simply asked her whether she had ever been to my house. He asked how she knew about the drugs. She said that she learned it from several sources. She heard it from her son, the one who stole her gun.

I wondered why, if they thought Beverly had this much credibility, they hadn't sought a search warrant. If they had, they would have found these legal substances and I would have taken them to task. I would hold them legally, civilly, and publicly accountable.

They called another witness, a sixteen-year-old girl, who I barely knew as a high school student. She knew Joey but never spent time with him. Perry asked her to explain the conversation that I had with her regarding Joey and the stolen gun. She replied that she did not have any conversation with me. Right away, I knew this was the classic witness telling them what they wanted to hear at the time. Perry continued, "Didn't Mr. Sanborn tell you that you would regret reporting Joey had the gun?" She replied no. Perry again pressed her, "Didn't you tell Sergeant James that Mr. Sanborn said that you would regret it if you told anyone Joey had the gun?" She replied, "He never told me that. He only loves Joey as a son." There were whispers and shuffling throughout the courtroom. It was obvious to me that she was like many witnesses seeking favorable consideration from police. Once sworn to tell the truth and to face the person whom they were accusing, people will more likely tell the truth. It was a major setback for the brain truss.

They presented only the Concord lie detector examiner. Somehow, calling it a polygraph added more credibility to it. He spoke about a single anomaly in his charts. He pointed to the chart where I held my breath. He said, "We call this holding and hoping." I thought to myself, *Hoping for what? That you would learn some psychology?* I thought maybe he could plug his fancy polygraph apparatus into a Ouija board and get the answer. When asked in cross-examination, "Holding for what?" He said, "Hoping for the question to go away." He successfully dodged any questioning because his certification was unquestionable. I was hoping that you would get enough education to realize your hocus-pocus is no better than card reading. We science people call it pseudoscience.

We tried to counter with a psychologist's testimony that perfectionists, such as me, often hold their breath to focus and search memory. The prosecuting brain truss energetically resisted. The therapist had no certification in lie detection. She was excluded.

This technique of automatically holding my breath while focusing is what has allowed me to be a highly skilled marksman. I often catch myself holding my breath when I run as I try to listen to traffic. Without looking, I can usually identify the type of vehicle, how many, and whether they are accelerating behind me. Holding my breath while running can affect my running performance if I don't notice it in time. I often hold my breath whenever I intensely focus on something. I challenge anyone to do this simple thing. Hold your fingers in your ears. Now hear your breathing. Breathe a few cycles.

Isn't this a lot of noise? That noise is there even when your fingers are not in your ears. Your brain filters them out. When I hold my breath, I temporarily quiet this distraction so my brain can process better on what I am intently engaged. It's embedded in my personality and has nothing to do with whether I am telling the truth. I am carefully listening to the examiner's potentially tricky questions, many with double negatives. I would like to add that I also closed my eyes. I do this for the same reason, to remove distractions from the tester, my attorney, and the shadows behind your one-may mirror. I would like to know what line in your polygraph shows that and how you interpret it? Perhaps you would say that I was closing and hoping you would disappear. I have firsthand experience that people like this examiner with narrow self-fulfilling views of their world are not well educated and use their simple certifications to discredit quality education. Sadly, they are most often successful in flexing the authority entrusted to them. My ethics would not allow me to be a lie detector operator, even if you call it a polygraph.

The brain truss put Walter Bean on the stand. Perry asked him about the conversation he had with me about Joey's innocence. Perry asked him for a direct quote of what I said. Since he couldn't remember it verbatim, Perry handed to him a copy of his report and asked him to read it. Walt questioned whether he wanted him to read it as it was written. Perry said yes. Walt said OK, then read, "Officer Sanborn said that Beverly is trying to frame Joey. Jerry took the gun. He said that he has to stay out of the investigation."

There was an immediate hush throughout the courtroom. The city attorney stood up and faced the audience. He said that they must not repeat what they just heard. What was read was accusing a juvenile of a crime, which is a crime if made public. He specifically told the newspaper reporter not to publish the names. To make these names and crimes public is a misdemeanor.

What was being overlooked is that the brain truss just committed a crime. I did not. Under Perry's direct order, Walt made these names and accusations public. The public is defined as any person who does have a right to the information. They just committed a misdemeanor subject to fines and even jail time. I committed no crimes and acted ethically, yet they just committed a crime by disclosing the delinquency of a minor.

Terribly embarrassed, Perry told Walt that he could step down. He called Joey's sixteen-year-old cousin Jerry to the stand. I was expecting Jerry to lie and say Joey stole the gun. Instead, I heard the stunning truth. When Perry asked Jerry if Joey stole the gun, Jerry replied, "No, I took the gun." Again, there was an audible gasp in unison across the courtroom. The city attorney stood up again and reminded the crowd that they must not make this information public.

The prosecution rested. The brain truss objected to the psychologist who could present qualified testimony countering the lie detector examiner. My lawyer explained to the commission that I could not testify to much of the juvenile information now publicly exposed. He referred to the accuracy of my reports and the prosecution's inability to establish any wrongdoing with them. He also explained that I handled the evidence in accordance with department police and legal chain of custody requirements.

The commission recessed very briefly and returned for a vote. Two voted in my favor. The one who voted against me bought Perry Allen's family business. I can't help wonder about that. I still wonder about how Perry and Darby questioned my ethics with no real evidence. Both took every advantage of their police employment they could. For example, they took a rent reduction from their landlord who wanted to encourage police officers to live in the complex to make it more secure. Rumors were that Damien regularly brought his kids to Burger King and flashed his badge to get half price. I also caught Damien's son with a stolen racing helmet and never brought any charges. Perry ran his personal errands with the unmarked police car and during his normal working hours.

I returned to work with several thousands of dollars in back pay. Most fellow officers avoided contact with me. They should have listened to the hearing to learn about how foolish, incompetent, and vindictive their leaders are. A position soon opened in the public works department to monitor industrial compliance. It paid considerably more and was a good use of my education. It was a good transfer for me.

CHAPTER 12

Professionalism

Professionalism Defined

We often hear police say that they will investigate with utmost professionalism. They seem to stress this most as they speak about complaints about themselves, peers, their department actions, or a brother agency. But just what does professionalism mean and why do we hear such promises mostly from police?

Simply defined, a profession is an organization whose members have special skills for which someone gets paid. It's very possible for someone to have the same skills or even greater and not be a professional because she or he doesn't get paid. We call them amateurs. The insinuation is that amateurs are not as skilled as the professional, which isn't necessarily the case. Sports are a perfect example of this. Sports are divided into amateur and professional categories with highly skilled people in both. Amateur sports have a code of standards that makes payments or favors for amateur athletes unethical. Some professions take many years to achieve the knowledge and skills required, such as a specialized surgeon. Some take only a few hours, such as a grocery clerk. Some have high ethical standards, such as lawyers. Others have vague and ambiguous standards, such as telephone solicitors.

Each profession has a hierarchy based on the knowledge and experience. When it is necessary for a professional to recite her or his credentials, I listen more for specialized education and types of experience. When the credentials are mostly the length of time in service, I value it less. Especially in police work, I have realized that to have longevity, one must avoid controversy. As one of my mentors said, "The more you do, the more likely you'll get in trouble." Though I liked and respected him very much, I felt sad that he felt this way. I felt an obligation to earn my salary.

Police seem to speak their own language or jargon. When I question it, I am abruptly told that it is professional and objective. Police are not alone in writing in the third person. I have seen science people use the third person for the same reason. However, I went to a good college and learned that it can have the opposite effect. "I" statements show more credibility by identifying ownership of my observations and actions. What is the advantage to writing "the writer" or "this officer" in the third person? It confuses the reader who must make the connection of the third-person identity to the author of the report. First-person writing clearly identifies the actor. Even worse is when someone writes with no person identified. An example could be "Then pepper spray was applied." In this case, who applied the pepper spray is in doubt. It is not professional and possibly deceptive. Third-person writings hurt credibility.

Similarly, identifying others as "perpetrator," "victim," or "witness" also erode credibility. When a reader must struggle or even guess the identity of these individuals, much is distracted from the quality of the writing. Each of these roles can be assigned to named individuals. A lengthy report could have a list of individuals involved. It can also have a list of dates and addresses if the report extends over a long time. It's best to use simple, direct language with the first person and names and without police jargon intended to impress or somehow elevate credibility in writings and testimony. I have seen reports when the victim is also one of the witnesses. This makes the report extremely complicated and confusing.

As a professional achieves experience, he or she usually rises in the hierarchy. One thing police officers with rank don't realize is that their rank is unimportant to most citizens. They don't care if you are a corporal, sergeant, etc. They see a cop. The shopkeeper and the person hanging on the street see no relevance in what is on the cop's sleeve or collar; they expect all to respond the same. They also don't care whether you are on or off duty or in uniform or not if they recognize that you are a police officer.

Every profession has a measurable set of knowledge and skills. It has specific requirements to be admitted to the profession. There is also a continuing education requirement. It also has a means to expel members who violate these professional standards.

Some professions require many years of education, skill building, internships, and rigorous testing and board approval. Other professions require very little education and easily met standards. An example of a profession with high standards is teaching. Most teachers have bachelor's degrees. Many have master's degrees. Teachers must complete a semester of internship in each of the certification areas. Police have relatively very low standards. Often, only a high school equivalency, some on the job training, then eventually a few weeks at the academy. Within three days of being hired, I was assigned a patrol assignment. I did this for four months until there was an opening at the police academy. Contrast this with nearly a year of training in the army before I was assigned to my first unit. I spent two months in basic training, four months in officer candidate school, and almost six months of artillery officer training. Especially compared to my college education, none of this police or army training was academically challenging.

Plato wrote about the difference between actors and artisans around 400 BC. He wrote in ancient Greek, and his analogies were more applicable to his era, but still relevant today. Plato described an actor. He could stand and move about before his audience and describe the actions, skills, and feelings of the chariot driver in battle even though he had never driven a chariot. The actor probably never even road in one nor witnessed its use on the battlefield. However, he could command the attention and awe of his audience. The chariot operator is the artist. He is the one that can operate the chariot in battle but probably could not impress an audience like the actor can. Plato's artist is a skilled professional.

I think about Plato's definitions sometimes when I listen to people when they speak about how great they are about doing their job.

I question whether they are truly as skillful as Plato's artist or are they a Platonian actor. I have worked with several professionals especially with municipal construction projects. We engaged civil, mechanical, hydraulic, and chemical engineers. We had surveyors and architects. We worked with grant writers, grant regulators, lawyers, and federal and state environmental regulators. We worked with property owners and politicians. Lastly, we worked with bonding agencies and payments scheduling. To manage all these experts, I have two science degrees and one in management. In my experience with police, I found great reluctance to engage outside expertise except in extreme cases, such as medical examiners in a homicide. I have never seen any police officer of any rank with a master's level degree in management. Police are more like Plato's actors than his artists when working outside the motor vehicle and criminal codes. Sadly, many believe they have expert knowledge in child development, parenting, domestic relationships, animal behavior, etc. Even worse, they usually dismiss the expertise others may have that is greater than theirs and rely on a two-hour class they had at the police academy.

Professionalism refers to a set of standards and practices in a profession. It is assumed that it includes ethical standards. When a spokesperson assures that an investigation within the profession will be conducted with professionalism, it doesn't give me much assurance. I not only saw firsthand how police cover for one another and even retaliate against other officers who do not. We hear that criminals don't "rat" on one another. Many cops have this same doctrine. I have worked with a criminal in jail who insists, "I am not a rat," as he or she refuses to cooperate with an investigation. I reply, "You're here because someone ratted on you." The criminal adheres to the brotherhood to take care of the errant informant. Some police do too. I shared several of these actions directed against me in this book. If leaders in this profession wish for a thorough and fair investigation, it should be done in whole by outside experts with no connection to the organization being investigated. It cannot be a "brother" agency.

When police refer to their professionalism, they imply that there are ethical standards. Ethical standards describe values of honesty, fairness, duty, and behavioral expectations. Each police organization develops their own set of standards in writing and/or in practice. Daily actions may or may not be consistent with written standards when they exist. Regardless, I challenge every member of every police organization to independently write the standards of practice in their organization, compare it with one another, then apply it to specific events. I guarantee numerous inconsistencies. With such inconsistencies, how do you expect to establish that high standards of professionalism when you cannot identify it?

The first consideration in identifying the ethical standards of a profession such as law enforcement is that one must accept that we are all humans. Humans have faults. Our faults can grow unchecked when power is concentrated and secrecy is allowed.

People also tend to behave as they are expected. Every organization grooms its newest members to perform in a certain manner. I remember what dominated my initial police days. I was expected to back up my fellow officer without hesitation. As time went on, I found officers with values that conflicted with mine. I would still back them up. I also felt the "no rat" expectation, so I seldom voluntarily reported injustices. When I finally rejected conformity and followed my own ethical standards, I was rejected. This was wrong. Why does it persist?

Knowing that we try to behave as expected, we need to identify expectations. Police work for a governing agency is subjected to changing leadership and funding. The common denominator that must drive police behavior is consistent service to the public—whether the individuals we serve are involved in politics or have money or social status. Everyone must be treated the same, fairly.

An organization must have a mission and a code of ethics. Communicating these values and everyday information is always a challenge in any organization. Communication only flows when people feel that they can share information and ask questions without retaliation. A good leader facilitates communication. She or he monitors communication to check its accuracy. A good leader also doesn't accept credit for things that go well, giving that credit to subordinates. He or she also accepts responsibility for what doesn't go so well and seeks systemic solutions. Individual blame is reserved for those who intentionally and purposefully violate ethics, rules, or standards for his or her own benefit or desire to retaliate.

So when you hear a police officer say that they will be acting with professionalism as they handle your incident, ask for the written standards to which they are acting. Ask if anyone outside the organization is overseeing the investigation. If they are unable to provide these, I suggest that you seek outside counsel.

A profession has a skill set, standards, and ongoing assessment of itself and its members. In keeping these requirements, there are gatekeepers who determine a person's entrance into the profession. For the police, this is often a panel of interviewers often called a board. People on this board are selected to assess recruits' ability to meet the standards of the profession. Members of the board represent past police skills of the organization to which they determine admission. They wish to maintain the status quo of the organization. They do not necessarily have expertise in human resources and organizational development. Hiring board members may see someone who might advance the profession as a threat, personally or organizationally. Most of these in my department had difficulty earning their high school diploma or had only an equivalency. College-educated people were rare in the police profession. Diversity in education is an organization's strength but is most often rejected within police applicants.

Similarly, the specialties within the department are guided this way. There is much value on seniority and less value on education. For instance, when an opportunity arose to attend a crisis negotiation training, I was rejected because I had less seniority than the one with the GED. It didn't matter that I had a master's degree with coursework in conflict resolution. I remember the rejection of my education. It wasn't relevant to law enforcement. My education was readily discounted by a ranking administrator with no college education. My forty hours of coursework and research was valued less than the five-hour training conducted by law enforcement people who were "certified" to do the training.

I was surprised and pleased to be selected for the two-week accident investigation training. I think it is only because it relied heavily on math skills that only I had. I learned many valuable techniques, but I also became deeply disappointed in how the instructors relied so heavily on their learning and could not accept any weakness in it. It frustrated me that they wouldn't even consider any higher level of physics.

In the two-week accident investigation class, one of my rejected questions involved the temperature of the pavement. They taught friction coefficients for skid marks and how to determine them but did not consider the different pavement at night and that heated by the sun. I pointed out how I can twist a marking into hot pavement with the toe of my boot but not at night. "It doesn't matter" was my response. I knew full well that it did, so in my investigations when skid marks were important, I always determined the coefficient of friction during similar conditions as the accident.

Another point that bothered me is that accident instruction readily accepted that motorcycles do not stop as well as cars, yet they refused to accept the difference in how a Corvette turns compared to a van. I asked, "Why do they build a Corvette wide and low?" I also asked about a car that came up on two wheels. My subsequent concern was that a vehicle with a high center of gravity would shift weight onto two wheels much like a motorcycle. The "certified instructor" angrily replied, "It doesn't make any difference." The response was obvious that I needed to be quiet, or they would report me to my chief.

I questioned the charts of the varying coefficients of friction with speed. The charts are bracketed from zero to thirty-five miles per hour, thirty-five to sixty miles per hour, and above sixty miles per hour. The coefficient of friction was less for the higher speeds. The instructors couldn't explain why. They said that a traffic investigator didn't need to know because the charts have been accepted by the state. That is all we needed to know. The reality is that friction is a force that opposes the energy of the fast-moving vehicle. Friction decreases exponentially with speed. The force is proportional to the square of the velocity. The charts were produced from a formula. The closer to the end of each range, the greater the margin of error. I used the original formula when I investigated serious accidents.

I always presented them with my calculations in my reports. I was never challenged in court while other investigators routinely had to defend their conclusions.

I was also much more versatile in determining speed from a collision. For instance, the speed of a car that drives directly into a telephone pole with no skid marks cannot be determined by these instructors. I could determine the speed by where a part such as a light lens first landed. Its velocity can be determined from the height from which it fell. I could determine the velocity for a car that vaulted from the road and how far it traveled before it hit the ground. I learned this in college, not from a certified accident instructor. I had credentials beyond most accident investigators. My reports were widely accepted by lawyers reviewing it. I was confident that any college physics professor would agree with my determinations. Had they presented it to any of my certified accident investigation instructors, they would have disqualified my report.

Traffic accident investigators primarily focus on collecting the evidence through techniques, including measurements, photographs, and interviews. It's important to collect all that is relevant or may be relevant to an analysis to be done later. I did respect this part very much as it was perfectly aligned with my science education. Different scientists can look at the same data and come to different conclusions based on their knowledge and experiences. It only bothered me that most evaluators don't understand their limitations on their ability to analyze data.

Another area that I appreciated was that as a radar instructor. We are taught that meaning of the acronym, radio detection and ranging. We were also taught that it operates on the Doppler principle, but we didn't need to understand it. We were also taught about how it measures only that portion of a car's speed that approaches us. Unless it travels directly at us or away, we only get a portion of the speed. It's called the "cosine effect." Police are firmly told that they do not need to understand this either. It seemed like they didn't understand either and were intimidated by a term intended to impress and intimidate others. They taught us to never allow an attorney to question these.

The gatekeepers, the board members selecting recruits, had no idea how well I understood these concepts and could explain them. I wondered why accident investigators used the cosine effect exclusively when I have never met a fellow police officer who had the most remote idea what cosine meant. I always believed that a simple explanation of vectors and the construction of a triangle can be easily understood and explained. Maybe I am wrong to assume gatekeepers can learn these math and simple physics concepts.

Police call it a polygraph. Somehow this makes it seem more scientific than calling it a lie detector. It, of course, requires certification to be qualified to operate it. I have watched it used on a criminal that I felt certain was guilty, but the polygraph expert determined he was truthful. My case went to a dead end and was never solved. I am sure it was because he was guilty that we could never find another culprit. He managed to pass the lie detector test because he took a sedative, but that was never proven.

I have always considered polygraphs as hocus-pocus or smoke and mirrors. More academically, I call it pseudoscience. "Pseudo" is Greek meaning "false." The best that it could prove was that a certain question stimulated a physiological response. What stimulated a physiological response is the problem within entire concept in the line of questioning. My burglar managed to sedate his physiology, or he is a sociopath without guilt. Either or both can defeat the examiner. No one truly knows who is truthful other than the one who answers the question.

When you sign on as a police officer, the policy is that you will take a polygraph if required. It is a condition of your employment. Refusal meant dismissal. I was ordered to take one. When I was found truthful, I was ordered to take another with a different examiner. He found that I was deceptive. I still cannot believe his presentation. He pointed to a tracing of the polygraph, the lines monitoring my pulse, skin conductivity, and breathing. All was normal except on one question that affected my breath rate. He said, "We call this holding and hoping," explaining it meant that I was deceptive. He had no idea that I commonly hold my breath when I focus intensely. I'll also close my eyes when listening intently. The questions were tricky double negatives and obviously meant to trick me into a desired answer.

Polygraphs are not allowed by law in many situations, except law enforcement on themselves. How strange. Someone with a GED and a little training on a device can be held in higher regard than professionals such as psychologists, psychiatrist, doctors, therapists, physiologists, and anyone with a real education outside the law enforcement "profession."

I have worked in and with many professions. I must say that the police profession has the lowest standards. It requires little education for entry; its certifications are easily attained in a short period of time. It discounts professions with higher standards and uses terms it doesn't require its members to understand to add credibility to their certifications. I have graduated from three colleges and have three degrees. Each time, I found the open intellectualism refreshing. Police seem to keep the door closed to such broader conceptual ideas.

A competent professional welcomes questions and challenges. Questions help me demonstrate how well I understand the topic and can do my job. If the question cannot be fully answered, it shows me an opportunity to seek the answer and possibly strengthen my professionalism. Take notice how an officer cites court case decisions so that he doesn't need to know the friction formula used to determine speed or how the cosine effect applies.

Truth

Especially since I am a science person, I describe our natural human desire to make sense of our crazy world as a lifelong endeavor. Science has a process of asking a question, developing a hypothesis, working out a possible solution, coming up with a repeatable testing procedure, collecting measurable and verifiable data, and comparing data to the original hypothesis, perhaps answering the question or asking new questions. The ultimate result is to answer the question by gaining a body of collective knowledge. A very key component to this process is that it is universal and all data is measurable and verifiable. If we repeat the procedure, we get the same result. If results vary, we troubleshoot the procedure.

The popular phrase "jumping to conclusions" is interestingly applicable to the science process. If we begin with a question, we develop a hypothesis, a possible answer to the question. If the process stops there, the hypothesis becomes the conclusion. The person jumped from hypothesis to conclusion with no testing and data collection. This happens a lot in everyday life. Someone thinks they "have it figured out," but they have not verified any data. Worse yet, they have no data to support their conclusion. It is illogical, absent of any logical process. A science person such as me recognizes this and issues the standard challenge, "Show me the data."

I like this science analogy. Truth is a solid. Lies are fluids. Sometimes we say "rock-solid." In science, it is quantifiable, measurable, factual, and does not change. At an accident scene, it is the measured distances of final vehicle positions and such things as vehicle final location and length of skid marks. Such competently collected data is solid. However, the event that got the vehicle to the final resting point can be open to different interpretations from differing viewpoints. Each viewer of data has their own biases based on previous experiences.

I have an interesting example of truth and education. It was an unremarkable arrest for shoplifting. The shopkeeper testified; then I testified to the arrest and subsequent search. I found in his pockets the merchandise identified by the shopkeeper. Then the shoplifter testified on his own, without a lawyer. He denied stealing the small tool that I found in its original packaging. He said that he had just bought it from a competing retailer. When he finished, the judge said, "I find your testimony to be incredible." The judge found him guilty and imposed a fine and a suspended sentence. As we left the courtroom, the shoplifter seemed unusually happy for someone to have lost a contested case. I heard him boast, "The judge said I was incredible." He was happy that the judge called him a liar. My thought was maybe, if he stayed in school longer, he might have learned that incredible is without credibility. The judge called him a liar, and he was so ignorant that he thought it was a compliment.

Statements, even written statements, may be the truth from the witness's honest account, but statements are observations. Science accepts observations that are verifiable and consistent with the measured data. Statements, or observations, that cannot be verified with measured data are less reliable. When viewed from differing perspectives and biases, statements become even less reliable. I was never comfortable bringing forward a case solely reliant upon witness testimony. I wanted some factual evidence to support witness statements.

Lies are fluids. Fluids flow. Fluids are gases and liquids. A liquid has a definite volume but takes the shape of the container. Gases have no definite shape or volume and take the shape and volume of the container. For whatever reason, we tend to rate lies. We even call some "white lies." White lies are supposed to be harmless. White lies are usually expected to be temporary, and the truth will eventually prevail. An example of a white lie might be about a birthday present, Santa Claus, or the tooth fairy. The white lie is exposed and disregarded with the presentation of the gift. I used to set a mousetrap to catch the tooth fairy. I showed the tripped trap to my daughter and later my grandchildren. I asked them to check and see if I caught the trespassing fairy. They closely examined the trap and assured me that I was unsuccessful again.

Lies of substance can also be classified as serious and less serious. Using my liquid example, the quantity remains constant, but its shape changes depending on the container, the circumstances, or location. A liquid lie can be brought back to its original container and appear to be the truth. Too great or many lies overflow the container. Gaseous lies are uncontainable once let out. It's nearly impossible to reconstruct them in the original container. Gaseous lies swell its container until it bursts; then they can no longer be contained. Very bad lies can be contained in a balloon. Balloons are easily blown away and soon pop or deflate.

Lastly, truth as solid as a rock is also not perfect. A rock can be broken. Rocks break along fault lines, the crystal's structure line. If there is a problem with the data, the crystal loses its integrity, and the rock breaks under pressure. Data collected based upon a lie will lack stability, like a boat on water. It moves with the waves and can be blown across the lake.

Honorable people seek the truth. Less than honorable people try to stabilize their boats. Truth on firm foundations maintains its credibility. Boats require a great deal of maintenance and eventually leak. A balloon will deflate quicker than a boat will sink.

In the army, we commissioned officers understood the importance of our personal integrity. It goes beyond telling the truth. It includes every part of our lives. We conduct ourselves with duty and respect. Never would we take advantage of someone. We are leaders who help people achieve their best. I cannot do my best unless those I lead do their best.

Our integrity included the knowledge and ability to perform our roles. We strived to constantly learn and practice skills to be our best. We also strived to remain at our best physical condition. All this fit well with my concept of being a police officer. I soon learned that other police officers did not share my concept of duty.

I worked with many police officers who relied only on their narrow police training. Rarely did any accept expert opinion. Even when they did, the legal definition of an expert is one who knows more than the average person. Most police officers by their training feel they know more than the average person in everything, even more than highly educated people in a specialized field. A former military police soldier who never attained any appreciable rank described his response to commissioned officers like me. His response was "Sir, you are confusing your rank with my authority." Army officers know full well the military police mission. We had to enforce nonjudicial punishment and serve in court-martial proceedings. The military police primary wartime mission is to handle prisoners of war. Their peacetime mission is not their primary mission. He was confusing my expertise with his mission.

A commissioned officer's personal integrity would never compromise her or his ability to function without influence. Never would we take any special favors even when there is no obvious advantage to the giver. We would not allow ourselves to be vulnerable for any reason at any time, present or future. I was very disappointed that I did not find the integrity I expected among police officers. Several took discounts in rent in exchange for the appearance of safety in the housing complex. Many took advantage of the half-price meals to uniformed officers at Burger King. At least one officer "flashed his badge" when he took his family there. Cumberland Farms provided free coffee to police officers. Both establishments liked appearing to be favorite places for police officers. They reaped the benefits of extra protection and promoted the idea that cops knew the best places to eat and get coffee. My personal integrity did not allow me to go to any of these places to conduct business, on or off duty.

My personal integrity extends into being physically fit to perform my duties. I heard many times, "I don't get paid well enough to…" followed by a task they didn't want to perform. If you accepted the position, you agreed to perform the job. If you think you can make more money doing something else, go for it. Most police officers will not be able to find a better job with their skills.

One of the things that bothers me greatly is seeing a fat cop. He or she is being paid well to perform a job that protects the people paying her or him. That includes running to the scene or chasing a criminal. I find it a little curious that even the army adjusts physical condition requirements for gender and age. The job is the same, regardless of age or gender. I remain in physical condition for the most stringent requirements of any position I held. When I was commissioned in the army, I was told that I could be called back to duty in a national emergency. I remain committed to this duty, and I am confident that I can still perform well in the army. I have strong negative feelings for those who collect a paycheck to perform a job that protects others yet cannot perform it. If you cannot physically perform your duties for which you are being paid, you are merely an actor described by Plato. You no longer have the skills to be the artist.

To Serve and Protect

A mission statement defines a profession. It states in the most direct way possible what the organization does. Typically, mission statements vary among the various organizations within a profession. Mottos are common short versions of the longer mission statements. They help unite the group and quickly relay its purpose to interested people. For the marines, "Semper Fi" and a guttural chant help bind them. Semper Fi is short for *semper fidelis*, always the brotherhood. Though marines like to set themselves above other branches of the services, we all share a common bond. We all endured a period that is unique. One that no one can truly understand without living it.

The police motto heard almost universally is "to serve and to protect." What does this mean? It's assumed that it would be further explained in the expanded mission statement. To serve is extremely broad. I am confident that most police department do not routinely deliver services provided by local vendors. Protection also has limits to their ability. That's why states have the national guard to mobilize during natural disasters. The coast guard protects our coasts and large bodies of water. Much is assumed with this simple motto. It's a motto that is very likely to be misunderstood and be mostly meaningless due to its ambiguity.

I have seen mission statements that were too long. A concise statement is much easier to understand and remember. It's a challenge to produce a concise statement that covers all that an organization does. It's an opportunity to examine what is most important and the greater role the organization has in the community. It examines the community's overall needs and how your organization meets some of these needs. No organization meets all of a community's needs. How it coordinates and fits into the grand scheme is important for its members to understand.

How a mission statement is developed is important if it is to be supported by the organization membership. The people who implement the mission will follow it best when they were part of its development. I like to say they take ownership of it. Others may call it "buy in." Buy in is acceptance of what was developed by others. One takes ownership when they created it. Mission statements should be regularly reevaluated and updated. Times change. Even when there is no significant change, being part of the renewal process helps with the changing membership's ownership.

I have also seen mission statements that seemed to include what belongs in a code of conduct. The code of conduct separately defines the values of the organization and how its members perform their duties. It is not a reference to laws that regulate the organization. Ethical standards are best worded positively. It defines the standards members of the organization strive to meet. Words like "professionalism," "integrity," and "ethical" are too general. Standards with measurable definitions are easier to follow. Positive language defines what to do. Negative language defines what not to do. Though it may have a place, it is very difficult and practically impossible to list all that should not be done. Such concepts remind me of a foster child I once had. When he did something obviously unacceptable, he said, "You didn't tell me not to do it," making me accountable for his misbehavior. I soon learned to respond with "Do nothing unless I say you can." I remember this when I see people in a profession stretching or exceeding its ethical limits.

Well-developed mission statements, mottos, and codes of conduct seek outside contributions. A knowledgeable facilitator can help tremendously. Remember, you develop a mission statement and motto to communicate it inside and outside your organization. It only makes sense that you include representatives from both to develop them.

Political Influences

Police should operate without pressures for desired outcomes of their work. One most direct factor is funding. If the governing body is happy with the police work, they are more likely to approve an increase in the budget. If they are unhappy, it's a struggle to maintain the present budget level or even prevent budget cuts.

One seemingly innocent function we performed was delivering packets to the city council members. Before each city council meeting, the city manager prepared a binder for the agenda items with supplemental information. The secretary prepared the nine copies and brought them to us for distribution. It was usually the night before the council meeting, so their delivery was a priority.

Complicating it was that it was at the end of the day, our busiest time for police calls. Perhaps it was good relations for the police to make these deliveries, but it took time away from our primary responsibility. The city manager disagreed. He said that we only needed to drop them off during our regular patrol. It was his way of justifying placing his department's responsibilities on us. Refusing or failing to make the deliveries due to a busy period to make these deliveries would have a negative impact on our performance. Inevitably, the deliveries took priority over some lesser duties.

The most sinister political influence in which I was involved was with the city manager's social habits. Malcolm McGoodwin was from Alabama. He stopped by a local restaurant and bar on his way home most every night. He drove the city vehicle, which was an old police car. Though technically wrong, few objected to the use of the city car since the restaurant was on his direct route home. The greater problem was that he was consuming a significant amount of alcohol. We all knew it but followed the directive to look the other way. We knew his schedule well. His arrival times at the restaurant varied with his workload. The departure times were consistently eleven thirty in the evening, one-half hour before closing.

During one very difficult budget preparation season, the chief was growing angrier with each meeting he had with the city manager. One day, the chief shocked us when he said, "Go get him." It was a simple matter to park down the street from the restaurant and stop him. We got him that night.

I was riding with Tom. Since he was assigned to the beat, he was the driver and wrote all the reports. I backed him up and wrote any necessary supplemental reports. For this arrest, I was only along as a witness. After all, we set out to arrest our top government employee. We didn't want any one of us exposed to a possible complaint of misconduct.

For a DWI conviction, the burden is on the police to show driver impairment when operating the motor vehicle. We followed Malcolm only a few yards and noticed that he was close to and wavering along the center line. This is typical of many impaired drivers. They try to use the center line as a guide to drive straight. It is also possible that he was paying more attention to us as we obviously waited for him near the restaurant.

Tom turned on the blue lights, and Malcolm pulled over. Jack approached the driver, and I took the standard position on the passenger side of the car. Malcolm presented his license to Tom but couldn't locate the vehicle registration. It was standard procedure to not place the registration of all city vehicles. They were kept by the city clerk. It was something the city manager should have known, but we were not surprised. We could easily run the check by computer to get the information we needed to the report and court summons.

Malcolm cooperated with Tom's instructions for the field sobriety. It always amazed me that individuals who have been drinking always try to beat this incriminating performance. They could simply refuse, and it cannot be held against them. Somehow, they think they will pass. Tom was building his case prior to arrest, to support the decision to make the arrest. Once arrested, the driver is required to submit to a blood alcohol test by providing a breath, urine, or blood sample as chosen by the officer. So the probable cause to make the arrest is the weak point in any DWI arrest that lawyers exploit.

Tom placed Malcolm under arrest. He followed procedure and applied handcuffs to Malcolm. Being a city car, we decided that we could leave it secured on the street instead of towing it as typically done. We do not want to leave a personal vehicle on the street where it could be vandalized, stolen, or have items stolen from inside. Our plan was to bring the car to city hall after processing.

At the police station, Malcolm cooperated with all the processing, including mug shots. It amazes me how many people smile for a mug shot. He agreed to the breathalyzer and tested two points above the legal limit. With processing complete, Tom asked him who he would like to call to come get him. We require a sober person who is willing to assume responsibility for his safety and to prevent him from driving.

Malcolm called the mayor. It was nearly one o'clock in the morning, but the mayor answered. Malcolm said that he needed to apologize and added, "My career is over." He started crying. I knew the mayor to be a kind and honest businessman. Malcolm spoke with him for several minutes; then we prodded him to seek a ride home, or he would have to spend the night in jail. He asked the mayor for a ride, and he agreed.

Malcolm took leave from his managerial duties until his court appearance. He surprised us with his guilty plea. Such high-profile arrests are usually challenged. Malcolm resigned from his post and moved back to Alabama to join his family.

In Malcolm's case, the political pressure was to avoid doing our job regardless of the individual's status. The advice from my respected mentor, "The more you do, the more likely you'll get into trouble," evolved from political pressure to avoid anything that might be controversial.

Dehumanization

It's very much universal that police will describe the gender of a person they are describing as either male or female. "Police are looking for a white male..." "The victim is a white female..." Why can't we say man or woman? I have a male dog or a female cat. It's how I describe my pets, creatures that are not human. The whole male-female concept is now very blurred with the nontraditional exclusive man-woman sexualities. In the broadest concept, gender and its identity doesn't really matter in most social interactions. Whether human or another animal or plant, gender roles only matter when reproducing.

We talk about preferred pronouns—he or she, his or hers. We only have gender-neutral pronouns in the plural. Their, theirs, they, and them are not appropriate pronouns for an individual. We shy away from using "it" as a pronoun for a human. It describes anything nonhuman. I try my best when I encounter someone who is unconventional. The easiest gender-neutral methods are to use that person's name and no pronoun. I have already written about the police desire to write in the third person. This is just another reason why I prefer using the person's name.

We have normalized the dehumanization of genders. As a biologist, I find myself looking at other beings and their development and evolution. What adaptations has the individual made and how has the species evolved over time? We can look at other species without dehumanizing ourselves but in a way to understand what we share with other beings to learn what is uniquely human.

In 1971, James Hammock wrote a thesis for his master of science in psychology at Portland State University titled "Behavioral Changes Due to Overpopulation in Mice." Homosexuality is not uncommon in many populations. In his study, he noticed an increase in homosexuality as mouse population density increases. Perhaps it's a mechanism Mother Nature uses to help control population density to avoid much more cruel mechanism, such as starvation, which adversely affects the entire population. As the population grows, less food is available, and the entire population is at risk. The parent does not want to waste precious resources on offspring that are not likely to survive, passing its genes to the next generation, assuring survival of the species. Kicking weak fledglings from the nest strengthens the species. Homosexuality may play an important role in reducing the number of offspring to feed, thereby increasing the survivability of the species.

There is also a darker side to the common species survivability first explained by Charles Darwin as the survival of the fittest. We humans often say, "Only the strong will survive." This isn't necessarily the case. Darwin said the fittest will survive. The advantage may be a decrease in size to a weaker body. This is clearly the case in the dinosaurs. Big animals need to eat a lot. If they cannot find sufficient food, they will starve. This is true today with large animals, such as elephants and polar bears.

We are very different from animals by protecting our entire gene pool. It's easiest to explain that a bird will kick a deformed chick from the nest so that it can better care for the ones most likely to survive. Some humans still practice similar behavior. The Ethiopian Kara tribe will abandon *mingi* (physically deformed) children in the jungle. A child can be considered *mingi* for several reasons, including top teeth that develop before the bottom teeth. Kara superstition is that the child is cursed, and it will bring bad luck to the remainder of the tribe.

This seemingly conflicting concept to abandon children in the jungle still does seem to align with human individuality and not with cruel nature. One unique characteristic is what I call the belief is something greater than us. Usually, it is religion, but it can also be our collective humanity being greater than the sum of our individuals. The Kara superstition is more a manifestation of a religious superstition than survivability due to dwindling resources.

Bullying may have its roots in selecting people out of the gene pool. Socially well-connected individuals are more desirable mates. Weak and abnormal ones outside the social class are rejected for breeding.

I see homophobia as having its roots in the most primitive survivability of the species. Primitive animals would not want to waste valuable resources on an individual that it not going to contribute to the survival of the species. We humans tend to protect our entire gene pool, and rightly so. Or survivability depends on our sum being greater than its parts. Our collective intellect is the reason we have survived and is key to our continuation. All members contribute to the greater whole far more than producing additional individuals. People who do not reproduce can very much contribute to our continued existence.

Of course, this gender designation difficulty and homophobia is prevalent everywhere, but I see it most embedded in police work. I see it in the officers and in the people with whom we interact. Calling someone "gay" is an attempt to incite a violent reaction. Sadly, I remember when gay meant happy. As a police officer, I tried to dismiss such provocations and focus on the reason why I was there. When the situation grew worse, I found a quick solution. I responded to the challenge by informing the provocateur that, if they were seeking a date, I was not interested. Only a few understood the reflection of the intended insult. Some who understood it attacked me. It was a quick resolution to a situation that had no solution. I brought closure with an arrest for assault and took the individual into custody.

We have a long way to go with racism. Morgan Freeman encourages us to stop talking about racism for it to go away. I preferred his comment, "If you don't want race to matter, stop notic-ing." Let me describe my entry into the army as to how I learned to see the person, beyond the appearance and unimportant behavior. Especially in the combat arms, nonwhites are the majority. I tried to learn the individuals, but first, you must be able to distinguish them. The hair, clothes, etc. are typical expressions of individuality. In the first few hours, I started making progress on learning about the forty widely varied personalities in my unit. I lost all what I learned when we were issued uniforms then brought to the barber-shop. Suddenly, we were all dressed alike and had the same hair-style. I had to start over. What I did learn most about this experi-ence was to study faces, body language, and verbal expression more. The downside is that I do not notice when someone changes her or his hairstyle. They may think I am insensitive. It's also a survival tactic. Complimenting a changed style when the person doesn't like it can be unwelcomed.

I would like to share my thoughts on race, but first, let me explain as a biologist. A species is a group of like individuals that can produce fertile offspring. There are distinguishable groups within a species I prefer to call variations but can be called races. It's this vari-ation that can assure the survival of the species when there is a devas-tating change in the environment. The more the gene pool is mixed, the stronger the species becomes. There are several cruel diseases that are inherited within a gene pool that have become isolated within populations—Tay-Sachs disease being one. It's found in the Hebrew community, and it is fatal at an early age. The more genes are mixed, the less likely the harmful ones appear.

Interestingly, some seemly harmful genetic conditions evolved to protect us. Sickle cell anemia is one. In its heterozygous (both the normal and sickle gene) form, it helps against malaria. The malaria protozoa invade the red blood cell. Its wastes are acidic. It causes the cell to distort to a sicklelike form. The body's immune system recognizes these cells as invaders and removes them, thereby con-trolling the malarial infection. Half the blood is still able to func-tion. This person may not even realize she has the gene. When the sickle cell gene is present in both chromosomes (homozygous) of the pair, any acidic condition of the blood causes all the cells to sickle, which can be fatal.

Dwarfism may be another advantage should our species survive until the next apocalypse. Being small allows you to occupy smaller dwellings, such as a cave. We may have to endure such conditions again.

Back to the police descriptions, you hear "black male" a lot. I would prefer "black man" if it's necessary to transfer such information. The officer's "black" description is almost universally understood as being guilty and likely violent. Because the police said it, you assume this man is a criminal. He may be a witness or a victim the police need to interview. We could describe dark or light skin. We could say African or European heritage. It's not his gender nor his skin pigmentation. It is his situation that caused him to be sought by the police and the assumption of guilt.

Let's consider biology again. I like to point out a fact to the white supremacists. All the supremacists I have known believe strongly in the Bible and take it literally. I establish agreement that science has established that humans began in Africa. I point out that Africans are all black. While they are processing this, I explain that humans migrated out of Africa into the Middle East, Asia, and Europe. As they migrated away from the intense sun, it was also colder. With less sun and more body coverings to stay warm, black skin didn't allow enough sun penetration to synthesize vitamin D required to build strong bones. As variations occur in a species, those with slightly lighter skin, less pigment to block the sunlight, produced more vitamin D. It's not necessarily that the darker-skinned individuals died out for lack of vitamin D. Those in the north with lighter skin felt better and more likely be interested in reproductive activities. It took several generations for this gradual change.

The melanin pigment is brown. When it's very dense, it can appear black. It is a pigment that is very common in nature. Humans have the same number of skin cells that produce melanin called melanocytes. Melanocytes are controlled by melanocyte-stimulating hormone produced by the pituitary gland at the base of the brain. Those of us who tan trigger the pituitary to produce more melanocyte-stimulating hormone. For this reason, skin grafted from an individual with a different amount of pigment will more closely match the receiving individual's skin after a period. The difference in skin pigment is the amount of hormone. The differences among groups is more cultural than physical. I am likely to share a very similar culture with most people with ancestral roots in New England. In the army, I became fascinated with learning about the various cultures and families of the men with whom I worked.

I am a bit dark for most whites. It may be because my grandfather's heritage was from Southern France. It could also be an infusion of genes that increase the melanocyte-stimulating hormone levels. It matters little to me. I especially enjoy tanning easily and getting sunburned rarely.

Being mostly white, I can easily challenge white supremacists. I don't care so much for upsetting them, though it may be my purpose when they are outrageous in their actions. I wish to challenge their flawed thinking. Having convinced them that migration explains the different amounts of melanin, they remain steadfast in their supremacist views. So I add the species thing. A species has similar characteristics and can produce fertile offspring. A mule is a cross between a horse and a donkey. It has identifiable common characteristics but is infertile. Mules will not sustain the herd by themselves. Obviously, our noted human differences are all the same species. Most recently, with the ancestral interests in DNA heritage, people are locating their global origins. Still, whites came from Europe. Many Europeans have DNA from Neanderthals. Most people believe Neanderthals are much more primitive than we *Homo sapiens*, but I'm not certain. Denisovan DNA from Siberia is also found in some Europeans. Denisovans were also very primitive. Neanderthals and Denisovans are considered different, more primitive species yet could breed successfully with modern humans. By the definition of species, we are all the same. Whites are carrying far more primitive genes than blacks. When I have had more than I find tolerable from a white supremacist, I caution him or her that her or his Neanderthal and Denisovan genes are showing. Finally, if humans came out of Africa and God created man in his own image, God is black. See you at the pearly gates.

Gatekeepers

Have you listened closely when someone provides his or her credentials when asked? Are you impressed when they disclosed the years in their position? Was that their only reference to credentials? Let me suggest that longevity alone is not necessarily competence. It is evidence of survivability. It does not distinguish how this person has retained this position, honorably or otherwise.

How broad and deep are the credentialing or certification requirements? I have found some organizations, especially the police and corrections, have annual recertifications such as use of force. It's done within the organization by instructors who are also certified instructors by a similar process. Change within such organizations comes only with outside pressure, rarely from within.

I am unimpressed when someone only cites the years of experience as expert qualification. Similarly, I am little more impressed when they cite training done within their own organization. An expert is defined as someone who has more knowledge than the average person. I like to hear some credentials such as a college degree or peer-verified research in the subject.

There is a huge difference between training and education. Training is that information and skills one needs to do a very specific job. An education goes in-depth. It would include the concepts behind the reasons and how we do things. A well-educated person has the knowledge and experiences to continually evaluate how something is done. Such a person has acquired the ability to research, experiment, and evaluate supporting and conflicting information. A technically trained person lacks these fundamental concepts to question and improve the job she or he performs.

In 400 BC, Plato explained the difference between actors and artisans. An actor can describe the actions very well. He used a chariot as an example. The actor can describe and act out the skills of driving and fighting from a chariot without ever having done it. Artists are the skilled people who do it. However, Plato stops here. There were no diversified in-depth schools. There were schools of philosophy that sought the reasons why we do things. We have a much more complex society, and in-depth knowledge is much more important.

Sadly, my experience in recruiting law enforcement personnel is more limited by their ability to pass the physical exam than intellectual requirements. Indeed, I worked with several who had general equivalency diplomas or barely graduated high school whose expertise was held in high regard by their peers. Years of experience is more valued than education. These gatekeepers have endured for whatever reason and have been promoted by elimination of the competition. Now they are the ones who decide who to hire and promote. They greatly distrust or feel threatened by educated people and discriminate against them. They are the gatekeepers that perpetuate organizational incompetence.

An officer who might have had an hour or two on how to handle juvenile delinquency at the academy will consider herself or himself more qualified to make decisions on a child's welfare than a parent, regardless of the parent's education, credentials, and experience. With similar training in domestic violence, such an officer may impose his or her will on resolving a potentially domestic violent situation. They will dismiss other professions, even the licensed therapist, as not applicable to police work. A serious concern for me is how officers arrest a parent and leave the child in the care of a family friend. This is technically a child placement activity reserved for human services. The officer has no idea that this is really a safe arrangement. Human services conduct a lengthy process before allowing a child to be placed with another person. The officer's quick assessment is frighteningly inadequate when the safety of a child is at stake.

Police often see themselves as better than others. They are no better than anyone else, and many times they are worse. I backed up many loud noise and disorderly conduct complaints. Citizens called in to complain about noise and foul language. No one liked these calls. The offending people were typically drunk, disliked cops, and had no regard for their neighbors. Only rarely did we deliver the complaint and achieve immediate and apologetic compliance. Often, we were assailed with a volley of insults and defiant language. I listened to many police officers attempt to quell the behavior with equal or greater obscenities. I had to think, who was the better person? We are no better than them if we become even more disorderly.

Similarly, I never understood why police broke up combatants by striking them with a baton, often called a nightstick. I soon learned that if you grabbed the dominant person in the fight, the other often took advantage of the opportunity to retaliate. After a few of these, I started using pepper spray. Again, I quickly learned that peppering the dominator gave the opportunity to the other one to reverse the roles. What I found worked best was to apply pepper spray to all participants, regardless of who appeared to be the aggressor.

Racism and classism are covert, subtle, and sometimes overt. It seemed to come naturally with people who felt that they were better than others. There were few minorities in our rural New Hampshire city. I did see a lot of what one of my respected college professors called classism. It's essentially the same as racial biases in another form. Even those of us who like to believe that we have no bias will refer to upper and lower classes of people. A typical member of the lower class is someone who has not done well in school and has less education. With less education, the lower-paying jobs are all that are available. The lower incomes limit housing options. Low-wage earners tend to be housed in neighborhoods of poorly maintained buildings. The class perpetuates itself as they are trapped in these conditions and teach their children how to survive in this environment.

I have had several friendly arguments with a judge I respect very well. When we met at social events and our conversations went generally in this direction, he sighed and said it's in their genes. I am the scientist with a degree in biology and favored genetics. I disagreed with him. I believed it was a learned behavior that trapped people into a way of life. Few felt that they had the ability to escape the environment into which they we born. Police unknowingly contribute as social gatekeepers, keeping people in the proper social class.

It's easy to identify the officers with classism bias. They refer to people as dirtbags, scumbags, pukes, etc. They don't use proper names. Nothing is more important to another person than someone who knows their name in a positive way. I live in this community and have always tried to accept people as they are and help resolve problems. Gatekeepers keep distance from the community. They use post office boxes, rarely disclose their address, and keep their phone numbers unlisted.

Teamwork for police is focused on whether someone is a reliable backup. Gatekeepers want colleagues who will come to their defense when the need arises. They seek blind support regardless of the circumstances and what led up to the incident requiring extra force. I can't say for sure that I knew anyone who didn't back up their fellow officer, though I heard how some would take an indirect route. I can attest that I answered the call for backup with determination. I didn't always agree with the officer's action that made the backup necessary, but it never prevented me from protecting my colleague.

Gatekeepers, those less educated officers with many years of experience, seem to be the ones most frequently calling for backup. They are less open to trying alternative resolutions. They expect the people to submit to their will immediately upon arrival to the scene. The more tolerant, competent, and confident officers will use the person's name. Many of our calls involved the same people, so it wasn't long before we learned many of their names. If we didn't know the name, simply asking in a manner one would in any social interaction helped gain a person's acceptance. I challenge you to approach someone by saying, "I am Officer Sanborn. What name can I use when I speak to you?" Now use your own name, not mine. It may seem strange that I say this, but I have seen officers give the wrong name more than their own. People become defensive if you have a notepad and demand names, like a gatekeeper. Remember, the gatekeeper is only comfortable in maintaining the status quo.

If you want respect, you must first give it. To retain respect, you must be broadly knowledgeable, not narrowly certified.

About the Author

George Michael "Mike" Sanborn was born into a classic fifties family with a working father and a stay-at-home mother. His family soon descended into alcoholism, domestic violence, divorce, and poverty. He and his siblings were never delinquent, but they were the stinky kids that moved a lot and had difficulty making and keeping friends. His family reminded him that other people could do things not available for him.

Mike found positive influence and encouragement from some people who believed in him. It was his high school math teacher who simply expected him to go to college and showed him how. Motivated to prove his family wrong, he graduated from Saint Michael's College with a strong education in the arts and sciences. Feeling guilty about avoiding the draft during the Vietnam era, Mike enlisted and obtained a commission in the army, achieving the rank of captain. The army encouraged him to obtain a master's degree in human resources from Pepperdine University, which included individual and organizational psychology and leadership.

After the army, he became a police officer in a small city, hoping to make a difference in his community, to help others who struggle like he had. He soon became very disappointed when he didn't find the same high ethical standards of his previous education and military experience. Only a few in the profession shared his high standards of integrity. After six years, he transferred to city administration and eventually became the water and sewer superintendent. Though he achieved the high standards for his department, other departments and the city manager often worked against him. After thirteen years with the city, he decided to go into education like he promised his math teacher.

He matriculated to Antioch University's environmental studies master's program with teaching certification. Mike became certified in biology and started teaching high school. Seeing the need for certification in the other sciences, Mike also became highly qualified in chemistry and physics, supported by his strong education at Saint Michael's College.

After teaching for many years, he did case management for people transitioning from county jail and led a juvenile diversion program. After thirty-two years of military and public service, he retired from direct public service. Mike continues his love of teaching in an online high school. Still wishing to do more, he now shares his experiences in his writings, hoping to benefit others.